Migration, Diasporas and Citizenship

Peter J. Aspinall • Martha J. Chinouya

The African Diaspora Population in Britain

Migrant Identities and Experiences

palgrave
macmillan

Peter J. Aspinall
Centre for Health Services Studies
University of Kent
Canterbury
United Kingdom

Martha J. Chinouya
Department of Public Health
University of Liverpool in London
London
United Kingdom

Migration, Diasporas and Citizenship
ISBN 978-1-137-45653-3   ISBN 978-1-137-45654-0   (eBook)
DOI 10.1057/978-1-137-45654-0

Library of Congress Control Number: 2016938240

Printed on acid-free paper

This Palgrave Macmillan imprint is published by Springer Nature
The registered company is Macmillan Publishers Ltd. London

*To my mother, for her innumerable kindnesses, and to Şenay
for her interest (PJA)
To my father, Aaron, Pasi Chinouya (MJC)*

INTRODUCTION

For a number of reasons it is timely to write a book on the Black African population in Britain. The 2011 Census revealed that the Black African population had grown to 1.0 million people, making it the largest Black ethnic group in the country and substantially larger than the Black Caribbean (0.6 million) and Other Black (0.3 million) ethnic groups. Moreover, with the release of nearly all tables from the 2011 Census, this has furnished the authors with a rich repository of data to provide a socio-demographic profile of the Black African group that will remain a key source of evidence until the first releases from the 2021 Census in mid-2023. Further, 2015 marks the beginning of the United Nations International Decade for People of African Descent and the African Union has declared the diaspora the sixth region of Africa. The African Union has also called for the diaspora to engage in Africa's 10-year Science and Technology Programme endorsed in 2014. It is therefore appropriate to celebrate these events in this way.

The main focus of this book is the population now generally known as 'Black African', with a few exceptions where a wider capture is justified. This term has been used in the three decennial censuses of 1991, 2001, and 2011 and is now salient across central and local government and other statutory bodies. Members of this ethnic group have also coalesced around this term as a satisfactory self-descriptor. The term captures those with African ancestral origins who either self-identify or are identified by others as Black African, but excluding those residents of Africa who are of European or South Asian ancestry and people of North African ancestry. It refers to people and their offspring with these African ancestral origins who migrated *directly* from sub-Saharan Africa (Agyemang et al., 2005; Bhopal 2004). It thus excludes 'Black Caribbeans' (another census category, sometimes referred to as 'African Caribbeans' or 'Afro-Caribbeans') who are defined as people with African ancestral origins who migrated via the Caribbean.

There are other terms for the 'Black African' population, such as 'African (origin)' and 'African British', but all, including 'Black African', are contested and most are technically ambiguous or problematic. The book engages with these debates. Some oppose the term 'Black African' as the use of the word black invokes the category of race, though cognitive research amongst community members indicates that the term is acceptable and does not cause offence. Attempts have been made to promote 'African British' but these have attracted only limited interest and the term is ambiguous with respect to specific origins in Africa. 'African (origin)', sometimes used as a synonym for 'Black African', as in the title of this book, also lacks specificity. Moreover, the term 'sub-Saharan Africa', widely used by international organisations, continues to be regarded as Eurocentric and racist.

The book's title also invokes the concept of 'diaspora'. The concept has traditionally been conceived in terms of a 'catastrophic' (Cohen 2008) and involuntary dispersion from a homeland in Africa associated with slavery. The new definition of diasporas has been widened to encompass recent and contemporary African migrations in pursuit of work, education, and asylum from civil strife and diasporas located in countries outside Africa and their interactions with processes of globalisations and associations with the broader concept of transnational communities. This focus on diasporas is particularly appropriate in the case of the predominantly migrant Black African population. The concept as used here focuses on the dispersion or the widely spread situation of a particular migrant group, the circumstances of these diasporic groups or communities, on recent flows of people across spaces and on their transnational activities. This shift in terminology in the 1980s and 1990s—from traditional approaches to *inter*national migration, invoking unidirectional flows and concepts such as 'assimilation' into the host culture, to diaspora studies on *trans*national experiences and communities—reflects growing interest in processes of globalisation as a sociological theme.

Developments in technology, notably the availability of cheap airfares across a widening network of routes and of electronic communications (electronic mail, Skype, the World Wide Web, satellite television, and methods of money transfer), have all made it possible for these scattered communities to develop and sustain their own particular genres of diasporic identities, economic types, and lifestyles. Accordingly, 'the rigid territorial nationalism that defines modern nation-states has in this way been replaced by a series of shifting and contested boundaries' (Scott and Marshall 2005). These are explored, for example, in the book's discussions on groups, categories, and national and transnational identities, that focus on the complexity, multidimensionality, fluidity, and diversity of diaspora identities.

It is within these broad debates and frameworks that such themes as population change, migration, the labour market, housing, health and social care, education, and social, cultural, and civic life are discussed. In the final chapter, attempts are made to draw out policy-relevant findings. Wherever possible we have tried to accord importance to the substantial heterogeneity concealed in the 'Black African' collectivity, though this has largely been limited to the different migrant communities or country of origin groups. The concealment of such contrasting groups as Somalis and Congolese on the one hand and Nigerians and Ghanaians on the other is one of the most important impediments to understanding the Black African diaspora. It is hoped that our analysis will add to evidence-based arguments for more finely granulated categorisation in the decennial census and surveys and to our understanding of the lives and diverse cultures of Black Africans in Britain.

ACKNOWLEDGEMENTS

We are grateful to a number of people who have facilitated this study. They include Professor Ludi Simpson for access to supplementary online materials that link to the population pyramids in Chap. 2 in Stephen Jivraj and Ludi Simpson (eds.), *Ethnic Identity and Inequalities in Britain*. Bristol: Policy Press, 2015 (Figs. 2.3 and 2.4 are from this source) and Dr. Stephen Jivraj for permission to use Table 13.1 in Jivraj and Simpson (2015). We thank Mr. John Eversley, London Metropolitan University, for access to language data from the Annual School Census and to *Language Capital* (London: CILT, 2010); Mr. Nick Fox, Workforce and Facilities Team, Health and Social Care Information Centre (HSCIC), for providing information on the number of qualified Black African nursing, midwifery, and health visiting staff, 2008–2014 (Table 6.9); and to staff at the Office for National Statistics for advice on various standard and commissioned table data. We also thank Mrs. Sandra Mather, of the University of Liverpool, for the excellent migration flow map (Fig. 2.1) prepared at short notice. We are also grateful to our university libraries: to the Templeman Library, University of Kent, for use of its extensive online full-text collections and to Lynne Meehan and Ruth Russell, of the University of Liverpool in London, for help in the procurement of books and other literature.

The book also draws on the findings of Lavinia Mitton and Peter Aspinall's Economic and Social Research Council (ESRC) Understanding Population Trends and Processes (UPTAP) project 'Black Africans in the UK: Integration or Segregation' (Grant Reference RES-163-25-0040) undertaken at the University of Kent from 1 April 2008 to 30 September 2009.

Use is made in the book of decennial census data that are Crown Copyright from the Office for National Statistics, National Records of Scotland, and Northern Ireland Statistics and Research Agency.

At Palgrave Macmillan, we thank our Editorial Assistant (Politics and Sociology), Dr. Judith Allan, for her expert guidance of the project and keeping us on track, and to the editors of the series 'Migration, Diasporas and Citizenship', Professor Robin Cohen and Professor Zig Layton-Henry, for taking an interest in the research and their informative comments on the manuscript.

CONTENTS

LIST OF FIGURES

LIST OF TABLES

CHAPTER 1

African Communities in Britain

The term 'Black African' first emerged in the 1991 Great Britain Census as a new official ethnic category, allowing people of this ethnicity to coalesce around this term rather than having to utilise residual 'other' categories. It has been utilised in the two subsequent decennial censuses. The 'Black African' group was the largest Black group in the 2011 Census. A total of 989,628 Black Africans were enumerated in England and Wales, substantially exceeding Black Caribbeans (594,825) and Other Black persons (280,437). Just two decades earlier the relative sizes of these groups was quite different: In 1991, Black Caribbeans numbered almost half a million (499,964) in Great Britain, substantially more than Black Africans (212,362) and the Other Black group (178,401).[1] How this group has evolved in Britain—from its earliest presence nearly two millennia ago to the country's largest Black group in the early twenty-first century—is the subject of this chapter.

There is evidence of a long history of a Black African presence in Britain, going back to at least the Roman times. Africans were first recorded in the north of the country 1,800 years ago, as Roman soldiers defending Hadrian's wall—'a division of Moors' said to number 500 (Fryer 1984; Killingray 1994). Some are reported to have held senior positions. There is evidence of Africans in York in the same period (Walvin 2000). Indeed, North Africans are well documented in the epigraphic record of Roman Britain (Thompson 1972; Birley 1979). However, the case of the 'ivory

---

[1] After adjustment for undercount (Sabater and Simpson 2009) these 1991 figures are: Black Caribbeans, 570,751, Black Africans, 258,746; and Other Black, 224,172.

© The Editor(s) (if applicable) and The Author(s) 2016
P.J. Aspinall, M.J. Chinouya, *The African Diaspora Population in Britain*, DOI 10.1057/978-1-137-45654-0_1

bangle lady' in York (Leach et al. 2010)—whose burial indicates she was from the higher echelons of society—challenges assumptions based on recent historical research that immigrants were of low status and male, and that African individuals are likely to have been slaves. Leach et al. argue that both women and children moved across the Empire, often associated with the military.

Some historians suggest that Vikings brought captured North Africans to Britain in the ninth century. After a hiatus of several hundred years, the influence of the Atlantic slave trade began to be felt, with the first group of West Africans being brought to Britain in small numbers in 1555. African domestic servants, musicians, entertainers, and slaves then became common in the Tudor period, prompting an unsuccessful attempt by Elizabeth I to expel the 'blackamores' from her kingdom in 1601. By the last third of the eighteenth century, academics have estimated that there were between 10,000 and 15,000–20,000 Black people in Britain, mostly concentrated in London and other port cities (Fryer 1984, p. 68).

The *scale* of this African presence, going back almost two millennia, is difficult to establish as few written records are available. However, a new type of evidence, based on the study of Y-chromosome and mitochondrial DNA, is beginning to provide the first genetic trace of a long-lived African presence in Britain, though such studies are still few. Among a set of 421 males who were analysed as part of an ongoing large British surname study, a relatively rare African Y-chromosome type, called haplogroup A1, was found in a Yorkshire man (King et al. 2007). Seven out of 13 men carrying this individual's same rare east-Yorkshire surname were also found to carry hgA1 chromosomes. The investigators argue that this chromosome was probably introduced to the genealogy several hundred years before the late eighteenth century. However, a survey of 1,772 Y-chromosomes from the British Isles found no examples of haplogroup E3a, by far the most frequent Y-chromosomal lineage in Africa, and they were also absent from the surname study sample. While there is evidence that a greater proportion of the African component of the hybrid population being contributed by females, a study of mitochondrial DNA sequence diversity among 100 'White Caucasian' British contained only one haplotype with a probable origin in West Central Africa. King et al. comment that this general rarity of African lineages may be due to a variety of factors, including sampling bias.

Other studies point to a similar rarity of genetic evidence of an African presence. The Oxford Genetic Atlas Project found a very small number of very unusual clans in Southern England, two from sub-Saharan Africa. Sykes (2006, p. 334) speculates that these 'slightest traces' or 'dustings' 'might be the descendants of Roman slaves, whose lines have kept going through unbroken generations of women'. It seems surprising, therefore, that in another source, *Bionews*, geneticist J.S. Jones is reported as suggesting a much higher level of population mixing, claiming that around one in five White British people has a direct Black ancestor (Anonymous 1999). The historical source to which this estimate is attributed includes British census data from the sixteenth century, which apparently shows that thousands of Africans who had come to trade in Britain had settled in London and the West Country, many of whom married into White families. This estimate has not been published in the peer-reviewed literature and seems improbable, given the lack of a commensurate genetic trace in the population.

The seventeenth, eighteenth, and early nineteenth centuries—from around the late 1620s to the early 1830s—are dominated not solely by the Black African presence in Britain but also by Britain's relationship with the peoples of Africa through the enslavement on an industrial scale of hundreds of thousands of Africans. Recent exploration of the Slave Compensation Commission records, a total of 1,631 ledgers, at the National Archives by scholars at University College London reveal the true extent of slave-owning in Britain at the time of abolition in 1834 through their listing of every British slave-owner, the number of slaves owned, and the amount paid for these slaves by way of compensation (Olusoga 2015). Slave-owners were to be found in every occupational and social group in British society, including estate owners, lawyers, doctors, clergymen, iron manufacturers and other industrialists, and even widows, the inheritance of slave income allowing slave ownership to spread across huge swathes of British society. Their ownership varied from just one slave up to 3,000. A total of 46,000 British slave-owners across the British Empire came forward to claim compensation, a sum of £20 million in total. However, the 3,000 of these who lived in Britain owned 50 % of all slaves in the Empire. They lived all over the country and in sizeable numbers in Bristol, London, and Liverpool, and disproportionately in Scotland.

Most of these slaves were used to develop the sugar plantations in Barbados but the practice spread across Caribbean communities, including Jamaica. The 24-hour shift system combined with a terror-based regime substantially reduced life expectancy on arrival. By the time of abolition, the roll call of slaves identified 800,000 separate names. Such slave-owning was a major engine of the British economy, creating huge wealth from the sale of sugar in European markets and spawning the creation of credit and investment networks. Lavish mansions and infrastructure projects were funded in this way. Many of the first wave of slave-owners were granted peerages. Of the 650 MPs in the early 1830s, more than 80 made compensation claims to the commission.

From the late seventeenth century there is archival evidence of Black Africans living in central London that is mainly associated with slavery. Parish registers often noted the race or colour of children being baptised: this source records the first birth of a Black person in Lambeth in 1669, when John, the son of Abimelech Potter, 'a blackamore', was baptised in St. Mary's church, next to Lambeth Palace (Newman and Demie 2006). By the eighteenth century, when the slave trade was well established in Western Europe, a small proportion of these Black people were free, most of whom remained slaves or indentured servants, and in cities like London, Bristol, and Liverpool, escaped slaves with no legal status. Parish registers and poor law accounts provide evidence of former slaves living in the parish. Between 1669 and 1812, more than 80 Black Africans are listed in Lambeth, most of whom were slaves or domestic servants baptised in later life. The absence of the parent's name, uncertainty about exact age, and the disproportionate number of men may indicate their slave origin. Some of them were described as the property of or servants of a master. The parish poor law accounts, recording payments of relief paid to sick and poor people, list four Africans in 1722–1723. Moreover, Black Africans were entering other services at this time. According to Gilroy (1993, p. 13), at the end of the eighteenth century, an estimated quarter of the British navy was composed of Africans.

In the eighteenth century, records of missionaries and ministers record conversions of Black Africans, living mainly in London, to Christianity. For example, John Wesley baptised two Black Africans in South London 'belonging to Mr. Gilbert, a gentleman lately from Antigua' on 29 November 1758. This led to many African kings sending their sons to London for a Christian education, including William Ansah Sessarakoo in the 1740s and a son of Naimbana, the ruler of the Koyo kingdom in Sierra Leone, in the 1780s. The latter came under the patronage of the 'Clapham sect', a group of wealthy evangelical Christians living in Clapham. One of the group, Zachary Macaulay, started a school, the African Academy, in Clapham to educate Africans and freed slaves, 24 such children being said to be under education in England by 1802. The Clapham parish registers chart the progress of the school, the Holy Trinity registers recording 18 baptisms of African boys and young men in Clapham as well as five burials between 1801 and 1805. There was a separate school for three or four African girls in the neighbouring parish of Battersea. There are records of other high-status baptisms of Black Africans in Clapham in 1836, including John Tootoo Quamina Comassee and William Accootoo Comassee, Kings of Ashantee in Ghana, baptised at Holy Trinity church. The Church Missionary Society's first African clergyman was ordained in London in 1841.

African performers appeared through the nineteenth century in local Lambeth theatres, many of the plays with a Black or colonial theme dramatising slavery and commentaries on current international events. Though many of these performers were 'blacked up' White people, there was also a developing tradition of Black African and African-American performers, including Ira Aldridge, Master Juba (William Henry Lane), 'The Algerine Family', and Princess Azahmglona (the niece of the Zulu King, Cetewayo). In the late nineteenth century, Afro-American speakers were appearing at clubs and halls in Lambeth to speak of their former lives as slaves in the Southern USA.

Once again, Britain's relationship with the peoples of Africa was dominated from the late nineteenth century by events taking place on the continent of Africa. Britain's colonial campaigns on the continent got under way around the 1870s and were substantially complete by a generation later. Britain by then had taken control of the Cape Province, the West African settlements of Sierra Leone, the Gold Coast, and Gambia, the Lagos Coast, and the upper valley of the Nile. This was followed by the declaration of protectorates over British Somaliland (1884); Bechuanaland and the Rhodesias (1885); the hinterland of the Gold Coast, Ashanti (1886); Sierra Leone (1889); Zanzibar (1890); Nyasaland (1891); and Nigeria (1900). By 1902, the British had complete control of South Africa. Colonialism in Africa was also practised by France, whose African empire in 1914 was even larger than that of the British. The Congo Free State, established as a neutral concession in 1884, was annexed as a Belgian colony in 1908. Germany's participation in 'the scramble for Africa' began in the mid-1880s when they took possession of Togoland and the Cameroons. Italy came late in the division of Africa and Spain and Portugal also played limited roles. The consequence of these colonial ventures was such that by 1914 the whole of the African continent—with the exception of Liberia and Ethiopia—was occupied or controlled by European powers. Just 50 years earlier Europeans had controlled around one-tenth of the continent.

This era of colonialism—the end of which was marked by the departure of European administrators in the post-1945 period—was accompanied by the settling of White populations in these territories and the exploitation of local economic resources by the colonising powers. The domination of these countries around the idea of the 'civilising mission', accompanied by Britain's policies of segregation, left its legacy in the rise of racism. Moreover, the replacement of old social, economic, and political systems by those of the colonising powers had long-lasting consequences. Britain's colonial experiences shaped subsequent migration flows from Africa to the UK from the early 1950s and, according to Gilroy (2004), have given rise to a state of 'postcolonial melancholia'.

An immediate impact of Britain's establishment of colonies in Africa was a growing presence of Black Africans in Britain. Before the First World War, a small number of Black South Africans arrived in Britain for the purposes of study or training: Alice Kinloch, Francis J. Peregrino, Henry Gabashane, and the first Black South African lawyers, Isaac Pixley Seme and Alfred Mangena (Killingray 2012). The importance of this group lay in their notions of pan-Africanism and their active involvement in pan-African organisations while living in Britain. With others, Kinloch's efforts resulted in the formation of the African Association in 1897 and then the summoning of the Pan-African Conference in London in July 1900, the first time that people of African descent from different parts of the world had organised a forum to discuss issues of common interest.

Other initiatives included the launching of the East London-based newspaper *Izwi Labantu* (Voice of the People) which became the organ of the South African Native Congress (SANC) formed in 1898. The Liverpool-based Ethiopian Progressive Association (EPA) was founded in November 1904 by West African students at various colleges in the city. The South African Isaac Pixley Seme and the African American Alain Locke founded a student group with pan-African ideas in Oxford, known as the African Union Society. The African Institute at Colwyn Bay was also part of the Black African network in Britain at this time, serving as a provincial meeting place for Black people. Finally, Alfred Mangena set up the pan-African United African Association in 1906, the year in which John Edward Quinlan from St Lucia founded the National Association for the Protection of Dark Races, both in London.

By the end of the century, the population of Black Africans in Britain was substantial. The 1901 Census recorded 12,706 persons born in the Cape of Good Hope and other colonies in Africa, as against 7,461 in 1891, though not all may have been Black Africans. In addition, 462 'foreigners' were reported as born in Africa. There are no estimates of populations by ethnic group at this time.

The First World War had a substantial impact on the size of the Black African community in Britain. By the end of the war, there was an estimated 20,000 Black people in Britain (Fryer 1984), numbers having risen through the recruitment of Africans as seamen and as labourers in chemical and munitions factories. Moreover, troops from Africa and the Caribbean fought bravely in several theatres of the war, many of whom were killed or injured. Sixteen members of the West African Frontier Force and the King's African Rifles were awarded the Distinguished Conduct Medal (DCM). The war was reported to have taken a huge toll on Black seamen in Cardiff, with 1,000 being killed at sea and another 400 injured. Many Black soldiers were demobilised in Britain.

There is a more comprehensive evidence base on Black Africans in Britain for the rest of the twentieth century and the unions they formed with White British population and the offspring of such unions. Before the mass migration of people from former colonial countries from the 1950s, there were significant settlements of African origin populations in the port cities of Cardiff, Liverpool, London, and South Shields which can be traced back to the years of the First World War, and a growing offspring population of 'mixed race' children.

The Second World War was another turning point, even though the experiences of colonial men and women in the Second World War have remained largely invisible. Killingray and Plaut (2010) have done much to redress this by providing an examination of the part played by African servicemen in the war. Some 1.4 million African soldiers served in the Second World War, 1.05 million under Britain as a colonial power. They included 289,530 in the King's African Rifles (from Kenya, Tanzania, Uganda, and Malawi); 243,550 in the Royal West Africa Frontier Force (from Nigeria, Ghana, Sierra Leone, and Gambia); 100,000 from Egypt, 77,767 from Lesotho, Botswana, Swaziland, Zambia, and Zimbabwe; and 334,000 from South Africa (though Black South Africans were prevented from serving as combatants). African soldiers served in Palestine, Ceylon, India, and Burma as well as on the African continent. The regiments were diverse, comprising different tribal allegiances, and African soldiers often maintained these tribal allegiances, though war experiences 'detribalized African minds' (p. 182). There were also Black Africans who served in air and naval forces, equally neglected and forgotten. The war signalled a major watershed in Britain's relations with African peoples. Financially depleted by the war, colonial powers including Britain embarked on their departure from the African continent in the post-war years. Contemporaneously, African migrants from these colonies began their migrations to Britain.

The era of mass migration to Britain started in 1948 with the voyage of the Empire Windrush and continued throughout the second half of the century. Before the time of government social surveys, commencing in the late 1970s, sources on Black Africans and their unions with the White population are few. However, in 1969, country of birth of parents was added to the birth registration data. Bagley (1972) uses this source to investigate patterns of interethnic fertile marriage[2] in Great Britain using the Registrar General's Returns for the second and third quarters of 1969. Of a total of 3,393 marital (or parental) units, involving one or two partners born in Africa, 633 (18.7 %) involved African/British or other European marital partners. Bagley (1972) inaccurately terms these 'black–white marriages', interpreting the country of birth as ethnic origin. For example, some of those born in Africa may have been ethnic Indians from East Africa and some of those born in Britain may have been from groups other than White (though very few in 1969): this data does not satisfactorily enable ethnic origins to be distinguished. Of these 633 unions, two-thirds ($n = 421$) involved a father born in Africa and a mother born in Britain (or elsewhere in Europe) and one-third ($n = 212$) involved a father born in Britain (or elsewhere in Europe) and a mother born in Africa. Given that these figures are based on just 2 years of data, it is clear that a significant African-White mixed race population was emerging by the early 1970s.

From the late 1970s, the government started to collect ethnic origin in government social surveys, and these provide a much more robust estimate of the size of the African and Mixed African and White population. In 1985, an estimated 102,000 Black Africans were resident in Great Britain, based on Labour Force Survey (LFS) data (the average numbers for 1984–1986 from this source were 103,000). Twenty-eight per cent were under the age of 16, 28 % aged 16–29, 36 % aged 30–44, and 7 % 45 to retirement age (64 for men and 59 for women). Fifty-seven per cent of the African population was male and 43 % female. Only 35 % were born in the UK, a much smaller proportion than West Indians (50 %). Black

---

[2] That is, where a birth was recorded for the parents in the second and third quarters, 1969.

Africans at this time were more concentrated in London than any other ethnic group, 64 % residing in the capital city compared with 57 % of West Indians.

By 1985, the African group was larger than Bangladeshis (99,000) but smaller than the Chinese group (122,000). In addition, there was a growing 'mixed' group that is likely to have contained a significant proportion of White and Black Africans. In 1985 it stood at 232,000 (235,000 in pooled 1984–1986 data), the fourth largest after the West Indian and Guyanese (547,000), Indian 689,000, and Pakistani (406,000) groups. While estimates are not reported for the African-White mixes, Muttarak (2004) provides data from the 1981 LFS. According to her estimates, 26.8 % of male Black Africans and 9.8 % of female Black Africans were intermarried, a similar differential to that reported in the parental unions' data for 1969. However, the truly large increases in migration of Black Africans to the UK were to take place from the mid-1990s and these are documented in Chaps. 2 and 3.

CHAPTER 2

The Changing Demography and Household Characteristics of the Black African Population

The key components of change in the minority ethnic group population are births, deaths, and international migration. The contribution of these components can be estimated by tracking the changing age structure of each ethnic group from the 2001 Census to the 2011 Census. Simpson (2013) has calculated the contribution of natural change (births minus deaths) and net migration (immigration minus emigration) to population change in England and Wales between 2001 and 2011. He estimated births as the number of children alive in 2011 aged under 10 and derived deaths by applying mortality rates to the age structure of each group's 2001 population. The remainder of the population change over the decade is the net impact of migration. With respect to the percentage increase since 2001, in the case of Black Africans, 38.2 % was contributed by natural change and 61.8 % by net migration, both net immigration and natural increase contributing significantly to the population growth. This placed Black Africans in the group of ethnicities where the ratios of natural increase to net migration favoured the latter: Indian, Other White, African, and Chinese. By contrast, natural change was more important than net migration for the Black Caribbean, Pakistani, Bangladeshi, and Mixed groups.

© The Editor(s) (if applicable) and The Author(s) 2016
P.J. Aspinall, M.J. Chinouya, *The African Diaspora Population in Britain*, DOI 10.1057/978-1-137-45654-0_2

11

THE SIZE OF THE BLACK AFRICAN POPULATION

The Black African population increased substantially between 2001 and 2011. In 2001, the England and Wales Census (after adjustment for undercount) recorded 494,669 Black Africans in England and Wales, 0.9 % of the total population. By 2011, this number had increased to 989,628, 1.8 % of the total population, a rise of 100.1 % over the decade. In addition, the Mixed White and Black African population (after adjustment for undercount) increased from 80,705 (0.2 % of the population) to 165,974 (0.3 % of the population), a rise of 105.7 %. The Black African population also increased substantially in the UK home countries. In Scotland, the numbers rose from 5,118 (0.1 % of the population) to 29,638 (0.6 % of the population). This represented almost a sixfold increase. In Northern Ireland, Black Africans increased from 494 (0.1 % of the population) in 2001 to 2,345 (0.1 % of the population) in 2011, almost a fivefold increase.

Little information is available on the size of the different communities of descent within this population of almost a million people, as the Census did not collect information on the ethnicity of subgroups such as Nigerians, Ghanaians, and Somalis. Moreover, those writing in such descriptions in the 'Any other Black/African/Caribbean background' free-text field (predominantly Nigerians and Somalis) substantially undercount the full size of these communities. As some two-thirds of the Black African population were migrants, countries of birth provide only an indicative measure of the size of some of the different ethnic subgroups. However, country of birth is in general a poor proxy measure for ethnic origins. For example, only 7 % of migrants from South Africa identified as Black, 44 % as White British, and 39 % as Other White in the 2011 Census. Sixty-two per cent of Zimbabweans identified as Black but 29 % as White British or Other White. High proportions of residents who were Kenyan, Tanzanian, and Ugandan born identified as Asian (69 %, 68 %, and 58 %, respectively) and substantially fewer as Black (16 %, 17 %, and 33 %, respectively). By comparison, 93 % of the Ghanaian-born and 92 % of the Nigerian-born identified as Black.

COUNTRY OF BIRTH AND MIGRATION

Of this population of 989,628 Black Africans in 2011, 323,276 (one-third or 32.7 %) were born in the UK, the so-called second generation, 607,566 (61.4 %) were born in Africa, mainly Central and West Africa

(340,390) and South and East Africa (250,145), but with 14,027 born in North Africa and 3,004 for whom Africa was not otherwise specified. In 2001, 33.8 % (162,330) of all Black Africans (479,665, unadjusted for undercount) were born in the UK and 62.6 % (300,046) in Africa. Those born in Central and West Africa numbered 166,271, South and East Africa 124,248, and North Africa 9,527.

For the 2011 Census for England and Wales, detailed tabulations of country of birth by ethnic group were released, enabling Black African migrants to be identified. For 2001, only a very limited number of countries of birth for Black Africans were released (only eight specific countries). The 2011 data are shown in Table 2.1, rank-ordered by the size of the country of birth group, with that available for 2001. Even these limited intercensal data show substantial increases in some of the country of birth groups.

Table 2.1 (and Fig. 2.1) shows that by far the largest Black African country of birth group is Nigeria, more than twice the size of the next largest group, Ghana. The Zimbabwe country of birth group has overtaken Somalia in size. There is a major gulf between the size of these four leaders (numbering between 68,000 and 169,000) and the next group of eight countries of birth (Kenya, Sierra Leone, Uganda, Democratic Republic of the Congo, Eritrea, Ethiopia, South Africa, and Zambia), which range in size from around 10,000 to 20,000 people. Also notable in this list of the top 40 countries of birth are the Netherlands (7,718), Portugal (3,939), Germany (3,610), Sweden (2,410), and Denmark (1,510): These are probably the children of Black African migrants, especially Somalis in the case of the Netherlands, Sweden, and Denmark, who have been born in these EU countries and undertaken secondary family migration to the UK.

In addition, the table shows that 60.5 % of migrants were recent (2001–2011). Amongst countries with around two-thirds or more Black Africans migrating during 2001–2011 were Zimbabwe, Eritrea, South Africa, the Gambia, Cameroon, Malawi, USA, Guinea, Botswana, Guinea-Bissau, and Senegal. All the EU countries with secondary migrations had high proportions: Netherlands (86.9 %), France (77.6 %), Portugal (82.8 %), Germany (79.1 %), Poland (95.5 %), Sweden (88.9 %), Italy (83.2 %), and Denmark (95.6 %). Individual country data, where available for both 2001 and 2011, show that the Zimbabwean country of birth group increased fourfold over the decade, while numbers in Nigeria, South Africa, and Zambia increased twofold or more, though there was significant under-enumeration in 2001.

Table 2.1 Countries of birth of overseas-born Black African residents in England and Wales, 2001 and 2011 censuses

	2011	% recent migrants (2001–2011)	% all Black Africans (incl. UK-born)	2001[a]
Total: Country of birth	666,352	60.5	67.3	
Nigeria	168,675	60.2	17.0	76,291
Ghana	82,937	48.0	8.4	
Zimbabwe	70,911	74.1	7.2	17,852
Somalia	67,783	56.3	6.8	
Kenya	20,143	55.8	2.0	13,421
Sierra Leone	19,302	36.8	2.0	
Uganda	19,091	43.6	1.9	
Congo (Democratic Republic)	16,701	61.4	1.7	
Eritrea	15,429	65.4	1.6	
Ethiopia	12,743	54.2	1.3	
South Africa	10,515	74.0	1.1	4,218
Zambia	10,014	62.8	1.0	5,008
Gambia, The	9,697	65.7	1.0	
Sudan	9,248	62.3	0.9	
Cameroon	8,672	73.4	0.9	
Angola	8,437	56.9	0.9	
Netherlands	7,718	86.9	0.8	
Congo	6,894	59.6	0.7	
Ivory Coast	6,611	58.2	0.7	
Tanzania	5,496	55.2	0.6	
France	4,981	77.6	0.5	
Malawi	4,625	77.9	0.5	1,810
United States	4,059	75.1	0.4	
Portugal	3,939	82.8	0.4	
Rwanda	3,721	53.9	0.4	
Burundi	3,659	61.6	0.4	
Germany	3,610	79.1	0.4	
Ireland	3,038	58.1	0.3	
Africa (Not otherwise specified)	3,004	44.1	0.3	
Poland	2,908	95.5	0.3	
Liberia	2,827	61.8	0.3	
Sweden	2,410	88.9	0.2	
Algeria	2,060	45.3	0.2	
Italy	2,054	83.2	0.2	
Guinea	2,025	89.0	0.2	
Botswana	1,669	85.0	0.2	1,020
Guinea-Bissau	1,615	81.2	0.2	
Denmark	1,510	95.6	0.2	
Senegal	1,466	74.0	0.1	

Source: Commissioned Table CT0263, Ethnic group by detailed country of birth, 2011 Census

[a]2001 data were drawn from Standard Table S102 and Neighbourhood Statistics, Country of Birth, Table UV08. Data for Botswana, Namibia, Malawi, and Zambia are contained in Commissioned Table C0568

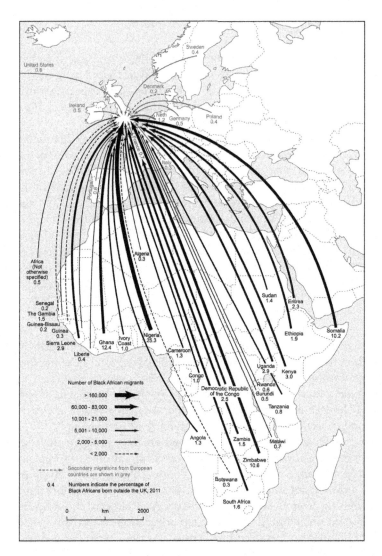

Fig. 2.1 Migrant flows from African countries and secondary flows from European countries amongst Black Africans born outside the UK: England and Wales residents, 2011.

Source: Commissioned Table CT0263, Ethnic group by detailed country of birth, 2011 Census.

Note: The flow lines indicate the African (and in the case of secondary migrations, European) countries of birth of Black Africans living in England and Wales in 2011 who were born outside the UK (thickness of flow lines indicate numbers and the numbers [e.g. 0.4] the percentages of Black Africans born outside the UK). Clearly, some migrants will be excluded: those who had died or emigrated before the 2011 Census enumeration.

Thus, while the first major immigration by Black Africans to Britain took place in the period after the Second World War, there has been very substantial recent migration since the early 1990s—and especially during the 2000s—which has been largely absent in the case of the Black Caribbean group (whose main migration was 60 years ago).

The data also show that for some countries in the latest Office for National Statistics (ONS) estimates of the most common countries of birth in Africa—and their rank amongst all countries of birth (Table 2.2)—country of birth is a very poor proxy for ethnic group. People born in South Africa were overwhelmingly White as were around a third of Zimbabweans. Those born in East African countries included Black Africans and African Indians. For example, only a small proportion (around 15.6 %) of Kenyan migrants was Black African. Nevertheless, it is notable that Nigeria now comprises the tenth largest country of birth group with an estimated population of 178,000 and that Somalia has now overtaken Ghana.

Components of Change

Figure 2.2 shows how ethnic group populations have changed over the decade (2001–2011) with respect to births, deaths, and the net impact of immigration and emigration. Simpson (2013) uses a simplified method to calculate these components, whereby births are estimated as the number of children alive in 2011 aged under 10, while deaths are derived by applying mortality rates to the age structure of each group's 2001 population. Births and deaths thus estimated are very close to the registered total births and deaths. The net impact of migration is the remainder of population change over the decade. Figure 2.2 shows that Black Africans grew most by net migration though natural change was also important, contributing around 40 % of the increase. An additional though secondary component of change to ethnic group populations is changes to individuals' ethnic identity between one census and the next (Simpson and Jivraj 2015a). The latter has only a limited impact on growth: There was a net transfer to the Black African group from other categories of –5 % between 2001 and 2011.

The dynamics of population change can be used to project the Black African population into the future, but such population projections are technically difficult to undertake. Several attempts have been made by teams in Leeds (Wohland et al. 2010) and Oxford (Coleman and Smith 2005; Coleman 2010) to undertake population projections by ethnic

Table 2.2   Estimated African-born population resident in the UK by sex and country of birth, January 2014 to December 2014 (thousands)

Country	Overall rank	All residents: estimate and CI	Males: estimate and CI	Females: estimate and CI
South Africa	7	201 (±10)	93 (±14)	108 (±15)
Nigeria	10	178 (±19)	88 (±13)	89 (±13)
Kenya	17	129 (±16)	61 (±11)	69 (±12)
Zimbabwe	21	120 (±15)	56 (±10)	65 (±11)
Somalia	23	114 (±15)	48 (±10)	66 (±11)
Ghana	25	92 (±13)	39 (±9)	53 (±10)
Uganda	40	51 (±10)	25 (±7)	26 (±7)
Mauritius	44	41 (±9)	21 (±6)	20 (±6)
Egypt	48	35 (±8)	20 (±6)	15 (±5)
Tanzania	50	34 (±8)	16 (±6)	18(±6)
Zambia	51	31 (±8)	16 (±6)	14 (±5)
Congo DR	57	24 (±7)	11 (±5)	13 (±5)
Libya	58	24 (±7)	15 (±5)	9 (±4)
Sierra Leone	60	24 (±7)	10 (±4)	13 (±5)

Source: Annual Population Survey (APS)/Labour Force Survey (LFS), ONS (released 27 August 2015). Accessed at: http://www.ons.gov.uk/ons/publications/re-reference-tables.html?edition=tcm% 3A77-376534.
Notes: African countries selected from 60 most common countries of birth

groups. For example, Coleman's (2010) standard population projection for population size is for the UK Black African group to grow to 2,093,000 by 2031, and 3,769,000 by 2056. The percentage of the Black African population aged 65+ is projected to increase to 4.2 % in 2031, 12.1 % in 2056, and 19.4 % in 2081.

AGE STRUCTURES

In 2011, Black Africans had a youthful age structure. Twenty-eight per cent were aged under 15, 45 % aged 15–39, 24 % aged 40–64, and 2 % aged 65 years or older. Mixed 'White and Black Africans' had an even younger age structure, with 47 % in the under 15 age group (the highest proportion of any ethnic group), 36 % aged 15–39, 15 % aged 40–64, and 2 % aged 65 and older.[1] This reflects both the high net migration for

[1] Note that a qualitative study with Somali people in Bristol found that the participants gave conflicting dates of birth (see Phillips-Mundy 2011), perhaps resulting from the use of different calendar systems.

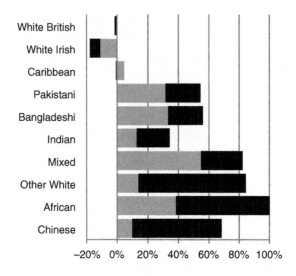

■ Births minus deaths (natural change)

■ Immigration minus emigration (net migration)

Fig. 2.2 Population change, 2001–2011, England and Wales (% of population in 2001).

Source: Simpson (2013). See also Simpson and Jivraj (2015a)

Fig. 2.3 Black Africans: age structure, 2001 and 2011.

Source: 2001 and 2011 Census, England and Wales population. Sourced from Jivraj and Simpson (2015), online materials (see http://www.ethnicity.ac.uk/dynamicsofdiversity/)

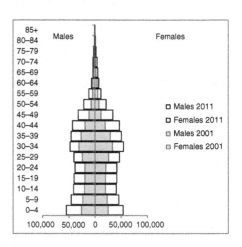

this group and the significant contribution of natural increase. The Other Black group had a similarly young age structure, with an even higher proportion in the under 15 age group (36 %). The four 'Mixed' groups have the youngest age structure with 39–47 % in the under 15 age group. By contrast, Black Caribbeans had a much older age structure, with 16 % aged under 15, 33 % aged 15–39, 37 % aged 40–64, and 14 % aged 65 or older. Such a young age structure with very small numbers in the old age groups is characteristic of a population that has grown substantially by immigration, half of all immigrants to the UK arriving when aged 15–29 (Simpson 2013). These young migrants result in a growing child population as most new migrants are of the age to start families.

Population Pyramids for the Black African Group

The first population pyramid shows the age structure for Black Africans in 2001 and 2011 by detailed age group and gender (Fig. 2.3).

It shows a wide base for the 0–4- and 5–9-year-olds and then narrows in the 10–14, 15–19, 20–24, and 25–29 age groups. The 30–34 age group bar widens and subsequent bars then show a progressive narrowing to the 85+ bar. In Fig. 2.4, using a method developed by Simpson (2013), the 2011 age structure is presented in bold outline and shaded (greyscale) bars that represent numbers of people in 2001, at the age they would have been in 2011.

For example, the shaded 30–34-year-olds are the number of 20–24-year-olds in 2001. The different size of a cohort in 2001 and 2011 shows whether it has grown from immigration or reduced from a combination of emigration and mortality. Children under 10 were born during this decade.

The Fig. 2.4 pyramid shows new births between 2001 and 2011 in the 0–4 and 5–9 age groups. The age groups 10–14 to 40–44 show significant growth mainly through net migration. The age groups 60–64 up to 85+ show little difference, except in the 85+ female age group, where the difference is mainly deaths.

Smaller Population Groups

ONS tables for small populations in merged local authorities with 200 or more persons in the specific groups provide a source of information on age at the level of selected individual countries of birth and ethnic

Fig. 2.4 The Black African
population in 2001 and
2011, age at 2011.

Source: 2001 and 2011 England and
Wales Censuses. Sourced from Jivraj
and Simpson (2015), online materials (see http://www.ethnicity.ac.uk/
dynamicsofdiversity/)

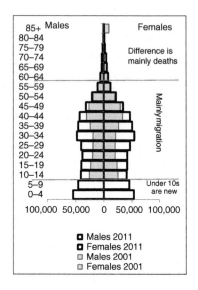

group write-in responses. These tables account for 91.8 % of all Nigerian
migrants, 87.3 % of all Ghanaian migrants, and 96.1 % of all Somali
migrants and 56.8 % of the Somali ethnic write-in responses and, therefore, provide strong indicative evidence of age structures.

These special population tables show marked differences across the
country of birth and ethnic groups (Fig. 2.5). Amongst Somalis, 15.4 %
of those in the Somali ethnic group (as measured by Somali write-ins to
the ethnic question) were aged 0–4 compared with 0.6 % who were born
in the Somalia group. Nigerians and Ghanaians have much higher proportions in the 25–29 to 50–54 age groups.

FERTILITY RATES

Fertility rates for many migrant groups in Britain, such as Indians and Black
Caribbeans, have declined to around the national average, and below it in
the case of Chinese and East African Asians (Coleman and Smith 2005).
However, over recent decades, Black African women have had higher total
fertility rates (TFRs) than most other ethnic groups, and in 2011 women
born in several African countries were featured in the top 20 for number
of births. A number of attempts have been made to calculate fertility rates
across ethnic groups, including approximate and robust methods. These

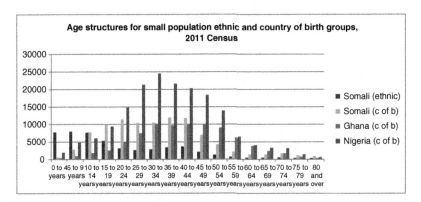

Fig. 2.5   Age structures for small population ethnic and country of birth groups, 2011 Census.

Source: ONS 2011 Census, Tables SP009 (Somali ethnic), Table SP019 (Ghana country of birth), Table SP023 (Nigeria country of birth), and Table SP028 (Somalia country of birth).

Note: Figures are for usual residents and 5-year age groups and summed for merged local authorities. Small population tables provide census data for some of the key characteristics of people in specific small population groups—for example, individuals of an ethnic group, a country of birth, a religion, or a national identity—in which the small size of the total population in that group means confidentiality constraints limit the release of more detailed standard statistics. These small population data are produced only for geographic areas in which the small population being counted is or exceeds a threshold of 200. Only the areas in which the population exceeds these thresholds are included in each table. This means that all tables do not contain the same geographic areas, because those exceeding the threshold will vary depending on the small population being counted. c of b = country of birth.

are frequently calculated around the time of the decennial census, as ethnic group is not recorded at birth registration. Simpson (2013) uses the child/women ratios method that compares the number of children born for a 5-year period before each of the 1991 (1986–1990), 2001 (1996–2000), and 2011 (2006–2010) censuses with the number of women at fertile ages (15–44) to provide estimates of TFRs. For the period 1986–1990, Black African women had a TFR of 2.25, the third highest after Bangladeshis (3.96) and Pakistanis (3.16) and higher than the White group (1.76). By 1996–2000, the Black African rate had fallen to 2.05 but increased to 2.37 in 2006–2010, remaining third in rank-ordered rates. One drawback of this approach, as Simpson acknowledges, is that some mothers in each ethnic group have children of Mixed or Other ethnic groups, probably lowering the rates a little. While there is a trend towards the convergence of fertility rates across ethnic groups, only the Black African group significantly increased its TFR between 1996 and 2000.

Simpson's findings are broadly consistent with those of other investigators (Coleman and Dubuc 2010; Dubuc 2009, 2012; Dubuc and Haskey 2010) who use the own-child method to calculate average period total fertility for 1996–2000 and 2001–2005 from the Labour Force Surveys (LFS). These investigations estimate a Black African TFR of 2.41 in 1996–2000, only exceeded by the Bangladeshi (3.43) and Pakistani (2.91) groups and higher than the TFRs for Black Caribbean (1.88), Other Black (1.87), and White British (1.71). By 2001–2005, the Black African TFR had fallen to 2.32 though the Other Black rate had increased to 2.23, against a stable White British rate.

Women living in England and Wales but born in Africa had a TFR of 2.76 in 2011, the highest TFR of women living in England and Wales but born in any world region. However, estimates of TFR for the African-born population conceal substantial heterogeneity (this can only be measured for migrants): Indeed, Africa had the highest variation across world regions. In 2011, TFRs for migrant women from across sub-Saharan African countries varied from 4.84 (Guinea) to 1.71 (Botswana) (Table 2.3).

Some of the largest migrant communities had some of the highest rates. For example, the 5,654 births amongst Somalia-born women yielded a TFR of 4.19, the second highest in sub-Saharan Africa.[2] The Democratic Republic of Congo (1,103 births) was third highest, Nigeria (7,476 births, 3.32) was the seventh highest in sub-Saharan Africa, and Ghana (3,328 births, 3.24) was the ninth highest, rates that were substantially above that for the UK-born (1.84) and more than twice the England and Wales average. Rates for Zimbabwe (2,837 births, 1.83) and South Africa (4,430 births, 1.79) were much lower but the data for these two countries would have included White as well as Black African women. These compare with significantly lower rates for migrant women born in Western countries, for example, USA, 1.83, Canada, 1.45, Australia, 1.31, and New Zealand, 1.36. These rates are, of course, only for migrant women. The lack of ethnic group data collection at birth registration precludes the derivation of fertility rates for 'whole' ethnic groups (including group members born in the UK).

In England and Wales in 2014, births to mothers born in Africa contributed 5.0 % of all live births (ONS 2015). The top ten non-UK coun-

---

[2] Coleman (2006) reported that the total fertility of women born in Somalia was around five in the year 2000.

Table 2.3 Total fertility rates for non-UK born women living in England and Wales, 2011, rank-ordered by mothers' country of birth in Africa

Mothers' country of birth	TFR 2011[a,b,c]	Number of births in 2011 in England and Wales
Libya	5.58	728
Guinea	4.84	171
Algeria	4.32	938
Somalia	4.19	5,654
Congo (Democratic Republic)	4.16	1,103
Gambia, The	3.82	584
Sudan	3.69	651
Morocco	3.61	747
Guinea-Bissau	3.42	99
Nigeria	3.32	7,476
Eritrea	3.26	808
Ghana	3.24	3,328
Ivory Coast	3.24	376
Cameroon	3.02	453
Sierra Leone	2.68	676
Liberia	2.67	103
Ethiopia	2.65	639
Rwanda	2.60	172
Egypt	2.57	361
Burundi	2.56	172
Namibia	2.52	97
Uganda	2.52	916
Malawi	2.48	373
Tanzania	2.35	431
Angola	2.31	461
Congo	2.13	264
Zambia	1.96	560
Kenya	1.89	1,402
Mozambique	1.86	127
Zimbabwe	1.83	2,837
South Africa	1.79	4,430
Mauritius	1.75	607
Botswana	1.71	72
Seychelles[b]	1.38	40
Africa (Other—not individually listed)[d]	2.22	658

Source: Office for National Statistics. Reference Table 1: referencetable1_tcm77-350670.xls. TFRs for non-UK born women living in England and Wales, by mother's country of birth. Released 4 February 2014
[a]TFR is the average number of live children that a group of women would each bear if they experienced the age-specific fertility rates of the calendar year in question throughout their childbearing lifespan. It provides a snapshot of the level of fertility in a particular year and does not necessarily represent the average number of children that a group of women will have over their lifetime
[b]TFRs based on less than 50 births in 2011, so they must be treated with caution
[c]The TRFs are derived from mothers' self-reported country of birth in 2011 Census returns and in-birth registrations
[d]'Other' groups include any countries not individually listed. The full list of countries can be found in an ONS attached grouping sheet

tries of birth of mothers have remained similar across the decade since 2003, Nigeria and Somalia appearing in this ranking in each year between 2003 and 2014 and Ghana between 2005 and 2010. In 2014 mothers born in Nigeria contributed 1 % (7,030) of all live births and Somalia-born mothers contributed 0.7 % (4,696). The age of African-born mothers is different to UK-born mothers: fewer are in the below 24 age groups (9.3 % vs 22.9 %) and more in the 35–39 age group (22.8 % vs 15.3 %). Where the number of previous live-born children were five and over, the proportion amongst African-born mothers was 3.2 % (and especially high, 6.6 %, amongst Eastern African-born mothers, the group containing Somalia) versus 1.5 % in UK-born mothers. Just over a third (35.2 %) of all live births to African-born mothers was outside marriage/civil partnership status, compared with 54.7 % of UK-born mothers. With respect to the spreading out from London of the Black African population (Chap. 5), 48.4 % of live births were to African-born mothers usually resident in London, down from 51.6 % in 2011 and 56.4 % in 2005.

MARITAL AND HOUSEHOLD CHARACTERISTICS OF THE BLACK AFRICAN POPULATION

This section considers the marital characteristics of the Black African population (though with limited census data) and household/family characteristics.

Marital and Partnership Status

While the decennial census collected information on the marital and civil partnership status of all respondents, no tables have been released from the 2011 Census for marriage/partnership status by ethnic group. It is therefore not possible to draw out relationships between marital/partnership status and household composition. However, data from the 2004 Health Survey for England (Karlsen and Nazroo 2008) show the marital status for Black African Christians and Muslims. Thirty-eight per cent of Black African Christians were single, 47 % married, 9 % separated, 3 % divorced, and 3 % widowed. A higher proportion of Black African Muslims, 63 %, were single, while 20 % were married. A higher percentage, 14 %, were separated, 1 % divorced, and 1 % widowed.

    An analysis of marital status using 2001 Census microdata (Mitton and Aspinall 2010) showed notable differences amongst Black African migrants by their country of birth. The proportion of widows and widowers was especially high amongst Somalis, Ugandans, South Africans, and Sierra Leoneans in England. It is possible that the death of some of these spouses in conflicts overseas may explain some of the differences. It is also difficult to interpret the high figures on those who are separated as Black Africans may have a different understanding of this term to that used in the census and surveys (i.e. separated for reasons of the break-up of the union, but still legally married). Some Black Africans may have understood separation as temporary due to force of circumstances, to earn and save before returning to the country of origin, or awaiting family reunification, rather than relationship breakdown. Reported separation in the 2001 Census microdata is high amongst Congolese (14.1 %), Sierra Leoneans (11.3 %), and Somalis (10.7 %), compared with just 2.3 % for the White British group. Divorce rates were higher than the White British group amongst Ghanaians, South Africans, Nigerians, and Black Africans born outside the UK and sub-Saharan Africa.

With respect to the research context, there may, in some contexts, be misreporting as a strategy to avoid stigma. A qualitative study of African women living with HIV found that although most had reported that they were single, the women were actually 'widowed', concerns about stigmatisation having led them to select the single category as this avoided further questions about the cause of death of 'husbands'. Again, some of the women used the word 'husband' to refer to men they were in sexual relationships with, but not legally married to.

There is a dearth of literature on same-sex unions/civil partnerships and households headed by Black African men and women who are in same-sex relationships (Aspinall 2009). Based on a review series on Black African men,[3] findings highlighted that being gay was highly stigmatised amongst African men, those who are gay or frequent public sex environments indicating that they did not wish to have their sexuality disclosed. The percentage of African respondents who declared a lesbian or gay sexual identity in the 2007 Citizenship Survey was just 0.26 %, perhaps providing indicative evidence that same-sex unions (especially those formalised) may be few or concealed, though perhaps more common amongst men. For example, the BASS line sexual health survey (Dodds et al. 2008) reported that same-sex attraction amongst African respondents was more common for men than women.

---

[3] A review of annual reports based on African men's seminar series in London that was organised by the African communities team within the Camden and Islington Community Health services, as part of health-promotion targeting.

Household Composition

However, census data on household composition (Table 2.4) provides information on different household types. There were around 88,000 one-person households where the household reference person (HRP) was Black African, which comprised a quarter (25.4 %) of all Black African households. However, only 7.9 % of these one-person households were persons aged 65 and above. 30.2 % of White households were one-person households with a much higher proportion (43.5 %) of persons aged 65 and older.

Amongst families with dependent children, where the HRP was Black African ($n = 185,319$), 70,515 (38.1 %) of these families were lone parent families. The proportions amongst Black Caribbean families (47.4 %) and Other Black (49.0 %) families were even higher. This compares with households with a White HRP ($n = 5,667,082$), where 1,398,919 (24.7 %) were lone parents.

These findings are broadly consistent with those of Platt (2009) using the LFS (October/December 2004–April/June 2008). Across all family types, where the head of the family unit was Black African, 44 % were single person family types, 9 % a couple with no dependent children, 25 % a couple with dependent children, and 22 % a lone parent. In this analysis, Black Africans had the third highest proportion of lone parent family type, after Mixed White and Black Caribbeans (29 %) and Black Caribbeans (28 %).

The census only enables household composition types like lone parent families to be distinguished for a limited number of Black African subgroups. In the 2011 England and Wales Census, lone parent families accounted for 18 % *of all families* but the proportion was highest for families with a Somali-born family reference person (FRP) (60 %), and also high for a Ghanaian-born FRP (40 %) (and Jamaican-born FRP (44 %)). Moreover, the highest proportions of lone parent families *with dependent children* were found for family reference persons born in Somalia (61 %), Other Central and Western Africa (56 %), and Ghana (44 %) (as well as Jamaica (55 %) and Other Caribbean (44 %)).

The reasons for the high proportion of lone parents amongst families with a Somali-born FRP may relate to the triggers and circumstances of their migration. Many Somali-born migrants arrived during the 1990s following the Somali civil war in 1991. Many women may have left Somalia without their partner during this period, possibly because of their loss in the civil war. This is reflected in the sex ratio of the Somali-born

Table 2.4   Household composition by ethnic group of household reference person (HRP), England and Wales, 2011

Household composition	All categories: ethnic group of HRP	White: total	Black African	Black Caribbean	Other Black
All categories: household composition	23,366,044	20,900,820	348,226	293,367	89,476
One-person household: total	7,067,261	6,457,444	88,369	111,690	32,006
Aged 65 and over	2,903,930	2,808,425	6,968	30,364	3,163
Other	4,163,331	3,649,019	81,401	81,326	28,843
One family only: total	14,448,646	13,032,088	197,721	152,690	45,461
All aged 65 and over	1,905,393	1,860,870	1,181	9,148	687
Married or same-sex civil partnership couple: total	7,757,255	6,886,394	91,155	51,375	15,297
No children	2,883,145	2,712,350	14,434	12,210	2,967
Dependent children	3,557,230	2,975,230	70,574	28,305	10,775
All children non-dependent	1,316,880	1,198,814	6,147	10,860	1,555
Cohabiting couple: total	2,298,234	2,162,037	22,167	20,974	6,244
No children	1,233,571	1,170,798	7,302	7,461	2,553
Dependent children	949,564	882,317	14,236	11,772	3,367
All children non-dependent	115,099	108,922	629	1,741	324
Lone parent: total	2,487,764	2,122,787	83,218	71,193	23,233
Dependent children	1,671,396	1,398,919	70,515	48,556	18,963
All children non-dependent	816,368	723,868	12,703	22,637	4,270
Other household types: total	1,850,137	1,411,288	62,136	28,987	12,009
With dependent children	612,625	410,616	29,994	13,912	5,625

(*continued*)

Table 2.4 (continued)

Household composition	All categories: ethnic group of HRP	White: total	Black African	Black Caribbean	Other Black
All full-time students	132,352	88,889	5,749	1,075	455
All aged 65 and over	66,167	63,381	154	753	88
Other	1,038,993	848,402	26,239	13,247	5,841

Source: 2011 Census, Table DC1201EW.
Note: The units are households

population, which, at 78 men per 100 women in 2011, was substantially lower than that of England and Wales (97 men per 100 women). Only 7.6 % of Somali-born lone parents were male, around half the proportion of all lone parents who were male. The other two countries of birth groups who also had high proportions of lone parents—the Jamaican-born and Ghanaian-born populations—also had low sex ratios at 81 and 93 men per 100 women, respectively.

Fragmented households and family break-up are widely reported amongst Somalis in Britain in other sources. In an analysis of the 2001 Census Controlled Access Microdata Sample (CAMS) data, the UPTAP project (Mitton and Aspinall 2010) found that the proportion of widows and widowers was especially high among Somalis (5.4 % of the over 16s[4]), as it was amongst Ugandans, South Africans, and Sierra Leoneans. A reported marital status of 'separated but legally married' is also high amongst Somalis (10.7 % of over 16s), Congolese (14.1 %), and Sierra Leoneans (11.3 %). Other data also indicate fragmentation of households. Twenty per cent of Somali couples are cohabiting and divorce is not noticeably lower amongst Somalis (4.9 % of over 16s) despite their Muslim culture. Fragmentation may also be due to absent family members. In a sample of 500 Zimbabweans living in the UK (Bloch 2008), nearly everyone (94 %) had close family in Zimbabwe: 15 % had a partner or spouse, 24 % a child or children, 70 % a parent or parents, and 50 % another close relative such as a sibling.

---

[4] According to 2001 Census CAMS data, 47.2 % of over 16s were single (never married) and 31.8 % married.

A number of researchers have indicated that there are a disproportionate number of single female heads of household in the Somali community (Demie et al. 2007; Rutter 2004). Rutter (2004, p. 4) suggested that 'between 20 and 70 % of Somali households are being headed by women'. This, again, 'may be as a result of men being killed in Somalia, families being split up as a result of working in the Gulf States and also divorce'. In their survey of Somalis in the London Borough of Hackney, Holman and Holman (2003) reported that more than 60 % of the 77 responding households were headed by single mothers. The research by Mitton and Aspinall (2010) also found a particularly high proportion of lone parents among Somali migrants: Using the 2001 CAMS, 35.3 % of Somalis over 16 were found to be female lone parents (just 2.6 % of over 16s were lone male parents). The likelihood is that unions have been split up in the process of fleeing the conflict in Somalia.

Household/Family Size

According to the 2011 Census data for England and Wales, average household size was 2.8 persons for Black Africans, 2.0 for Black Caribbeans, and 3.1 for Other Black (based on the proxy measure of ethnic group of household reference person and population count). Platt's (2009) analysis of the LFS shows that average family size for Black Africans was 2.4 persons, higher than for Black Caribbeans (2.1), Other Black (2.3), and White British (2.2). Only the South Asian groups had a larger average family size. Moreover, 24 % of Black African families had four or more people, a higher proportion than for Black Caribbeans (16 %), Other Black (21 %), and White British (16 %). Again, only the South Asian groups had a higher proportion. Karlsen and Nazroo (2008) found some differences in household size between Black African Christians and Muslims. Amongst Black African Christians, 18 % were one adult only, 12 % two adults only, 29 % a small family, 22 % a large family, and 19 % large adult households; African Muslims had fewer one adult only (15 %) and two adult (9 %) households, similar proportions of small family (27 %) and large family (23 %) households, and more large adult households (16 %).

However, there is evidence that average family or household size and a number of other size characteristics vary across more granular African subgroups, with Somalis being a notable outlier. The 2011 England and Wales Census showed that families including three or more dependent children accounted for 7.0 % of all families in England but families with a Somali-born FRP had the highest proportion (47 %). Conversely, a Somali-born FRP had the lowest proportion with no dependent children (15 %). Further, 93 % of stepfamilies with a Somali-born FRP included dependent children (and this also applied to Afghani-born FRPs) (ONS 2014a).

Several other sources provide similar findings. According to 2005/2006 LFS data (IPPR 2007), the average household size of Somali migrants was 3.8 persons, smaller than that for Nigerian migrants (4.0) but larger than for Ghanaian migrants (2.7). The average number of families in Somali migrant households was 1.2. The analysis of the LFS for Mitton and Aspinall's (2010) research found that around a quarter (24 %) of Somalis were in families with four or more dependent children. Congolese and Sudanese also had relatively large numbers of children, in contrast to migrants from Zimbabwe and Southern Africa who had the smallest families. In Hackney, 20 % of the households of respondents had six or more members, compared to just 2 % in Britain as a whole (Holman and Holman 2003).

Several factors may account for the large number of dependent children in Somali families. Those populations which have more recently arrived in Britain and which have a younger age structure—as is the case with the Somali-born population—are more likely to have higher numbers of dependent children in the family. In the 2011 England and Wales Census, the Somali-born population was younger, with 79 % aged under 45, compared with 58 % of the population as a whole. Moreover, more than half (57 %) of the Somali-born population in 2011 had arrived since 2001, with one in four having arrived between 2001 and 2003, following instability in the country. For these reasons, those born in Somalia are less likely to have *adult* children living in the family. The large number of dependent children may also be related to cultural differences in desired and actual family size.

Distinctive Black African Practices

While Census and survey data provide some measure of different marital statuses and household compositions, they tell us little about distinctive Black African practices which are not measured in surveys. A historical glance at African marriage in the continent shows that marriage and family life were dynamic institutions that were subject to changes brought on by colonialism and its repercussions such as rural–urban migration, Western education, and the commodification or monetisation of goods and services. Oheneba-Sakyi and Takyi (2006) write that the context for understanding African marriages and families is embedded in the fusion and resistance by Africans of foreign ideologies brought in through religions, in particular Christianity and Islam. Thus, rights of marriage in Africa include 'integration of traditional African and Western family modes' (Nzira 2011, p. 80). Most Black Africans value marriage. The marriage ceremony is conducted in the presence of a large extended family, marriage practice being 'an exchange of relations between families who can then establish and secure useful alliances. It is like two clans coming together through the institution of marriage and hopefully look after each other's interests' (Nzira 2011, p. 67).

The groom's family is expected to provide a so-called bride price to the bride's family, comprising stipulated resources such as the exchange of goods and/or money. The bride price or bride wealth varies according to the lineage system. Amongst the Southern Africa Zulus, the process is known as *Lobola*, amongst the Igbo tribe of West Africa *Ikpo Onu aka Nwayi*, in the East African state of Tanzania *Mahari*, and in the Shona culture *roora* (including *mbereko*, a blanket which acknowledges the mother carrying her daughter on her back, and *majasi*, for their wedding clothes worn at the religious wedding ceremony) (Mhende 2013). A wedding represents the loss of a daughter to a family and so a loss of labour and someone to tend to younger children within the family. Nzira (2011) notes that this is a 'standard practice although variations are emerging and critics of bride-price arrangements see it as an out of date practice as it interferes with the balance of power between couples' (p. 67). Bride price remains common not only in African homelands but also in the diaspora in Britain.

Strong views are now voiced amongst community members in both the UK and sub-Saharan Africa for and against the bride price. As an example of the former, Mhende (2013) argues that the bride price serves to protect women as it prevents marital dissolution and shows honour and high regard to the family of the bride (Mhende 2013). Obbo (1980) similarly considers the practice strengthens marriage and Nangoli (1986) concurs, seeing it as a way of showing respect and gratitude. However, critics of bride price argue that it affects the power dynamics in African families, creates tensions amongst practising Christians, and commodifies women, making them dependent on men for recognition and status. However, external influences like formal education, engagement in economic activity, and equality legislation may be diluting the practice.

Polygamy (polygyny), or having multiple wives, like bride price, is key to the dynamics of the descent system, but it is a characteristic of selected African countries rather than diaspora populations, though probably declining because of the increased cost of marriage and a more educated and economically independent population (Oheneba-Sakyi and Takyi 2006). Such customary unions still have saliency in West Africa (40–50 %), particularly in rural areas of Ghana, traditional Nigerian cultures, and in Senegal and Côte d'Ivoire, East Africa (20–30 %), and Southern Africa (10–15 %) (Hayase and Liaw 1997).

The practice of polygamy only intersects with the life of Black Africans in Britain when a husband who has more than one wife settles in the UK. A marriage celebrated in England and Wales between persons domiciled in this jurisdiction must be monogamous (Gaffney-Rhys 2011). However, a polygynous marriage celebrated outside England and Wales is not void if the parties were not domiciled in this jurisdiction at the time. Parties to a polygamous marriage are allowed to claim ancillary relief if the relationship breaks down, a measure designed to ensure that a vulnerable wife will be supported by her (former) husband. UK immigration policy is designed to prevent the formation of polygamous households in this country by restricting settlement to one wife only: The UK will recognise a second wife for immigration purposes but this does not mean that several wives can be admitted for settlement. Like bride price, formal education and economic independence are placing pressure on the practice.

With regard to the family and child rearing, some patterns and practices are considered more common in Africa (Nzira 2011). These include the diversity of family types; the extended family as the norm, including the sharing of child rearing amongst extended family members and kinship foster care (a role replicated in the diaspora by community and faith groups); the importance of remittances to extended family members; the expectation that children will show respect to their elders in culturally specific ways; and the importance of discipline. Also, roles within African households appear to be gender specific and co-resident men remain heads of households. Some of these practices were referred to in the Victoria Climbié enquiry, including private fostering arrangements and the timidity and submissiveness of the child. There has been some stereotyping and stigmatising of Black African child-rearing practices based on the publicity that resulted from the death of this child and police investigations into possible ritual assaults and killings, such as the 'Adam's torso' case (Hoskins 2012). As Nzira (2011) indicates, 'these publicized cases of child abuse

within the African community do not represent the reality of the experience of most African families'. Rather, that experience might encompass
shared experiences of discrimination and disadvantage while using social
care services; poverty; the difficulties of combining work, study, and family
life; the lived experience of African children in local authority care; changing family compositions, including interethnic unions and their offspring
with a racialised mixed race heritage (Ifekwunigwe 1999; Aspinall and
Song 2013); and blended families.

CHAPTER 3

Patterns of Migration

An act of immigration may be defined as crossing a national border and going through customs with the intention to stay. This act and the acquisition of immigrant status can have a varying impact on migrants. Jivraj (2013) has written:

> '[I]n public policy, and especially in politics, immigration is a label that can stick for much longer. If you were an immigrant at some point, then that can be taken as an indication you will need support and advice, such as English language classes, for a period of time. For some, immigrant status, as felt by the individual and wider society, is of no importance and lasts for a very short period. For others, the status can last for life, even when naturalised, or even longer through their offspring.'

However, it is clear that immigrant status has, to an extent, become a racialised term that has been used as a synonym for 'not belonging', 'requiring services to help integrate', and having 'other' status. Many attributes frequently applied to the 'born outside the UK' population—such as not speaking English well, not speaking English as their main language, being a foreign national, and having a foreign national identity—do not apply to all people born abroad (Jivraj 2013).

A variety of data sources provide several ways of counting the immigrant population. The decennial census asks: 'What is your country of birth?', enabling persons to be identified who were born outside the UK. Similarly,

© The Editor(s) (if applicable) and The Author(s) 2016   35
P.J. Aspinall, M.J. Chinouya, *The African Diaspora Population in Britain*, DOI 10.1057/978-1-137-45654-0_3

the 2011 England and Wales Census asked for the first time: 'If you were not born in the UK, when did you most recently arrive to live here?' The census question on 'One year ago, what was your usual address?' can be used to count people resident outside the UK a year before the census. The census question 'What passports do you hold?' (again, asked for the first time in the 2011 England and Wales Census) identifies persons who hold a foreign passport. All these definitions refer to persons who are part of the usual resident population. It excludes those who intend to stay in England and Wales for less than 12 months (captured by the England and Wales 2011 Census question: 'Including the time you have already spent here, how long do you intend to stay in the United Kingdom?'). The latter accords with the UN definition of a long-term international migrant, that is, 'A person who moves to a country other than that of his or her usual residence for a period of at least a year (12 months), so that the country of destination effectively becomes his or her new country of usual residence.' This definition is used in the Long-term International Migration estimates produced by the Office for National Statistics to monitor inflows and outflows of migrants to and from the UK. Citizenship is defined as the nationality of the passport which the traveller is carrying.

AGE OF ARRIVAL OF POPULATION BORN ABROAD

The 2011 Census asked respondents who were not born in the UK when they most recently arrived to live here (not counting short visits away from the UK). These data clearly do not measure how many people have *ever* arrived during past years as they exclude those who have died or who have emigrated. It only includes the time of arrival of those residents in England and Wales in the 2011 Census. Nevertheless, it enables statistics to be compiled for this population, including age of arrival in the UK. Around half the persons born abroad arrived in the UK when they were between the ages of 15 and 29 (Jivraj 2013).

Figure 3.1 shows that the age structure of the Black groups at the time of arrival was somewhat different, being skewed towards the younger age groups, especially the 0–15 age group. There was a lower proportion of 0–15- and 16–24-year-olds at the time of arrival amongst Black Africans compared with Black Caribbeans. However, significantly higher proportions of Black Africans were aged 25–34 and 35–49 than Black Caribbeans.

Fig. 3.1 Migrant Black groups in England and Wales in 2011, by age at time of arrival. *Source*: Census Table 2801EW ethnic group by age of arrival in the UK. ONS Crown copyright reserved (from Nomis on 22 May 2015)

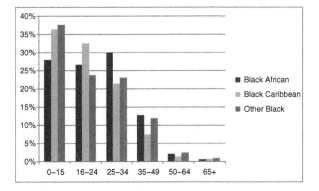

YEAR OF ARRIVAL OF BLACK AFRICANS BORN ABROAD

The census question on when the person most recently arrived to live in the UK also enables which year (or range of years) migrants from Africa arrived in the UK to be identified. However, routine data are only available by African region of birth—North Africa, Central and Western Africa, South and Eastern Africa, and Africa not otherwise specified—rather than by ethnic group. Counts for South and East Africa will contain some White and Indian migrants, so Central and Western Africa probably best represent the Black African group.[1]

Figure 3.2 shows that Africans from Central and Western Africa have arrived since before 1961 and in relatively modest numbers in the 1960s (1961–1970, 13,063) and 1970s (1971–1980, 16,266). However, these numbers increased substantially during the period 1981–1990 (49,764) and reached a peak in 1991–2000 (94,611). In the first decade of the twenty-first century, the numbers plateau—61,071 (2001–2003), 70,505 (2004–2006), and 61,575 (2007–2009)—but fall to 24,964 in the last 2 years. For South and Eastern Africans,[2] the numbers are higher in all periods (except 2010–2011), rise earlier from 1961 to 1970, and also reach

[1] The countries of birth for Central and Western Africa are Angola, Cameroon, Cape Verde, Congo, Democratic Republic of Congo, The Gambia, Ghana, Guinea, Guinea-Bissau, Ivory Coast, Liberia, Nigeria, Senegal, Sierra Leone, St Helena, Togo, and Other Central and Western Africa.

[2] The countries of birth for South and Eastern Africa are Botswana, Burundi, Eritrea, Ethiopia, Kenya, Madagascar, Malawi, Mauritius, Mozambique, Namibia, Rwanda, Seychelles, Somalia, South Africa, Swaziland, Tanzania, Uganda, Zambia, Zimbabwe, and Other South and Eastern Africa.

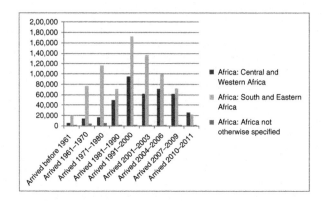

Fig. 3.2   Country of birth (Central and Western Africa, South and Eastern Africa, and Africa not otherwise specified) by year of arrival in the UK, England and Wales, 2011.

Source: Table LC2804EW: country of birth by year of arrival in the UK. ONS Crown copyright reserved (from Nomis on 22 May 2015)

their peak in 1991–2000. However, they fall more steeply from their peak than the Central and West African figures.

However, commissioned table data for the 2011 England and Wales Census allow a much more exact measure for the Black African population. This enables Black Africans to be identified by individual country of birth for four periods of arrival (pre-1981, 1981–2000, 2001–2006, and 2007–2011). The statistics in Fig. 3.2 are broadly consistent with the more detailed data on a broader range of dates for migrant Black Africans living in England and Wales in 2011 (so relating to country of birth embedded in ethnic groups rather than country of birth alone as in Fig. 3.2). A total of 30,559 migrants arrived before 1981 (4.6 %); 232,614 during 1981–2000 (34.9 %); 263,168 during 2001–2006 (39.5 %); and 140,011 during 2007–2011 (21.0 %).

However, the composition of these migrant flows changed dramatically by country of birth over these four periods. Migrants arriving before 1981 were dominated by Black Africans born in Ghana and Nigeria (Fig. 3.3).

The composition of Black African migrants arriving between 1981 and 2001 changes dramatically (Fig. 3.4). While Black African migrants born in Ghana and Nigeria still dominate the composition, the contribution of Ghanaian migrants falls from 30.5 to 14.5 % and Nigerian migrants from 33.9 to 24.4 %, although the numbers of both increase

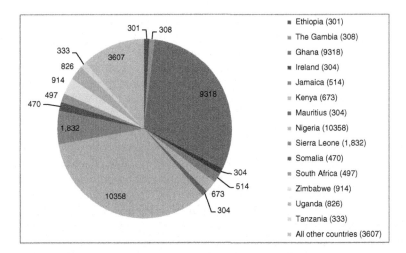

Fig. 3.3   Black African migrants arrived before 1981: countries of birth.
Source: 2011 Census commissioned table CT0263—Country of birth by year of arrival by ethnic group.
All countries contributing 1 %+ of migrants are shown

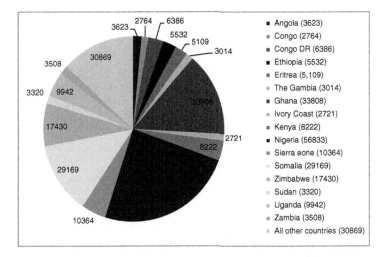

Fig. 3.4   Black African migrants arrived 1981–2000: countries of birth.
Source: 2011 Census commissioned table CT0263—Country of birth by year of arrival by ethnic group.
All countries contributing 1 %+ of migrants are shown

substantially. The major change is in Somali migrants who increase their share from 6.0 to 12.5 %. Also, many new countries make their appearance, including Angola, Congo, Congo DR, and Eritrea which were not former British colonies, unlike Sudan. Zimbabwe increases its share from 3.0 to 7.5 % (masking an almost 20-fold increase in numbers). The increased numbers from the Netherlands (from 11 to 998) and Sweden (2–265)—in contrast to the small numbers from Norway (60), Finland (31), and Denmark (66)—probably reflect the migration of second-generation Somalis to England and Wales from these countries.

The period of arrival 2001–2006 also saw notable changes (Fig. 3.5). Ghana and Nigeria continued to contribute falling percentages of Black African migrants. Ghana's contribution fell from 14.5 to 10.4 % and Nigeria's from 24.4 to 20.3 % (and numbers also fell). However, the major change was in the increase of Black African migrants from Zimbabwe, up from 7.5 to 16.5 % (and with a commensurate increase in numbers from 17,430 to 43,518). Numbers increase more modestly for the DR Congo and Zambia. Black African Somali migrants maintained their proportion and numbers. There is a substantially increased secondary migration of

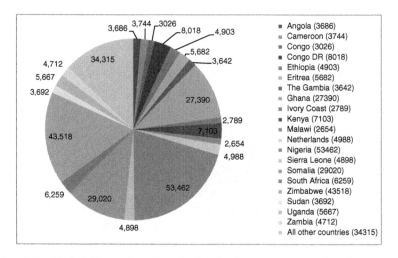

Fig. 3.5 Black African migrants arrived 2001–2006: countries of birth.
Source: 2011 Census commissioned table CT0263—Country of birth by year of arrival by ethnic group. All countries contributing 1 %+ of migrants are shown

Black Africans born in the Netherlands, up from 998 to 4,988, and a less steep rise in Black African migration from Sweden, from 265 to 1,475 (which sources suggest in both cases comprise Somalis). Some new countries enter the 1 %+ threshold: Cameroon, Malawi, and South Africa. In other countries, numbers and proportions fall, including in particular Sierra Leone and Uganda.

In the final, most recent period (2007–2011), the number of Black African migrants fell from 263,168 to 140,001 (albeit for a slightly shorter period) (Fig. 3.6). Migrants from Nigeria increased their share from a fifth to over a third (34.3 %). However, migrants from Ghana fell from 10.4 to 8.9 %. The proportion contributed by Somalia fell substantially from 11.0 to 6.5 % (from 29,020 to 9,124). There was also a dramatic fall in Black African migrants from Zimbabwe, from 16.5 to 6.4 % (from 43,518 to 9,049). Some new countries come into the 1 %+ threshold, including France, Portugal, Tanzania, and the USA. Indeed, secondary migration from EU countries continues to be important, though the contribution of the Netherlands falls from 1.9 to 1.2 % and Sweden from 1,475 to 668 (<1 %).

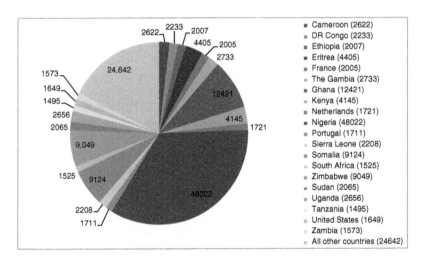

Fig. 3.6   Black African migrants arrived 2007–2011: countries of birth.
Source: 2011 Census commissioned table CT0263—Country of birth by year of arrival by ethnic group. All countries contributing 1 %+ of migrants are shown

ONWARD MIGRATION

As the above census data on period of arrival for Black Africans by country of birth revealed, an important recent characteristic (in the period 2001–2011) has been the onward migration of Black Africans from EU countries, especially the Netherlands, France, Portugal, Germany, Poland, Sweden, Italy, and Denmark. The migration of Somali refugees from EU countries, especially the Netherlands, Sweden, and Denmark, to the UK has formed an important part of this onward migration. A variety of evidence has been assembled by Lindley and Van Hear (2007)[3] on Somalis' countries of departure. With respect to those leaving Denmark, estimates range from 1,000 (2001–2005) to 3,000–4,000 (2002–2004). Estimates of Somalis leaving the Netherlands for the UK also cover a wide range: 10,000, one-third of all Dutch Somalis (1998–2003) (Van Liempt 2007, citing Van den Reek and Hussein 2004); 10,000–20,000 by government representatives (Moret and Van Eck 2005); and 20,000 (2000–2004), including a half of Tilburg's 3,000 Somalis (Evans-Pritchard 2004).

There is also a small evidence base on the arrival of Somali refugees from EU countries in the UK. Momatrade (2004) estimated that in the period 1998–2004, 18,000–22,000 Somalis had moved to the UK from the Netherlands and Scandinavia. Leicester seems to have been one of the main destinations. A report commissioned by Leicester City Council from the Improvement and Development Agency (IDA) (2003, p. 17) on community cohesion in the city stated that 'within the last few years Leicester has experienced a sudden arrival of Somali migrants from EU countries—in particular The Netherlands. Variously, this new community is estimated at between 8,000 and 10,000 people.' It also mentioned that the recent arrival of Somali families from the EU had added 'over 900 children—2 % to the school population' (IDA 2003, p. 29). This figure is consistent with that given by one of the city's MPs in the House of Commons (2002): 'Some 900 Dutch Somali children of school age have arrived in Leicester over the past 18 months, with 488 of them—54 % of the total—arriving since September 2001.' The city council's own estimate is of some 6,000–10,000 Dutch Somalis arriving in Leicester or 2 % of the city's population (LCC and Leicester Partnership 2007). A figure of an estimated 10,000 arrivals of Somali Dutch citizens during 2001–2004 was also given by Leicester City Council to the UK Parliament's Select

---

[3] See their Appendix 1: Estimates of Somali Europeans' onward migration, p. 22.

Committee on Home Affairs. Press sources (cited by Lindley and Van Hear 2007) indicate that Birmingham was also a destination, with over 200 Somali Dutch families arriving in 9 months in 2001–2002.

Van den Reek and Hussein (2004) carried out their research on Dutch Somalis in England in these two cities—Birmingham and Leicester—and found that hardly any of the adults had plans to move back to the Netherlands, although the young people wanted to. Precipitant factors for the move were dwindling tolerance, limitation of freedom with respect to religion and moral standards, and limited possibilities for developing one's own (Islamic) identity. They also reported that the Dutch regulated care system was in conflict with the national character of the Somalis.

A variety of other data point to the importance of onward Somali migration to the UK from EU countries. A survey of the identities of young Somalis in Sheffield (Sporton et al. 2006; Valentine et al. 2009) found that around a quarter (27.6 %) of respondents came to the UK directly from Somalia or Somaliland, a third (33.1 %) migrated to the UK via another European country, and 6.2 % arrived in the UK via, or from, a Middle Eastern country. Their data on country of birth of these young Somalis showed that, whilst most were born in Somalia, the UK had the largest share of those born in Europe, followed by the Netherlands and Scandinavia. A small proportion of respondents was born in the Middle East. The investigators identified three different cohorts of arrivals. Those who had lived in Sheffield for longer than 8 years were most likely to have been born in East Africa (Ethiopia, Djibouti, and Kenya) or the Middle East, through which countries asylum seeking was staged. Of those young Somalis who had lived in Sheffield between 4 and 7 years, the majority were born in the Netherlands or Scandinavia. Many of the young Somalis were granted refugee status in these European countries, subsequently being involved in secondary migration to Sheffield. Sporton et al. (2006) attribute such movement to family reunion in Sheffield and an increase in negative feelings towards asylum seekers in these European countries. The most recent wave of arrivals of young Somalis in Sheffield have mainly come directly from Somalia/Somaliland, where they were born, indicating an increase in asylum seeking.

School data also provide evidence of significant migrant flows of Somalis from European countries. An OFSTED (2003) publication states that a 'primary school, located near the centre of a Midlands city, has 491 pupils on roll, with 34 % eligible for free school meals and just over three-quarters speaking English as an additional language (EAL)'. At the time of the Her Majesty's Inspectors (HMI) visit, the families with pupils at the school represented 32 languages. There were also 24 pupils on roll who were from asylum-seeker families and, in addition, 61 children of EU habitual residents, predominantly Somali speakers from the Netherlands or Sweden. According to the *Daily Telegraph*,[4] 'OFSTED was unable to identify the schools involved, though they are thought to be in the Leicester area, where many Somalis from Holland have settled. Since the 2001 Census, more than 500 Dutch Somali asylum-seeker pupils have joined the town's school register.' Finally, 902 pupils of 'Black African' or 'Mixed: White and Black African' ethnicity in the 2008 School Census were recorded as having Dutch as their first language: 236 (26.2 %) of these were coded as 'Black Somali' and other Somalis may have been concealed in aggregate categories like 'Black African'.

MAIN REASONS FOR MIGRATION

The reasons underlying these Black African migration flows are complex and may include economic migration (work permit holders, au pairs, seasonal agricultural workers, and others), forced migration (as asylum seekers/refugees), family reunion, and migration for education (student visa holders). Moreover, though largely unrecorded in census statistics, there are likely to be significant numbers of undocumented Black Africans in the country illegally and young persons being trafficked.

Asylum Seekers

Asylum seekers have contributed significantly to these migration flows. Overall, around 315,000 people from these 20 sub-Saharan countries sought asylum in the UK over the last 25 years (1989–2014), the vast majority of whom are likely to have been Black Africans. The largest numbers of asylum seekers were nationals of Somalia (67,230), Nigeria (35,146), Zimbabwe (33,967), Demographic Republic of the Congo (27,993), and Eritrea (22,375). Figure 3.7 shows flows of asylum seekers to the UK from the 20 sub-Saharan African countries over the period 1989–2014.

The figures relate to asylum applications from main applicants (excluding dependants) by nationality. The countries in Home Office tabulations are grouped into African regions based on the ONS National Statistics

---

[4] Telegraph 22 October 2003. 'School has taken 300 pupils from families granted asylum in EU.'

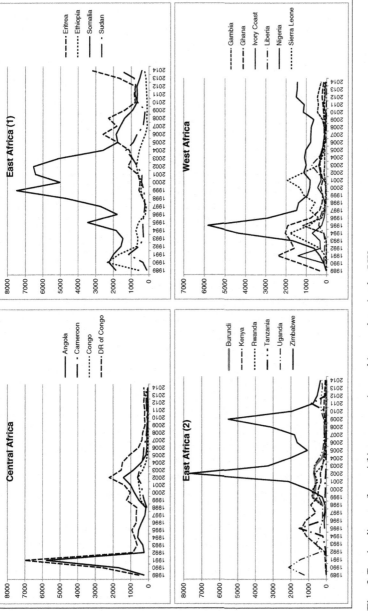

Fig. 3.7 Applicants from African countries seeking asylum in the UK.
Note: East Africa (one)—includes Sudan from North Africa group

Country Classification (Groupings and Correspondences), with all countries in sub-Saharan Africa being included.[5] The data may be interpreted as expressed demand amongst forced international migrants for refuge or protection, though only a proportion of applicants are successful. The graphs clearly show that the number of applications by specific country nationals changes over time and often reflects wars and civil disturbances in the countries of origin.

In Central Africa, asylum-seeker flows from the Democratic Republic of Congo and Angola have approximately tracked each other since 1989, both peaking in 1991 (7,010 and 5,780, respectively) but falling away subsequently. There was a much smaller secondary peak in 2002 with numbers falling substantially since 2005 and 2006. The trend in flows from Angola stem from the civil war which did not come to an end till 2002, with human rights abuses, poverty, and reliance on food aid being exacerbating factors. The Democratic Republic of Congo's civil wars (1996 to present) have been accompanied by marauding militias, resulting in death, disease, rape, malnutrition, and civilian displacement.

In East Africa, Somalia has contributed large numbers of asylum seekers throughout the 25 years, rising to a peak of 7,495 in 1999 and a secondary peak of 6,540 in 2002. However, numbers have fallen substantially since 2009. Somalia was without formal governance for two decades (until 2012), during which there was lawlessness and clan warfare, a situation exacerbated by drought and poverty. Eritrea has become one of the main contributing countries for asylum seekers, numbers peaking at 3,275 in 2014. These high levels of applicants from the late 1990s and especially from 2012 reflect Eritrea's civil wars with Yemen and Ethiopia, its poor human rights record, including alleged extrajudicial executions, torture, and an open-ended national service programme, and high levels of poverty, including soaring food prices, poor job prospects, and lack of basic services. Eritreans were the second largest group of fleeing nationals (22 %) entering Italy by boat during the first 10 months of 2014. Over 237,000 Eritreans having applied for asylum in 38 European countries over this period compared to about 13,000 in the same period in 2013. Numbers of asylum seekers from Sudan have also attained significance, also peaking in 2014 with 1,621 applicants. For much of its recent history, Sudan has suffered ethnic strife, two civil wars, and the war in the Darfur region. The country also suffers from poor human rights with respect to

---

[5] For reasons unknown, the Home Office locates Algeria in this grouping. This country was excluded.

ethnic cleansing and slavery. However, the number of asylum seekers from Ethiopia has gradually fallen from a peak of 2,340 in 1990 to 200 or fewer annually during the period 2006–2013.

The rise in the number of asylum seekers from Zimbabwe has been dramatic, with a surge from under 150 annually before 1999 to the two peaks of 7,655 in 2002 and 5,540 in 2009, since when there has been a marked falling-off in numbers. Post-independence Zimbabwe has experienced numerous problems, including a deep economic crisis (related to the seizure of White-owned commercial farms), endemic poverty and unemployment, a decline in living standards, food shortages, poor public health, the 2005 slum demolition drive, the policy of indigenisation, and a precarious humanitarian situation, all contributing to population outflow. Most of the other East African countries in this subgroup have seen numbers of asylum seekers plateau since 2005.

The main West African country contributing asylum seekers is Nigeria, with numbers peaking at 5,825 in 1995, but remaining high subsequently and with an increase since 2010. Ghana experienced a peak in numbers seeking asylum in 1991 (2,405) and 1994 (2,035) but with a marked fall-off over the last decade. Sierra Leone has experienced peaks in asylum-seeker outflows in 1994 (1,810) and 2001 (1,940) but with a subsequent fall-off. These high proportions in the 1990s and early 2000 reflect the Sierra Leone Civil War of 1991–2002.

Dispersal of Asylum Seekers

The government's programme of dispersing asylum seekers across the UK has had a number of consequences, including where asylum applicants live in the UK. Statistics on the location of asylum seekers in the UK are linked to available information on the support that the asylum seeker receives, the location of those asylum seekers not in receipt of support being unknown. For those in receipt of support, the government publishes statistics broken down by government office region, local authority, and parliamentary constituency, with these breakdowns being available from December 2002. At September 2009, for example, 24,000 asylum seekers were supported in dispersed accommodation across the UK (Aspinall and Watters 2010). The government office regions with the largest number were in the North-West (6,460), followed by Yorkshire and the Humber (3,795), and West Midlands (3,655). Scotland had 2,650, Wales 1,695, and Northern Ireland 260 asylum seekers. Four cities had a thousand or more asylum seekers in dispersed accommodation: Glasgow (2,650),

Birmingham (1,370), Liverpool (1,270), and Manchester (1,000). This dispersal process has undoubtedly led to a presence of Black Africans in parts of the UK where they had only a limited presence before the 2000s, although the lack of data by ethnic groups precludes estimation.

The dispersal programme has had a number of consequences for the public services. When asylum seekers and refugees were substantially concentrated in London and the South-East, a number of specialist services were developed in this area, including those to treat the victims of torture. Dispersal has had the effect of distributing incoming asylum seekers across the UK to give a much more even spatial pattern but with the consequence that for some these specialist services were no longer readily accessible. The Medical Foundation for Care of Victims of Torture has opened offices outside London. However, some regions have reported low provision of specialist expertise around unaccompanied asylum-seeking children.

Outcomes

Only a minority of asylum-seeker applications are accepted. For example, between 1995 and 2008, the proportion of initial decisions that recognised asylum applicants as refugees and granted as asylum varied between 3 and 19 %, exceeding the latter in only 1 year (Aspinall and Watters 2010, citing Home Office 2009). Moreover, across these 14 years, the proportion of initial decisions that did not recognise asylum applicants as refugees but were given leave to remain varied from 9 to 24 %. Those refused asylum during the period 1995–2008 varied from 52 to 88 %. The most common countries of origin of those granted asylum in 2008 were Eritrea (30 %), Zimbabwe (14 %), and Somalia (13 %). At the end of 2008, there were 10,600 cases awaiting an initial decision.

In the period 2009–2013, total asylum applications varied from 17,916 (2010) to 24,487 (2009). Total initial decisions varied from 16,774 (2012) to 24,287 (2009). Annual grants of asylum varied from 5,195 to 6,742, that is, between 26 and 37 % of initial decisions. Refused applications exceeded 10,000 in every year, refusals varying from 63 to 74 % of initial decisions.

MIGRATION FOR STUDY

Formal study (respondents who arrived in the UK for study) was the main reason for migration given by 14.2 % (171,000 ± 18,000) of the sub-Saharan Africa-born population in the UK in 2014. Students have always formed part of the Black African population in Britain since their arrival in the late nineteenth century (Chap. 1). From the 1960s young Black Africans, especially from West Africa, began to arrive in Britain in large numbers to study for academic and other qualifications. The Black African student population tended to be a transient one, as those who gained higher qualifications found good employment opportunities in Africa. However, many of the Black Africans enumerated in the Census and surveys in the early 1990s were 'students who stayed' (Daley 1996). Li (n.d.) has suggested that the 'amazing educational achievements' of Black African men and women in 1991 and especially 2001 reflect the importance of parental cultural capital, as their parents were very highly educated as students themselves who had remained in Britain.

The position since the early 1990s has changed. Study is no longer an effective route to settlement in the UK. Over three-quarters of migrants issued a study visa in 2004 no longer had valid leave to remain 5 years later.[6] The proportion has increased in each cohort from 2005 onwards (to 84 % of those issued a study visa in 2008). Conversely, only very small proportions were granted settlement. For people issued a study visa in 2004, only 3 % had gained settlement 5 years later and of those arriving in 2008 only 1 % had been granted settlement. Applicants (including dependants) with a sub-Saharan nationality numbered 17,477 in the 2004 cohort, 9.5 % of the total. At year 5, just 717 main applicants (4.1 %) had been granted settlement. Of the 2008 cohort, 16,335 (7.7 %) were of a sub-Saharan African nationality. At 5 years, only 618 applicants (3.8 %) had been granted settlement. Nigerians accounted for over a third of the applicants in 2004, rising to over a half in 2006.

In the 2011 Census, *all* full-time students[7] comprised 73 % of the Black African population aged 16–24. This was the third highest proportion across ethnic groups, after Chinese (87 %) and Arabs (76 %), and above the Black Caribbean (55 %) and Other Black (63 %) proportions. By contrast, only 44 % of White British young people were full-time students (the second lowest after Gypsies and Irish Travellers [30 %]).

Amongst the wider Black African population, aged 16–74 (684,636), there were 161,560 (23.6 %) full-time students. The proportion for those born in the UK (36.9 %, 38,256/103,557) was substantially higher than those born outside the UK (21.2 %, 123,304/581,079). Economically

[6] The cohort analyses for migration for study, work, and family migration are based on: Home Office. *Migrant journey: fifth report.* London: Home Office, 18 February 2015, and online data tables at https://www.gov.uk/government/statistics/migrant-journey-fifth-report-data-tables
[7] Students here are defined as full-time students who were economically active or inactive and part-time students who were economically inactive.

inactive full-time students (92,783) outnumbered economically active full-time students (68,777), and this was also the case for both those born in the UK (25,617 vs 12,639) and outside the UK (67,166 vs 56,138). Other measures of the size of the student population are revealed by the Higher Education Statistics Authority (HESA) figures. The ethnic group of UK-domiciled students is aggregated to the 'Black' group. The 'domicile' field in the data collection is the country code of the student's permanent or home address prior to entry to the programme of study. Data for this field, too, are subject to only limited release in routine statistics. In 2012/2013, there were 425,265 non-UK domicile students studying at UK higher education (HE) providers.[8] For non-UK students at UK HE providers in 2012/2013, Nigeria was the third ranking country (out of the top ranked 20) of domicile by student numbers with 17,395 students. There were no other African countries in the top 20. Nigeria was the third largest non-EU source country (after China and the USA) contributing students ($n=2,000$) to HE institutions in Scotland in 2012/2013 (Tindal et al. 2014).

MIGRATION FOR WORK

Work related (respondents who arrived in the UK for employment reasons) was the main reason for migration given by 15.0 % ($180,000 \pm 19,000$) of the sub-Saharan Africa-born population in the UK in 2014. There are specific visa arrangements for two types of workers. There is a potential path to settlement for people issued with a skilled worker's visa. For people issued with such a visa in 2004, around a third (30 %) had gained settlement 5 years later, and a further 15 % still had valid leave to remain in the UK. This had fallen to 20 % in the 2008 cohort. The proportions were similar for non-European Economic Area (EEA) skilled workers. South Africans ($n=4,448$) were amongst the top five nationalities in the 2008 cohort issued skilled worker visas. Indeed, in this cohort South African nationals considerably outnumbered Nigerian nationals ($n=1,236$) by a factor of 3.6. While 36.7 % of South Africans were granted settlement 5 years later, the proportion was 34.3 % for Nigerian nationals.

By comparison, temporary work visas do not generally lead to settlement. Of those issued with temporary work visas in the 2008 cohort,

---

[8] See International Students. Non-UK domicile students studying in the UK. 14 November 2014. Source: HESA student record 2012/2013. Accessed at: https://www.hesa.ac.uk/blog/3343-blog-post-0004

5 years later only 4 % had valid leave to remain in the UK and 2 % had been granted settlement. The majority of migrants who entered the UK in this route appeared to stay for a relatively short period of time (up to 2 years). In the 2008 cohort, South African nationals ($n=8,003$) were amongst the top five nationalities issued temporary work visas, just 5 % of whom were granted immigration status 5 years later. This total outnumbered Nigerian nationals ($n=709$) by a factor of 11.3, with a lower proportion of Nigerians being granted settlement (2.5 %).

These findings are broadly consistent with other data. The England and Wales 2011 Census shows that the South African country of birth group had the second highest level of employment (78 %). With respect to National Insurance number (NINo) registrations,[9] for non-EU citizens, the number of registrations in the year ending March 2015 was 193,000, Nigerian (12,000) along with Indian (35,000), Pakistani (14,000), Chinese (13,000), and Australian (12,000) forming the top five non-EU nationalities for NINo registrations.

FAMILY MIGRATION

For people issued a family visa in 2004, over half (63 %) had gained settlement 5 years later. This proportion increased for those in later cohorts, with over three-quarters (77 %) of those issued a family visa in 2008 granted settlement 5 years later. Over half of these had gained settlement after just 2 years. In the 2008 cohort, Somali nationals were amongst the top five nationalities for visas issued through the family route (the others being Pakistani, Indian, Bangladeshi, and American nationals). The proportion who had settled within 5 years differed by nationality. Somali nationals had the lowest proportion who were settled after 5 years (43 %), compared with 93 % of Bangladeshi nationals, 88 % of Pakistani nationals, and 87 % of Indian nationals. Somalis were different in another important respect. Only 2 % of all nationals were dependants but 19 % in the case of Somali nationals.

---

[9] National Insurance numbers are issued to non-UK nationals immigrating for work. The number of NINos will include people who are coming to the UK for short periods or temporary purposes, as well as long-term migrants. The figures are based on recorded registration date on the national insurance recording and pay as you earn system (NPS), that is, after the NINo application process has been completed. This may be a number of weeks or months (and in some cases years) after arriving in the UK.

Dependants joining or accompanying include those respondents who arrived in the UK as a spouse/dependent of a UK citizen or as a spouse/dependent of someone coming to the UK. Accompany/join was the main reason for migration given by 39.9 % (480,000 ± 31,000) of the sub-Saharan Africa-born population in the UK in 2014.[10] For people issued a dependants joining or accompanying visa in 2004, more than a third (35 %) had gained settlement in the UK 5 years later, and a further 15 % still had valid leave to remain. In the 2008 cohort, 46% had been granted settlement 5 years later. In the 2008 cohort Nigerians were amongst the top five nationalities issued dependants joining or accompanying visas. There were 2,265 Nigerian nationals in the 2008 cohort, 51 % of whom had been granted settlement 5 years later (5 percentage points above all migrants).

UNDOCUMENTED/ILLEGAL MIGRANTS AND TRAFFICKED POPULATIONS

It has been estimated that there are around 800,000 undocumented migrants living in the UK, 500,000 in London, based on research published by the London School of Economics (Woodbridge 2005). There are no robust data on the ethnic composition of this group, as they are not registered in routine data sets. It is therefore not possible to estimate the prevalence of Black Africans amongst these migrants. People staying in the country when their visas have expired or remaining after their asylum application has been rejected could account for a proportion of them. Others may have entered the country illegally without going through checks at the UK borders. Some studies have been undertaken on this group by the Paul Hamlyn Foundation with City University and at COMPAS (Centre of Migration Policy and Society).

These problems of capture also apply to human trafficking, that is, 'the recruitment, transportation, transfer, harbouring or receipt of persons, by means of the threat or use of force or other forms of coercion, or abduction, of fraud, of deception, of the abuse of power or of a position of vulnerability or of the giving or receiving of payments of benefits to achieve the consent of a person having control over another person, for

---

[10] A fourth main reason for migration amongst the sub-Saharan Africa-born population in the UK in 2014 was 'Other'. This includes those respondents who arrived in the UK to either get married/form a civil partnership, to seek asylum, as a visitor, or for other stated reasons. This category comprised 30.9 % of main reasons for migration (371,000 ± 27,000).

the purposes of exploitation' (UN protocol). In 2009, the UK established the National Report Mechanism (NRM) which is a system of identifying individuals who are potentially victims of human trafficking. This enables the victims 'to be offered support and protection which they are entitled to under the Council of Europe on Actions against trafficking in human beings'. Between January and March 2015, 731 individuals were referred to the NRM as potential victims of human trafficking. Nigeria was named as one of the common countries of origin of the people referred to the NMR and also the country of origin for some of the victims of sexual exploitation. The report by SOCA (2013) also states that Nigeria was the most common country of origin for those who were in domestic servitude.

According to the CEOP (2011) report, in total, 202 children were identified as trafficked into the UK during January–September 2011. Sixty-seven children from African countries were trafficked into the UK over this period, including 29 victims from Nigeria, mostly girls, trafficked for the purposes of sexual exploitation. Other victims from Africa came from Angola (1), Botswana (1), Burundi (1), Congo (8), Eritrea (3), Ethiopia (2), Gambia (2), Ghana (6), Guinea (6), Kenya (1), Mauritius (1), Morocco (2), Seychelles (1), Somalia (2), and Uganda (1). Victims from Africa were mostly female (48 female, 19 male). Most victims were aged 14–16 but some African victims falling into the younger age groups (8–10 and 11–13). Nigerian victims often report meeting a Westernised person who promised them a better life in Britain, through education and employment and facilities to travel. Overall, with respect to exploitation type, 68.2 % of experiences of domestic servitude were from African countries, 21.7 % of benefit fraud, and 56.8 % of cases of sexual exploitation. According to SOCA (2013), almost a quarter (24 %) of potential victims of trafficking were children and that, for trafficked children in 2012, Nigeria was the second largest country of origin of the children trafficked.

WHAT HAPPENS WHEN INTERNATIONAL BLACK AFRICAN MIGRANTS SETTLE OR REMAIN

This section looks at some of the consequences when international Black African migrants settle or remain in the country as, for example, in the case of visa overstayers or failed asylum seekers. Many encounter significant language difficulties and substantial poverty, together with financial and other problems related to living in deprived areas and in some cases in dislocated, transnational families. The focus is on adverse consequences, such as homelessness and destitution. Other outcomes, such as entering education and the labour market, are discussed in Chap. 6.

Homelessness

In 2009, Broadway and NatCen published a report on how the rough sleeping population in London had changed over the 8-year observation period 2000/2001–2007/2008, analysing information from the CHAIN database to establish trends in the number of rough sleepers and the profile of first-time rough sleepers (Cebulla et al. 2009). Over the period, an increasing proportion of people of Black British ethnicity (mainly non-British nationals, including a high number of refugees from African countries) had been reported. In 2004–2005, people of Eritrean nationality comprised 1.0 % of the total of first year recorded sleeping rough, rising to 3.1 % in 2005–2006, 5.0 % in 2006–2007, and 10.1 % in 2007–2008.

In-depth interviews were conducted with nine Eritrean rough sleepers. Nearly all had become homeless after their asylum claim had been accepted and they were asked to leave their asylum support accommodation to which they had been dispersed initially, across the UK. The majority moved to London to escape loneliness and racism in the dispersal areas, to join relatives in London, to be near Eritrean communities and Eritrean Pentecostal churches in London, and to find work. Eritrean rough sleepers reported depression, feelings of suicide, physical health and alcohol problems, and experiences of crime and harassment. Many did not have the support needs that would provide access to short-term hostel accommodation, did not have the money to enter the private rental market, and reported a sense of extreme helplessness.

The most recent data for rough sleeping shows that numbers have remained significant for some African national groups over the years 2012/2013 to 2014/2015 (Table 3.1). Eritreans were the largest group in 2012/2013 and 2013/2014. In 2014/2015, Somalians were the largest group. However, other sub-Saharan communities are represented, including Nigerians, Sudanese, Ghanaians, Ethiopians, and South Africans. Black Africans comprised 7 % of people seen rough sleeping in 2014–2015, larger than the Black Caribbean (4 %) and Other Black (2 %) groups.

Immigration statuses amongst the 'Rest of the World' (i.e. non-UK and Europe) nationality group ($n=781$) were dominated by indefinite leave to

Table 3.1 People seen rough sleeping in the year: nationality and ethnic group, Greater London: 2012/2013–2014/2015

Nationality	2012/2013		2013/2014		2014/2015	
	No.	%	No.	%	No.	%
Somalia	54	0.9	66	1.0	66	0.9
Eritrea	59	0.9	72	1.1	62	0.8
Nigeria	40	0.6	53	0.8	41	0.6
Sudan	24	0.4	11	0.2	31	0.4
Algeria	21	0.3	31	0.5	26	0.4
Ghana	13	0.2	11	0.2	18	0.2
Ethiopia	14	0.2	20	0.3	15	0.2
South Africa	13	0.2	8	0.1	15	0.2
Other African countries	132	2.1	141	2.2	119	1.6
Africa subtotal	370	5.9	413	6.5	393	5.3
Ethnic group						
Black African						7.0

Source: CHAIN Annual Report, Greater London, 2012/2013–2014/2015

remain (ILR) (279), followed by overstayer (59), limited leave to remain (56), refugee (36), illegal entrant (32), asylum seeker (25), failed asylum seeker (19), and student visa (11). Lukes and Perry (2014) have estimated that, amongst new rough sleepers from outside the EU recorded by CHAIN during the first 9 months of 2013, about 40 % of the 487 cases had insecure immigration status.

Destitution

The Asylum Support Partnership's 'destitution tally' revealed high proportions of visits by sub-Saharan African nationals (Smart 2009). Of a total of 1,972 visits by destitute people, Eritreans accounted for 176 visits (the third highest total), and others came from Zimbabwe (162), Sudan (98), Democratic Republic of Congo (93), Somalia (68), Ivory Coast (26), Angola (25), Nigeria (23), Ethiopia (21), Congo-Brazzaville (20), Kenya (5), and a further eight sub-Saharan African countries each with four or less. If the measure is taken of all countries of origin cited in visits by refused asylum seekers destitute for over 6 months, then a total of 731 visits were made. Again, sub-Saharan African countries were substantially represented: Democratic Republic of Congo (60), ranked third, Sudan (48),

Eritrea (38), Zimbabwe (27), Congo-Brazzaville (19), Somalia (16), Angola (15), Ethiopia (11), and seven other sub-Saharan African countries with three or less each.

Similar findings are found in other destitution audits. Brown's (2008) report on Leeds was carried out by five agencies, each destitute client attending the agency being recorded in the city over 4 weeks in April–May 2008. A total of 331 individuals were identified as destitute, including 51 dependent children. Twenty-one per cent of the destitute people came from Zimbabwe, 12 % from Eritrea, and 8 % from the Democratic Republic of the Congo. Compared with a 2006 survey in the city (Lewis 2007), the number of destitute Zimbabweans had increased substantially from 4 (2006 survey) to 56 (2008 survey). The Democratic Republic of Congo also showed a significant increase (from 8 in 2006 to over 20 in 2008). Eritreans and Sudanese, ranking first and second country of origin in 2006, slightly increased their numbers. The survey showed that people were destitute at all stages of the asylum-seeking process, 75 % being refused asylum seekers, 19 % asylum seekers, and 4 % refugees.

Factors contributing to severe poverty and destitution may include poor English language skills, the inability to work or difficulties in securing employment, and barriers to the housing market. Findings from the *Survey of New Refugees in the United Kingdom* provide some evidence (Cebulla et al. 2010). Amongst the countries of origin of new refugees, 17 % were Eritreans, 16 % Somalis, 7 % Zimbabweans, and 7 % 'Other Africa', out of a total of 5,600 new refugees who participated in the first sweep (Eritrea and Somalia accounting for one-third of all new refugees in this survey). Differences in refugees' English language skills at the time of the asylum decision by country of origin were most notable. Almost 90 % of refugees from Zimbabwe had a high level of self-reported English language skills, compared with 54 % of 'Other Africa', 37 % of Ethiopians, 22 % of Democratic Republic of Congo/Congo, 20 % of Eritrean, 12 % of Sudan, and 8 % of Somali refugees. Refugees from Zimbabwe also reported the highest rate of employment among refugees: at 8 months (sweep 2), 60 % of Zimbabwean refugees were employed compared with 45 % of Other Africa, 26 % DRC/Congo, 25 % Sudan, 20 % Somali, and 18 % Eritrea refugees. Eritrean and Somali refugees were also most likely to need housing support in the form of National Asylum Support Service (NASS) accommodation at the time of their asylum decision (sweep 1), whereas Zimbabwean refugees were among the least likely to do so. In the *Survey of Refugees Living in London* (Ipsos Mori Social Research Institute

2010), North/East African refugees were proportionally more likely to have no qualifications than the refugees overall (22 % compared with 15 %), and more likely to say they are not working in the UK or there is no work here (22 % and 21 %, respectively, compared with 15 % on average).

INTEGRATION

Achieving integration of minority ethnic groups and migrants in British society and reducing social exclusion of these communities has been at the forefront of policy debates over the last decade or so. However, progress in attaining these objectives has been impeded by the kind of data policy-makers and service providers have access to, which is mainly for the 'Black African' collectivity that contains heterogeneous subgroups. There has been relatively little research that has investigated the Black African group at a finer level of granularity, such as country of birth groups, cohorts of arrivals of migrants and their routes taken, and their language skills. This was one of the main aims of Mitton and Aspinall's (2010, 2011) ESRC UPTAP Project (ESRC, Economic and Social Research Council; UPTAP, Understanding Population Trends and Processes) on 'Black Africans in the UK: Integration or Segregation', in taking account of these finer subgroups. For example, migrants from some African countries appear to have a good level of fluency in English, such as Nigerians and Zimbabweans (whose main language is Shona). Their position is very different from Somalis and Congolese, for example.

Indeed, amongst migrants aged 3 or over in England and Wales in 2011, those whose main language was English varied from 90.1% in the Zambia, 86.0% in Nigeria, 77.4% in Zimbabwe, and 77.1% in Ghana country of birth groups to 34.9% in Congo, 34.0% in Democratic Republic of Congo, and just 27.1% in Somalia country of birth groups. Amongst those who did not have English as a main language, the proportion of migrants who could not speak English well or at all was largest in the Somalia (26%) and the two Congo (17.6%) country of birth groups.

Operationalising the concept of integration is problematic as many of the optimal measures do not have commensurate data to support the measures. Indicators of integration have been advanced by Castles et al. (2002), the Council of Europe (1997), the Home Office (2004), and Ager and Strang (2004), amongst others. Any one of the indicators they advance is probably not satisfactory when taken as a stand-alone measure, as the measures may operate differently across ethnic groups and subgroup population (Mitton and Aspinall 2010, 2011). For example, refugees and other migrants may find that they have access to the labour market but are excluded or disadvantaged in the welfare and education sectors. Often it is measurement across multiple indicators (multidimensional measurement) and the relationship between indicators that may be important and will offer the greatest potential to deepen our understanding of integration experiences (Phillimore and Goodson 2008). For example, inability to secure housing or poor health could influence a refugee's ability to progress in other areas, such as employment and education. In terms of operationalising the concept, the long-term nature of integration processes makes them difficult to measure. Most studies focus on those indicators where there are adequate data, such as labour market participation and progress towards equality in employment and education.

Much less attention has been accorded to how refugees and other migrants, themselves, feel about integration. Refugees are often presented as rather passive recipients of interventions designed to integrate 'them' (Rutter et al. 2008a, 2008b). Moreover, ethnic minority groups may attach different priorities to the integration indicators compared to the White group. For example, the host society may attach importance to unemployment and consequent welfare dependency, while ethnic minority groups may focus on their lack of legal status and their eligibility for and problems in accessing services.

Jivraj (2013) has suggested some indicators of 'foreign identity' or integration that can be derived from the 2011 England and Wales Census, and for which he provides proportions of the resident population in England and Wales: other than White British ethnicity (20 %), born abroad (13 %), other than British national identity (9 %), overseas passport (9 %), foreign main language (amongst resident population aged 3 and above) (8 %), and does not speak English well in the same age group (2 %). Not all these measures are relevant as indicators of integration when applied to the Black African group, such as born abroad (when two-thirds—67.3 %—of the community were born outside the UK in 2011). Others, such as a non-British national identity, a foreign main language, and proficiency, vary enormously by Black African subgroup. The UPTAP project (Mitton and Aspinall 2010, 2011) considered a number of measures, most by Black African subgroup, including geographical concentration, English language fluency, educational attainment, employment, housing tenure and mobility, and disadvantage as measured by receipt of benefits and eligibility for free school meals.

Amongst the key findings of this research (Mitton and Aspinall 2011), Black Africans from different countries of birth groups and of different ages when they arrived in the UK had different integration experiences when compared with the aggregate Black African group. Second-generation Black Africans were, as might be expected, more integrated than Black African migrants. UK-born Black Africans had high levels of educational attainment. There was no evidence of this group having language difficulties in their education or in finding or holding down a job. Some were thriving, in managerial and professional jobs, and had been able to secure a mortgage. However, many second-generation Black Africans were bringing up children alone, affecting their ability to earn. Rates of unemployment were substantially higher for UK-born Black African females than their White counterparts. Some Black Africans were struggling to translate their qualifications into higher-skill jobs. Many were working in low-pay sectors or were overqualified for the jobs they were in.

Zimbabweans and Nigerians had high levels of qualifications, employment, and English language competence, suggesting greater social inclusion and integration than Black Africans in general. Somalis and Congolese were the most disadvantaged and least integrated of all Black African subgroups, and even to a greater extent than Bangladeshis on some measures. This is likely to be linked to their status as refugees and the high proportion (14 %) with language difficulties in education and in finding or keeping a job (17 %).

The UPTAP project was undertaken before the 2011 Census. Data on country of birth groups who held a UK passport exemplify the problems of relying on just one indicator of integration.[11] The Somali country of birth group had one of the highest proportions (71.5 %) holding a UK passport. Only the Kenya country of birth group had a higher proportion (86.9 %). The long-established and large country of birth groups, Nigeria and Ghana, had 41.9 % and 48.9 %, respectively, holding UK passports. The Zimbabwe country of birth group, comprised substantially of recent migrants, had 50.5 % who held a UK passport. These data are broadly in accord with official statistics for the overseas-born population in the UK by nationality held for the UK, January–December 2014, derived from the Annual Population Survey. British nationals (as opposed to nationals of the country of birth or other nationalities) comprised 48 % of the Nigeria country of birth group, Kenya 87 %, Zimbabwe 57 %, Somalia

[11] These proportions are based on the 2011 Census, table DC2208EWr.

54 %, Ghana 55 %, Uganda 82 %, Tanzania 94 %, Zambia 81 %, and Sierra Leone 50 %,[12] though estimated with less precision for the smaller country of birth groups.

While citizenship is defined as the nationality of the passport which the traveller is carrying, this is an unduly narrow definition of citizenship. What is now termed 'inclusive citizenship' or 'full citizenship' amounts to a recognition of a community's identities and of full cultural participation. The ideas that Africans hold in their claims to recognition and citizenship in the diaspora are complex and encompass conceptualisations of multiculturalism, cosmopolitanism, human rights, transnational identities, and diaspora loyalties (Fumanti and Werbner 2010). Ong's (1999) definition of 'cultural citizenship' invokes 'subject-making in relation to power inequalities and normative reconfigurations of race, class and culture'. Werbner's idea of 'cosmopolitan ethnicity' (Werbner 2002) sought to capture an understanding of post-colonial elite citizenship that is both ethnically rooted and multicultural, transcending ethnic difference and promoting a universalist consciousness of justice and the public good. In Chap. 9, we see how the role of home associations, churches, and community organisations mediate notions of belonging and citizenship. These more nuanced conceptualisations of citizenship elude ready capture in censuses and surveys.

[12] See Table 1.6. Overseas-born population in the UK, by nationality held, January–December 2014: http://www.ons.gov.uk/ons/publications/re-reference-tables.html?edition=tcm%3A77-376534

CHAPTER 4

Categories and Group Identities

A number of themes have been addressed in the literature on categories and identities for the Black African population: the use of the term 'Black African' in the last three decennial censuses and in official data collections; the acceptability of a colour-based term, incorporating the descriptor 'black'; the heterogeneity concealed within the 'Black African' collectivity; the invisibility of distinct national origin populations; the concealment of disparities in health, healthcare, and determinants of health; the capture of the 'Black African' populations in the censuses of other countries; and possible alternatives for classifying this population in official data collections.

Analyses of the data show that the term 'Black African' conceals substantial heterogeneity with respect to national origins, religion, and language. It includes many who have come to the UK since the 1960s from former colonies but also sizeable groups arriving as refugees and asylum seekers from a wider range of African countries. Moreover, its boundaries are fuzzy, especially with regard to those originating in Horn of Africa countries. Marked variations are found in the (albeit limited) available disaggregated data on health and the determinants of inequalities. Given the substantial increase in the size of the group, the extent to which such heterogeneity can continue to be tolerated in a single term must be questioned. The 'Black African' collectivity merits categorisation that addresses this issue.

© The Editor(s) (if applicable) and The Author(s) 2016   61
P.J. Aspinall, M.J. Chinouya, *The African Diaspora Population in Britain*, DOI 10.1057/978-1-137-45654-0_4

CENSUS CATEGORISATION

'Black African' was a category in most of the census tests and trials between 1979 and 1989 and in the 1991 Census. 'African' was an option (along with West Indian) in the question recommended following the first field trials of a census question in 1975–1977 (Sillitoe and White 1992). The question used in the April 1979 Census Test also included 'African' and 'West Indian or Guyanese' categories. Although no ethnic question was asked in the 1981 Census, the House of Commons Home Affairs Sub-Committee recommended a question structured by broad ethnic groups (White, Black, Asian, and Other), the Black heading encompassing British, West Indian, African, and Other tick boxes. A further question, tested in October 1985, offered Black British, West Indian or Guyanese, and African tick boxes and a further Black category—an open response Other Black—was added to the question tested in January 1986. Another version, tested in that month, reduced the options to Afro-Caribbean, African, and the open Other Black. Perhaps, the least satisfactory of all the options was the October 1986 test which offered a single box for 'Black, West Indian or African' and the question proposed in July 1988 that offered a single 'Black' box.

Finally, 'Black African' was adopted as a group in the 1991 Census in a set containing nine categories in all (including three Black groups: Black Caribbean, Black African, and Black Other, *please describe*), the question that had been successfully tested in the April 1989 Census Test. There were no categories in this census for people who were 'Mixed', the question instruction stating that 'If the person is descended from more than one ethnic or racial group, please tick the group to which the person considers he/she belongs, or tick the "Any other ethnic group" box and describe the person's ancestry in the space provided.'

Over the last two decades or so, 'Black African' has become the standardised term to describe communities in Britain who are Black and have origins in sub-Saharan Africa. It has been used by officialdom in three decennial censuses (1991, 2001, and 2011) and the 'Mixed' category 'White and Black African' was introduced in the England and Wales 2001 Census and repeated in the 2011 Census. Given the 'gold standard' status accorded to the census ethnicity classifications, 'Black African' has been adopted as a standard category for data collection across government. The Department of Health, the National Health Service (NHS), and Social Care, for example, have all adopted 'Black African' as the generic label for this population. The term is also gaining currency as a political tool to mobilise Africans living in the UK 'diaspora' to think about responsibilities for contributing towards developing the African continent and to lobby for social justice in HIV services (AHPN 2007; Save the Children 2006). However, its utility—and, indeed, validity—has increasingly been challenged, even if only limited efforts have focussed on how people with these origins regard the term and might best be described and captured in data collections. On the use of the term, the Parekh Report commented: 'people of African origin in Britain...appear in official statistics as a single group. In fact, however, their diversity is such that official statistics are virtually meaningless as a basis for analysis' (Parekh 2000, p. 35).

The use of the term has also been contested in health research: 'Black Africans are an extremely heterogeneous group, survey evidence showing that they will identify their origins (for example, as "Nigerian" or "Ghanaian") when such options are offered' (Aspinall 2000, p. 36). While analysing ethnic inequalities in Camden, Mateos (2014) found that Somalis 'complained of not getting the same level of resources (as officially recognised ethnic groups) because they were "statistically hidden" under the all-encompassing "Black African" group'. Mitton and Aspinall (2011) found that 'groupings such as "Black African" used in official surveys are of limited usefulness' given the diversity concealed within the label. 'Black African' has been criticised as 'very broad' and 'unrelated to ethnicity', a term that 'may be both offensive and inaccurate' and to be avoided if possible (Agyemang et al. 2005). Other commentators have voiced concern in a range of specific contexts, arguing with respect to drug misuse needs, for example, that 'ethnic monitoring systems are rarely sophisticated enough to record particular ethnic groups within wider categories such as Black African' (Bashford et al. 2003, p. 12). Moreover, others have warned against an overemphasis on Black shared experiences that reproduce homogeneity. For example, Audre Lorde has observed that 'within Black communities where racism is a living reality, differences among us often seem dangerous and suspect. The need for unity is often misnamed for homogeneity' (Lorde 1984, p. 119).

The unsatisfactory position of having a single term to describe this population has become increasingly evident over recent decades. The 'Black African' community has rapidly increased in size over the last two decades (1991–2011). In the 1991 Census, 212,362 persons (258,746 after adjustment for undercount) were enumerated as 'Black Africans' in Great Britain (England, Wales, and Scotland), 0.39 % of the population. By 2001, the

'Black African' population in the UK (Northern Ireland included an ethnic group question in its 2001 Census) had increased to 485,277 (500,281 after adjustment for undercount), 0.8 % of the population. This UK figure had risen to 1,019,266 in the 2011 Census, 1.7 % of the population, or an increase of 110 % over the decade. Having a highly diverse population of almost a million people in England and Wales captured by a single term (the 2011 Scotland Census contained, under the label 'African', the categories 'African, African Scottish, or African British' and 'Other, please write in' with 29,186 and 452, respectively, enumerated in these categories) is clearly unsustainable. This population, with origins in a major part of continental Africa, shows substantial diversity in demographic, cultural, and socio-economic terms (Elam et al. 2000; Mitton and Aspinall 2011). Moreover, compared with some other ethnic groups, a disproportionate number of 'Black Africans' have come to Britain as asylum seekers and refugees and whose needs for services are likely to be different from other migrant groups and those of African origin born in Britain.

Some of these concerns were evident when the categorisation for the ethnic group question in the 2011 Census was being decided. The process of reviewing classifications provided an opportunity for data users to express their concerns. Indeed, the General Register Office (Scotland) (GRO[S]) advocated a radically new approach in its 2006 Census Test questionnaire (GRO for Scotland 2006). The ethnicity question eschewed colour terms ('White', 'Black') for a conceptual base of *ethnic background or culture*. The 'African or Caribbean' set contains seven options: 'North African', 'East African', 'Southern African', 'West African', 'Central African', 'Caribbean', and 'Other, write in'. 'North African' is also an ethnic background option under 'Arab'. In England and Wales, there was extensive consultation on the topics to be included; however, the questionnaire for the 2007 Census Test (Office for National Statistics 2006e) showed no change for the 'Black or Black British' categories compared with 2001. A question tabled in the House of Commons, asking the Chancellor of the Exchequer 'what plans he has to include a self-definition question for Somali people in the next census' (UK Parliament 2006) had presaged the decision: It evoked the National Statistician's response that 'there are currently no plans to include a tick-box for "Somali" but people who wish to identify themselves as Somali are likely to be able to do so through a "write-in" response option'.

The responses to the consultation on 2011 Census topics in England and Wales (Office for National Statistics 2006d) belied concerns with the term 'Black African' that were primarily about masked heterogeneity, as the submissions by around a dozen bodies—including the NHS Sickle Cell and Thalassaemia Screening Programme, London Borough of Tower Hamlets, Sheffield and Cardiff City Councils, Archbishops' Council of the Church of England, and Sahil Housing Association—consistently illustrated, for example:

> [T]he question and the categories have to be correct. A wider range of ethnic group categories is required for 2011 to reflect recent immigration of asylum seekers and refugees. Sheffield has several generations of Somalis and of Yemenis ... These two groups are never reflected in the Census because their numbers are not significant nationally. There should be a more sophisticated collection and presentation of the data to allow numbers to be reported in areas where they are significant and suppressed where they are too small. (Sheffield City Council)
> Consideration should be given to the subdivision of the African category to give information on backgrounds in, for example, Somalia, Nigeria and West Africa. (Archbishops' Council, Church of England)

The only option carried forward in the England and Wales Census Development Programme (CDP) was to provide the 'Black African' category with a free-text box, so that people could write in more information about their ethnic group. The ONS investigated the feasibility of this option through its 'Prioritisation Tool' (ONS 2009). It took the decision that a maximum of 2 new categories could be added to the 16 asked in the 2001 Census ethnic group question, out of the 22 candidates that had been identified (Gypsy or Irish Traveller, Arab, African plus write in, Kashmiri, Eastern European, East African Asian, Black and Asian, Jewish, Latin American, Polish, Cornish, White and Asian, Sikh, Vietnamese, Iranian, Kurdish, Non-European White, Black British, Greek/Greek Cypriot, Nepalese, Sri Lankan, and Turkish/Turkish Cypriot). Seven criteria were selected and each was scored as low, medium, or high level of evidence and with an unweighted and weighted overall score (the criteria relating to the adequacy of write-in answers and other census information were given a weighting of 2.5). On this basis, 'African plus write in', ranking third, only just missed out on inclusion in the 2011 Census question for England and Wales. In the event the 2011 England and Wales Census used the same categorisation as that for 2001, listing 'African', 'Caribbean', and 'Any other Black/African/Caribbean background, write in' under the overarching label 'Black/African/Caribbean/Black British' label.

The 2021 CDP is now under way. Without an informed debate 'Black African' may, again, be the category chosen for this group, yielding data that would be used throughout much of the 2020s. While populations with origins in the Indian subcontinent have been differentiated by national origin in the last three decennial censuses, the very heterogeneity of the 'Black African' collectivity has meant that it has been treated like a 'black box', unopened and unscrutinised. Indeed, the term itself describes a racialised pan-ethnicity rather than an ethnic group as usually defined, that is, 'a collectivity within a larger population having real or putative common ancestry, memories of a shared past, and a cultural focus upon one or more symbolic elements which define the group's identity, such as kinship, religion, language, shared territory, nationality or physical appearance' (Bulmer 1996).

Census Practices in Other Countries

How 'Black Africans' are captured in censuses and other data collections has been a concern for other states where, too, terminology is embedded in distinctive historical contexts. These experiences are examined to assess what they can contribute to practices in Britain. In the USA, the 2000 Census used the collective term 'Black, African Am., or Negro' ('Black or Negro' in 1990 and 1980, 'Negro or Black' in 1970) for African-origin populations. Research evidence indicates that for persons of distant African ancestry (who arrived as part of the slave trade), 'Black' competes on an equal basis with 'African American' as the preferred term (Sigelman et al. 2005). In addition, many recent African migrants and people with origins in the Caribbean find 'African American' an unacceptable descriptor (Wingerd 1992), a situation ameliorated only by the inclusion of 'Black' in the label. The free-text 2000 Census question on 'ancestry or ethnic origin' had the potential to capture national origin, the question examples including 'Jamaican', 'African Am.', 'Cape Verdean', 'Dominican', 'Haitian', and 'Nigerian'.

Canada's 2001 Census question on population group offered just 'Black', although 'Black (e.g. African, Haitian, Jamaican, Somali)' in 1996. As in the USA, a free-text question on ethnic or cultural group(s) the person's ancestors belonged to was asked, examples including 'Jamaican' and 'Somali' (and, additionally, 'Haitian' in 1996). 'Black' was first added to the ancestry question in 1986 (then also comprising a mark-in list) and, when repeated in 1991, generated public debate. Several Black groups viewed the term as a racial designator that denied them an ethnic heritage. The *1991 Census Guide* did not provide a specific instruction for African-origin respondents, and Statistics Canada indicated that 'in hindsight, it would have been helpful to have informed these respondents that they were to mark the box "Black" and, in addition, to report in the spaces provided their ethnic background as being, for instance, "Somalian", "Afro-American" or "Afro-Caribbean"' (White et al. 1993, p. 231). However, more recent research has shown that 'Black' is the most preferred term amongst African-origin populations in Canada, even if different label preferences are associated with different measures of social identity (Boatswain and Lalonde 2000).

Few other examples are available in national censuses: in 2001, those of Australia and New Zealand did not have African-specific categories and—across Europe—Portugal's alone included such categories ('Angola', 'Mozambique', and 'Cape Vert') in the context of questions about places of residence. Only the 2006 Census of Population of Ireland offered a relevant example, that of 'Black or Black Irish: African'. Thus, the limited international evidence—primarily North America—points to one solution, that of asking about ethnic origin or ancestry in addition to population group, although there has been no such tradition in official data collection in Britain.

Approaches to Classifying Black Africans in Future Censuses and Surveys

The current critical challenge is how to classify 'Black African' heterogeneous groups in surveys and the upcoming UK censuses. For migrant communities, the 'Black African' collectivity can currently be broken down by country of birth. In the case of second and subsequent generations, the focus needs to shift to the country(s) of family or ancestral origins. While few attempts have been made to disaggregate the African origin population in routine data sets, several approaches merit exploration.

Firstly, the use of African regions, as exemplified by Scotland's 2006 Census Test, represents a major advance compared with use of the undifferentiated colour term 'Black African', although it was not used in the 2011 Census. The five African regions (and additional free-text 'Other' option) are similar to the UN geographical subregions of Africa, Northern, Eastern, Southern, Western, and Middle (UN 2007) which have been used by the Health Protection Agency (now part of Public

Health England) in HIV/AIDS surveillance. This approach is probably impractical for a decennial census, given the current length of the ethnic group question. The 5 'ethnic background or culture' categories for the 'African' ethnic group and an additional one ('North African') under the 'Arab' group would have increased the classification to 27 categories, up from 14 in 2001.

However, this approach is far superior to the much cruder breakdown of 'North Africa' and 'sub-Saharan Africa', the UN noting that the latter is commonly used to indicate all of Africa except Northern Africa, but with the Sudan included in sub-Saharan Africa. The use of 'sub-Saharan Africa' has been found in just two routine data collections (the Neonatal [Hubbard and Haines 2004] and Maternity Core Data Indexes) and does not take us beyond the current status quo. With respect to Mixed White and Black African populations, England and Wales retained its 'Mixed' predesignated category for this group in the 2011 Census. Separate enumeration of the mixed population is important given its distinctiveness and the principle of ethnic self-identification and does permit the counting of the population with *any* African ancestry.

Moreover, the Scottish Census Test approach abandoned colour terms including 'Black' which for some 'Black Africans' and their organisations are regarded as offensive. These terms also reinforce linkages to racialised thinking and the disputatious meaning of 'race' in healthcare and other settings. With the omission of these 'colour terms'—a source of context and orientation for respondents in the 1991 and 2001 classifications— there were reported errors in how respondents interpreted such questions. For example, some of those who were White with origins in South Africa appear to have selected the 'Southern African' *ethnic background or culture* category. It is also unclear how consistently respondents would interpret—and therefore self-assign to—the five African regions. Users require data that are statistically stable, that is, data that give a robust count of the different communities and do not change significantly in test–retest surveys. However, cases of misinterpretation (where they arise) may be amenable to detection through other data collected.

A second approach that merits serious consideration would be to ask an additional question that accesses the dimension of family ethnic origins, as in other national censuses. The US census has traditionally asked questions on 'race' *and* 'ancestry or ethnic origin', whilst that in Canada has included questions on 'population group' *and* 'the ethnic or cultural origins of the person's ancestors' (an ancestor being defined as 'usually more distant than a grandparent'). Both the ancestry questions are open response and permit multiple reporting, the examples given in the question instructions being primarily country origins. Such a question would clearly provide this information for the 'full size' of the 'Black African' community (including the second generation). An alternative method of capture would be to ask specifically about the ethnicity or country of origin of parents and grandparents. Such questions have worked less well in census trials because of their complexity, birthplace of parents and grandparents yielding non/partial response rates of 6.5 % and 11.5 %, respectively, and marked differences compared with ethnic origin, in Canada's 1998 National Census Test. Given additional difficulties of processing, they are unlikely to be taken forward at this stage in the CDPs.

With respect to both approaches (and, indeed, the 'status quo'), greater use could also be made of mapping the data forward through cross-tabulating the census ethnic/cultural background categories with one or more of the others in the 'cultural' question set (country of birth, national identity, religion, and language). This derivative approach would give a more comprehensive picture of the self-assigned group by offering the additional perspective of measurement on the multiple dimensions of ethnicity. Hitherto, standard census output has been parsimonious in this area. The scope to offer separate predesignated tick boxes for the largest groups—Nigerians, Somalians, Ghanaians, and Zimbabweans—in the decennial census would seem limited as the 2011 England and Wales Census already offered 18 tick options.

Surveys and research data sets clearly offer more scope and the ability to tailor the classification to the particular purpose of data collection. For example, in using the UN subregions, the Health Protection Agency subdivides 'Eastern Africa' to create a 'South-Eastern Africa' grouping ('Malawi, Zambia, and Zimbabwe') as this was an emerging area of high prevalence of HIV/AIDS (UK Collaborative Group for HIV and STI Surveillance 2004). The Mayisha II study, also focusing on AIDS/HIV, usefully extracts an additional 'Horn of Africa' subgroup comprising Djbouti, Eritrea, Ethiopia, Somalia, and Sudan (Sadler et al. 2005). Investigators (Agyemang et al. 2005) have indicated that the word 'African' or 'African origin' is a suitable prefix for a more specific subpopulation, for example, 'African Kenyan' (hence different from 'Indian Kenyan') or 'African Nigerian'. Where research focuses specifically on African origin populations, it may be feasible to use such country of origin terms in a classification (the ethnicity question in the Black and Ethnic Minority Health and Lifestyle Survey, 1992, included the options 'Nigerian', 'Ghanaian', and 'Zambian', as well as 'Black African' and 'Black British'). The question syntax of the Health Survey for England lends itself to such adaptation: '[If African] What is your cultural background? Is it...?'

Clearly, the challenge of heterogeneity in the 'Black African' group needs to be addressed from an evidence-based perspective, including the establishment of a knowledge base on the preferred terms in the different 'Black African' communities, their acceptability of categories chosen by census agencies, and their views on the acceptability of the colour term 'black'. This is substantially lacking at present but could be provided through cognitive research and small-scale testing, minimally including the use of a 'Black African' free-text field to identify the range and frequency of terms used.

EMERGING PATTERNS OF NATIONAL IDENTITY

While ethnic group had been the only cultural identifier (along with religion) in the 2001 Census, the 2011 England and Wales Census for the first time asked a question on national identity: 'How would you describe your national identity?' Respondents were invited to 'tick all that apply' from the response options of 'English', 'Welsh', 'Scottish', 'Northern Irish', 'British', and 'Other, write in'. A similar question was asked in the 2011 Scotland Census.[1] Forty-three per cent of Black Africans in England and Wales gave a British identity only, a proportion that was lowest amongst the Black groups and 12 percentage points below the Black Caribbean group (Fig 4.1). It was also substantially lower than for the three Asian groups (58–72 %). Forty-one per cent of Black Africans gave a foreign identity only, substantially more than Black Caribbeans (12 %) but similar to the Other Black group. Only 10 % of Black Africans gave an English identity only, substantially fewer than Black Caribbeans (26 %) and the Other Black category (27 %). Finally, 5 % of Black Africans chose an other UK or UK combination identity.

---

[1] The 2011 Scotland Census asked: What do you feel is your national identity? Tick all that apply. Response options: 'Scottish', 'English', 'Welsh', 'Northern Irish', 'British', 'Other, please write in'.

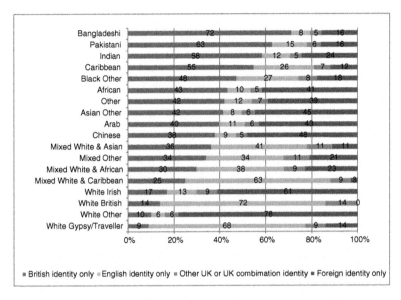

Fig. 4.1 Responses to the 2011 England and Wales Census question on national identity by ethnic group.

Source: ONS, 2011 Census, Table DC2202EW. National identity by ethnic group.

Note: The typology is as used by Jivraj and Byrne (2015)

Detailed information is available on those who gave a foreign identity only, though not tabulated by ethnic group.[2] A total of 489,457 persons in England and Wales gave an other identity only that was African, including 39,296 North African identities, 222,252 Central and West African identities, and 227,909 South and Eastern African identities. Named individual country identities yield information on those Census respondents who eschewed the British and home country options in the Census to write in the national identity associated with their community of descent: Ghanaian (41,195), Nigerian (93,506), Kenyan (14,115), Somali (42,555), South African (59,357), and Zimbabwean (51,366). Clearly, some Kenyans may have been African Indians and some South Africans and Zimbabweans White but the number of Somalis identifying only with their home country is notable.

[2] ONS. 2011 Census. Table Q5214 England and Wales. National identity (detailed). Local authorities. See also ONS. 2011 Census. Table CT0061. National identity (detailed), London.

Results for Scotland indicate stronger support for non-UK identities only. Only 12 % of the 29,600 Black Africans chose a Scottish identity only, one of the lowest proportions of all ethnic groups and well below Black Caribbeans (27 %) and the Other Black category (27 %). Seventeen per cent chose a British identity only, again smaller than the Black Caribbean (23 %) and Other Black (24 %) categories, and well below the proportion for Black Africans in England and Wales. However, over half (56 %) of Black Africans in Scotland chose a non-UK identity only, compared with 24 % of Black Caribbeans and 28 % in the Other Black category. In addition, small proportions chose Scottish and British identities only (3 %), Scottish and any other identities (6 %), and all other involving UK identities (5 %). No trend data are currently available from the census to track changes which might be taking place.

These findings are broadly consistent with those from the Citizenship Survey. As in the Census, respondents in the Citizenship Survey could select more than one identity. Eight per cent of Black Africans selected English, the lowest portion (apart from Bangladeshis) of any ethnic group (Communities and Local Government 2009). Forty-four per cent selected British, only the Chinese and White groups having a lower proportion. Over half (52 %) of Black Africans gave an 'other' national identity, the highest proportion (along with Chinese) across all ethnic groups.

While the 2011 Census does not give a breakdown of national identity by African subgroups, Mitton and Aspinall (2010) undertook an analysis of British and other national identities for people of Black African ethnicity by country of birth and age groups using the Labour Force Survey (Q2 2005, Q3 2006, and Q4, 2007 pooled). Around 91 % of those Black African adults born in the UK identified with a British/English/Scottish/Welsh national identity, around only 7 percentage points below the White British group. Proportions were very different for those Black Africans born outside the UK. Kenyans (56 %), Nigerians (46 %), and Ugandans (44 %) identified most strongly with a British/home country identity. Sierra Leoneans, Ghanaians, Congolese, and Somalis oscillated around 40 %. Zimbabweans (23 %) and other Black African migrants from Southern Africa had a low level of British/home country identities. This may reflect their relatively recent arrival. However, as Mitton and Aspinall (2010, p. 190) note, 'a drawback of this LFS data is that they do not allow us to gauge how many people have dual identities, such as British-Ghanaian,[3] as this is not an option in the survey questionnaire'.

There are also important age differences in national identity amongst Black Africans (Mitton and Aspinall 2010). In the 20–24, 25–29, and 30–34 age groups, other national identities substantially exceed British/ English/Scottish/Welsh national identity, especially in the 25–29 age group. In the 16–19 age group, there is only a few percentage points difference between the two identities. Younger generations have a greater affinity with mainstream London culture and many feel they have more in common with people of their age rather than people of their ethnic background (Elam et al. 2001). Nwajiaku-Dahou's (2013) study of Black African young Nigerian migrants in two London boroughs (Southwark and Haringey) found that amongst these minorities there was no deep appropriation of terms like 'Black British' ('black' being perceived as an imposed term by the police), reflecting weak affective ties to the nation. Instead, 'Nigerian' is increasingly worn as a trendy identity, associated with films and Nigerian music in clubs, and is about a London identity. However, there is a stark crossover in the 35–39 and older age groups where British/English/Scottish/Welsh national identities exceed other national identities (especially in the 60–64 age group). Some of these young adults may have been born in the UK or arrived here as migrants while older people may be more likely to identify as British as they have been in the UK longer.

The measure of national identity in the decennial census and general and social surveys may not satisfactorily capture how Black Africans construct their national identity. It prioritises UK home country identities (English, Welsh, Scottish, Northern Irish, and British), leaving only a residual write-in 'Other' option as the last in the classification for those who wish to declare some other national or cultural identity. It therefore conceptualises as discrete a British national identity and, say, a Nigerian national identity, even though respondents can multitick across all options. This kind of thinking is also implicit in various government statements on race equality and community cohesion. For example, the Home Office's 2005 report, *Improving Opportunity, Strengthening Society*, talks about

---

[3] One of Hickman et al.'s (2008) respondents—a long-term settled, minority ethnic Indian woman in Leicester—made a similar point: 'Where do I feel I belong? That's a split between Britain and India. Both places, yeah. That's why I said that I'm a British Indian' (p. 168).

the development in young people of 'an inclusive sense of British identity alongside their other cultural identities'. Again, we are informed: 'Today, Britishness encompasses the collective contribution diverse communities make to the country. People should not need to choose between their British identity and other cultural identities. They can be proud of both.' These sentiments were reiterated in the 2006 House of Lords Debate on British Identity and Citizenship. They see British and other cultural identities as compartmentalised and separate, sitting alongside each other.

However, testimony from Black Africans indicates that these two identities are mutually and reciprocally entailed in each other. Mercer and Page (2010) speak of the claim of their Cameroonian and Tanzanian members of home associations in Britain 'that their "Britishness" and their "other cultural identities" are in fact inseparable. In their reformulation, integration and acceptance in Britain is achieved through, indeed *because of*, a sense of security derived from a Cameroonian or a Tanzanian identity. Home association members thus articulate an alternative vision of diasporic identity, one which affirms an "African" identity but which also expands what it means to be "British".' This reading is somewhat different to what one might infer from multiticking of the 'British' and 'Other' options in the Census national identity question.

The Citizenship Survey corroborates these findings. Thirty-eight per cent of Black Africans 'strongly agree' that 'maintaining a separate cultural or religious identity is possible in Britain' (the highest proportion across the Black groups and more than twice the rate of the White group), whilst 43 % tended to agree (Communities and Local Government 2009). While the proportion of all Black Africans who agreed was lower than for the South Asian and Chinese groups, it was higher than the Mixed (76 %) and White (67 %) groups. This feeling does not differ by UK or non-UK national identity or by length of time spent in the UK. These responses 'suggest that a proportion of Black Africans believe they can integrate without sacrificing their religious or cultural identity, and are confirmed by the findings of Hickman et al. that it is possible to have diasporic ties without this being at the expense of belonging to Britain' (Mitton and Aspinall 2010, p. 193).

Gilroy opens up this debate about a British or home country identity and its relationship to the identity a migrant might hold with the country of origin and whether they can be constructed as discrete entities independent of each other. Indeed, the concept of 'transnational identities' (an identity running across different nations at once) has been the subject of extensive scholarly enquiry. Gilroy argues that migration may be 'an opportunity to rework a national identity' (Williams, p. 38) that may strengthen a migrant's ties to his country of origin. In William's words, 'models of belonging and culture that are rooted in one place ignore how migrant cultures infuse the identity of their host society'. This perspective goes hand in hand with a recognition that Englishness or Britishness is irrevocably heterogeneous and influenced by factors outside the nation-state's borders. Moreover, when national identity is liberated from the constraints of attachment to territory, it is also freed from claims about belonging.

Identity and Belonging to Britain

The different and complex meanings of 'belonging to Britain' have been explored by Hickman et al. (2008) in detailed interviews. They found that minority ethnic groups tended to be more openly appreciative of belonging to Britain because of the opportunities available, the existence of the welfare state, and the legal system. These narratives were sometimes tempered by the awareness of hierarchies of inclusion and dynamics of exclusion at work within Britain and Britishness. New arrivals in particular were grateful for the opportunities provided by living in Britain, as well as viewing Britain as a place of security and fairness. Many minority ethnic long-term residents had a sense of belonging to Britain as well as to their country of origin, even if they were born in Britain, with respondents reporting different degrees and intensity of multiple belongings.

The Citizenship Survey provides some measures of this sense of belonging. Eighty-four per cent of Black Africans indicate that they strongly belonged to Britain, the same proportion as Black Caribbeans and the White group but higher than the Other Black group (69 %) (Communities and Local Government 2009). Only the South Asian groups had higher proportions. Moreover, 91 % of Black Africans indicated that they feel a part of British society, 2 percentage points lower than Black Caribbeans, Other Black, and the White group. The South Asian groups (other than Bangladeshis) also had higher proportions. There were some differences by age. Young (aged 18–29) Black Africans had the lowest proportion indicating that they strongly belonged to Britain (83 %), though those aged 30–49 and 50+ were only marginally higher (84 %). Ninety-three per cent of those aged 18–29 reported that they feel part of British society, higher than those aged 30–49 (90 %) and those aged 50+ (92 %). More male Black Africans (85 %) than females (83 %) reported that they strongly belonged to Britain. Similarly, more males (93 %) than females (89 %) said that they feel a part of British society. A higher proportion of Black Africans born in the UK (85 %) reported that they strongly belonged to Britain than those not born in the UK (83 %). This also applied to those reporting that they feel a part of British society (95 % vs 91 %).

Transnational Identities

There is evidence for the growing importance of transnational identities in some communities of descent. African families in Britain are frequently transnational exchange networks with geographically dispersed kin, across and within the African continent and Britain, with members also having an attachment with places such as their home countries. There is a growing literature on transnational families and the moral duties that exist as webs of exchange between those left behind and Africans in Britain. Within these informal exchange networks, there are expectations from various kin dyads of the relevant type of support, or what Cattell refers to as family contracts (Cattell 1997). The flow of resources and the negotiation of obligations and responsibilities have long been identified as the basis for family life (Finch and Mason 1993) with such negotiations for African families taking place across national and international boundaries. These transnational moral economies of kin care and welfare support involve migrants' continuous involvement with politics and economics in their countries of origin (Levitt 2013). They are also sources of emotional labour as family members are constantly engaged in negotiating the physical absence of family members in their lives.

Despite their reasons for migrating to Britain, Africans continue to send remittances back home (Bloch 2008). Indeed, after social contact with close family members, economic remittances form the most regular exchanges. However, the context can be extended beyond a focus on financial transfers by a healthy migrant community. There are flows in the opposite direction, of prayers, emotional support, and herbal remedies, particularly around times of illness. A study with HIV-positive Zimbabwean women found that the women negotiated these family contracts with kin, including children who were left behind in Zimbabwe (Chinouya 2010). In this study, Zimbabwean Christian women relied on those left behind to offer emotional support and prayers in managing illness: local churches where their families were members were involved in sending biblical verses and words of worship to the women in England. With improvement in technologies, the means of transmission have extended to text messaging and visual media like Skype. There are also reports of African medicines and herbal remedies being delivered from Africa to family members in England. Technology, in particular tele-evangelism, also enables Africans living in Britain to 'participate' with worshippers in their countries of origin, in some cases through dedicated TV channels where prayers are made for global viewers including Africans in Britain.

RELIGION

An understanding of religion as a dimension of identity amongst Black Africans has been facilitated by questions on religion in the 2001 and 2011 England and Wales censuses. The voluntary question—'What is your religion?'—offered a range of response options: no religion, Christian (including Church of England, Catholic, Protestant, and all other Christian denominations), Buddhist, Hindu, Jewish, Muslim, Sikh, and an open response (Any other religion). This question enables the main faith groups—particularly Christian and Muslim—in the 'Black African' population to be identified (Table 4.1).

Thus, over two-thirds (69.9 %) of Black Africans were Christian and a fifth (20.9 %) Muslim. These figures were similar to those for the 2001 Census which enumerated 479,665 Black Africans in England and Wales: 68.9 % identified as Christian, 20.0 % as Muslim, 8.1 % as religion not stated, and 2.3 % no religion, no other census category individually accounting for more than 0.2 % of the total (as was also the case in 2011). The very small proportion giving 'no religion' is notable. It is only possible

Table 4.1 Black African: religion, England and Wales, 2011 Census

Religion	No.	%
All categories: religion	989,628	
Christian	691,482	69.87
Buddhist	933	0.09
Hindu	1,879	1.19
Jewish	618	0.06
Muslim	207,201	20.94
Sikh	554	0.06
Other religion	1,560	0.16
No religion	28,528	2.88
Religion not stated	56,873	5.75

Source: Table DC2201EW: ethnic group by religion

to explore religious diversity at a country of birth level through standard tables (2011) and commissioned data (2001: Office for National Statistics 2006c). The 2011 England and Wales Census provides only a limited regional breakdown that has little utility for identifying a proxy Black African population.

However, in the 2001 Census, a commissioned table yielded information on religion for individual African countries: 50.1 % of all persons born in African countries were Christian and 17.9 % identified as Muslim. In seven countries of birth, more than half the population identified as Muslim: Sudan (50.5 %), Tunisia (53.7 %), Libya (55.9 %), Gambia (65.9 %), Morocco (76.9 %), Algeria (77.9 %), and Somalia (89.3 %). Other countries with between a fifth and half their population identifying as Muslim were Senegal, Malawi, Egypt, Burundi, Eritrea, Tanzania, Sierra Leone, Mozambique, and Mauritius. Even in countries of origin like Nigeria, where 87.7 % of migrants identified as 'Black African' and 81.1 % of all migrants were Christian, 8.7 % of persons born in this country identified as 'Muslim'.

Religion is widely reported to be a key dimension of Black Africans' identity. Religion and spirituality are important to a significant number in this collectivity and have an important bearing on how they deal with mortality and death (Nzira 2011). Amongst 13 identity dimensions, Black Africans ranked religion the sixth most important factor that was important to identity, 87 % of Black Africans selecting this dimension (Communities and Local Government 2009). By comparison, Black Caribbeans ranked this dimension 11th, 73 % selecting it. In the White group, religion was ranked bottom, only 44 % of respondents selecting it. Further, amongst the most important values for living in Britain, 'freedom to follow a religion of choice' was selected by 32 % of Black Africans (the second highest after Pakistanis [38 %] across census ethnic groups). Moreover, Black African people (40 %) were more likely than White people (31 %) to mention respect for all faiths as amongst the five most important values for living in Britain. Sixty-seven per cent of Black Africans indicated that there was never a conflict between their national and religious identity, the highest proportion across the census categories.

LANGUAGE

The important variable of language—another measure of diversity amongst 'Black Africans'—was first asked in the decennial census in 2011: The England and Wales question was: 'What is your main language?', the response options being 'English' and a write-in 'Other' box. Those whose main language was not 'English' were asked: 'How well can you speak English?' (with response options of 'very well', 'well', 'not well', and 'not at all'). Thus, census statistics will undercount all speakers of specific languages as only *main language* is captured.

Main language was asked in the 2011 Census and data were released by ethnic group. Of 924,836 Black African residents aged 3 and over in England and Wales, 664,887 (71.9%) had English (English or Welsh if in Wales) as their main language[4]. There is detailed information on the other main languages of Black Africans: 30,805 French, 12,620 Portuguese, and 12,530 Arabic and 182,115 speakers of African languages (Table 4.2). For Black Africans we have main language information broken down by religion only for Swahili/Kiswahili (12,353), of whom 5,020 were Christian and 6,720 Muslim.

There are also counts of speakers of African languages (Table 4.2), that is, all persons whose main language was an African language whatever their ethnic group. African main languages accounted for a total of 244,057 speakers (of whom 74.6% were Black Africans), including almost 86,000

Table 4.2 People whose main language was an African language, England and Wales, 2011

African languages	No. (all)	No. (Black African)
Amharic	8,615	7,821
Tigrinya	12,443	11,455
Somali	85,918	55,448
Krio	1,192	1,084
Akan	18,417	16,965
Yoruba	14,914	13,732
Igbo	7,946	7,075
Swahili/Kiswahili	15,059	12,353
Luganda	3,445	3,212
Lingala	4,914	4,459
Shona	21,395	19,958
Afrikaans	11,247	277
Any other Nigerian language	6,639	4,544
West African language (all other)	9,402	7,648
African language (all other)	22,511	16,084
African language: Total	244,057	182,115

Source: 2011 England and Wales Census.

[4] ONS. 2011 Census. Commissioned tables CT0341 (Religion by ethnic group by main language) and CT0517 (Sex by age by ethnic group by main language).

Somali speakers, over 21,000 Shona speakers, over 18,000 Akan speakers, and around 15,000 (each) Swahili/Kiswahili and Yoruba speakers[5]. Detailed information is also available for Black African pupils in the Annual School Census (ASC), especially in London (Baker and Eversley 2000; Eversley et al. 2010; Mitton and Aspinall 2011; Mitton 2011). For example, in 2008, 30 % of Black African pupils in London spoke English at home, 20 % Somali, 9 % Yoruba, 6 % Akan, 5 % French, 2 % Lingala, 2 % Igbo, and 2 % Arabic (Von Ahn et al. 2010a, b). A total of 179 other languages were spoken by fewer than 2 % each of London's Black African pupils. While most Nigerians, Ghanaians, and Ugandans can speak English, many new migrants have only their own language. Amongst the Somali population in the UK, a large proportion—especially women and older people—speak only Somali, a factor which contributes to a low employment rate (e.g. just 12 % amongst migrant Somalis, compared with 62 % for all other new migrants, according to Kyambi [2005]). Few social and general-purpose surveys collect comprehensive information on the dimension of language as there are so many African languages, indeed too many to have made translation a viable option in the 2004 Health Survey for England (Nazroo 2005). However, eight African languages (Akan, Igbo, Lingala, Luganda, Shona, Somali, Swahili, and Yoruba) were supported by written translation in the 2011 Census (Hopper and D'Souza 2012).

The relationship between language and identity is complex and varies across languages. Some such as Swahili/Kiswahili—a 'main language' for around 15,000 speakers in the Census and around 5,900 pupils' 'first language' (including variants) in England in 2011—foster a sense of community in Britain. Swahili became Tanzania's adopted national language after independence, and Mercer and Page (2010) note 'the binding work done by Swahili' amongst Tanzanians in the UK. The Afro Culture Association in Leicester brings together Swahili speakers from across East and Central Africa and seeks to preserve the Swahili language among members and their children. Leicester Swahili Speakers Association[6] provides advice sessions, public local meetings, get-together events for families, after school clubs/sessions and other youth activities, burial services, and fitness and sports sessions. Amongst similar associations, the Leeds Swahili Cultural

---

[5] ONS. Table QS204EW. 2011 Census: Main language (detailed). Local Authorities in England and Wales.
[6] Charity Commission. Register of Charities.

Community provides after and out-of-school educational and socio-cultural support for migrant children and parental activities which aim at reaching out to other communities and engaging with local schools. The Coventry Muslim Swahili Association similarly offers help with funeral services and classes and short courses for young people.

However, it is frequently a desire amongst parents to maintain a knowledge of language and culture in their children—maintaining a sense of belonging in Africa and in the diaspora—that defines Swahili's binding potential. One of Mercer and Page's (2010) informants, a Tanzanian mother, explains:

'You should not lose [your national identity] simply because you are here. When you're together [i.e. in organised associational life], your children will find some kind of identity. But when you're not together children just grow up in a community that is so diverse, they have nothing to identify with. They do not identify with Tanzania, they cannot identify with the UK, where do they belong ... when you meet a Tanzanian child here who ... doesn't even speak Kiswahili, then you get worried ... it looks like that child doesn't know anything about Tanzania. That child is completely gone.'

The extent to which other home languages contribute to a sense of group identity is probably limited. For example, people whose main language was Shona, a native language to the Shona people who predominantly reside in Zimbabwe and Zambia, had a 98.4 % proficiency level in English.[7] The Communities and Local Government (2009) report did not include language amongst the 13 factors important to identity, suggesting that it is of limited importance as a cultural factor to identity.

OTHER IDENTITY DIMENSIONS

The Citizenship Survey asked respondents about 13 factors important to identity. Black African responses are shown in Table 4.3.

While family was the most important factor to identity for people across all ethnic groups, there were numerous differences in the other important factors. Compared with White respondents, Black Africans were

[7] This includes people who selected 'very well' or 'well' for qn. 19 on the 2011 England and Wales Census form 'How well can you speak English?' (very well, well, not well, and not at all). See ONS. Detailed analysis—English language proficiency in England and Wales. Main language and general health characteristics. London: ONS, 2013 (August).

substantially more likely to say that ethnic/racial background was important to their identity. This also applied to national identity, gender, level of education, level of income, family's country of origin, age and life stage, occupation, social class, and religion. The desire amongst Black Africans to see their children achieve academically is highly prized as parents associate academic achievement with improved prospects in the labour market (Nzira 2011).

STABILITY AND CHANGE IN ETHNIC GROUP IDENTITY

Amongst the many factors circumscribing the meaningfulness to respondents of category-driven ethnicity data collection is the fluidity of ethnicity. It is well established that ethnic identity is dynamic and changes over time for a variety of reasons, including personal shifts in preferred terms, shifts in fashion for particular labels, and the political context. In addition, changes in the range of options and in their acceptability will also result in changes in self-assignment across censuses, as might misinterpretation of the question or errors in assignment in one or both enumerations. However, the scale of change is difficult to capture as it involves multiple measurements. Such change is usually measured in longitudinal studies or repeated cross-sectional surveys where records can be linked. In addition,

Table 4.3 Factors important to identity amongst Black Africans, Citizenship Survey 2007–2008

Factors	% Black African	% White
Family	98	97
Interests	86	87
National identity	87	83
Level of education	88	81
Gender	86	77
Level of income	79	74
Family's country of origin	88	71
Age and life stage	82	72
Occupation	79	70
Where you live	70	70
Ethnic or racial background	91	65
Social class	64	54
Religion	87	44
Respondents	808	8,015

Source: Communities and Local Government (2009)

the comparing of linked responses in different surveys undertaken at the same time can provide an insight into the consistency of responses about ethnic identity.

The ONS Longitudinal Study (LS) of England and Wales has particular efficacy in exploring ethnic identity as it records ethnic group across successive censuses. Analyses are available for change across the 1991 and 2001 censuses and also the 2001 and 2011 censuses (when the ethnic classifications were the same). Platt et al. (2005) used the LS to analyse change in ethnic group identification for the same individuals between 1991 and 2001. Of the 1,235 LS members who identified as 'Black African' in the 1991 Census, only 77.4 % identified as 'Black African' in the 2001 Census (6.8 % as 'White British', 2.4 % 'Black Caribbean', 3.4 % 'Other Black', 1.9 % 'Indian', 3.3 % 'White and Black African', and 1.1 % 'Other Mixed'). Of the 1,152 LS members identifying as 'Black African' in the 2001 Census, 83.0 % so identified in the 1991 Census, both sets of data revealing significant fluidity. The intercensus stability of the Black African group has increased between 1991–2001 and 2001–2011. During 1991–2001, the stability in the Black African group (77.4 %) was the same as for Black Caribbeans (77.2 %), and substantially higher than for the open response 'Other Black' group (8.3 %). These proportions may have been influenced by differences in the ethnic group classification between 1991 and 2001.

Between the 2001 and 2011 censuses, stability in the Black African group had increased to 83.1 %, the two classifications being almost identical for the Black groups (Simpson 2014). Again, Black Africans had the highest stability of all groups with Black origins, higher than Black Caribbeans (81.1 %), Mixed White and Black Caribbeans (76.4 %), Mixed White and Black Africans (56.8 %), and the Other Black category (29.2 %). These percentages compare with proportions of over 99 % in the White group and 88–97 % in the Asian (including Chinese) categories over the two periods. Of the 2,842 Black Africans who identified as 'Black African' in 2001, 2,383 (83.8 %) did so in 2011. However, 2.1 % identified as White, 1.2 % as White and Black African, 0.5 % as Other Mixed, 1.2 % as Indian, 1.1 % as Other Asian, 1.1 % as Black Caribbean, 6.8 % as Other Black, 1.0 % as Arab, and 1.1 % as Any Other. The 2.3 % who identified as Asian were likely to have been African Indians. Similarly, 88.3 % of the 2,699 participants who identified as Black African in the 2011 Census did so in 2001. Of the others, 3.8 % identified as White, 2.9 % as Mixed, 0.8 % as Asian, 1.3 % as Black Caribbean, and 2.9 % as Other Black.

Responses in the 2011 Census were also compared with those in the 2011 English School Census through record linkage for school pupils (ONS 2014b). Linkage was achieved for 6.7 million children. Broadly, similar findings to those in the ONS LS analysis were found, even though this study compared different sources for the same years. The consistency level for Black Africans was 83 %, higher than for Black Caribbeans (77 %), White and Black Caribbeans (62 %), White and Black Africans (55 %), and Other Black (20 %). Of those recorded as Black African in the 2011 Census but not in the English School Census (17 %), the largest groups were 'Other Black' and 'Other Mixed' responses.

WHO IS 'BLACK AFRICAN': GROUP MEMBERSHIP AND FUZZY BOUNDARIES

'Black African' is a term that was first widely used following its inclusion in the categorisation for the 1991 Census ethnic group question (in a set containing 'Black-Caribbean', 'Black-African', and an open response 'Black-Other'). Its position as an ethnic group or category has been further consolidated by its status as a category option in the 2001 and 2011 censuses and its widespread adoption across government data collections. It has become part of our standardised terminology to describe ethnic groups. Moreover, the way in which categorisation and group identities become entailed in each other is likely to have increased the saliency of 'Black African' as the self-descriptor of choice. It was Petersen (1987, p. 218), for example, who suggested that 'few things facilitate a category's coalescence into a group so readily as its designation by an official body', while 'making race groups beneficiaries of policy can itself intensify group identities' (Prewitt 2013, p. 11).

Census terms are usually reasonably efficient at capturing their intended ethnic group as they are the product of cognitive research, small-scale tests, and large-scale field trials. However, there is a degree of fuzziness at the boundary of most ethnic groups. Heath et al. (2013), for example, commented that their interviewers' experience did 'bring out the fuzzy nature of the official categories' in their survey, remarking in particular that 'the distinction between black and mixed white and black and white have become rather fuzzy ones in the British context, unlike the US context where the "one drop" rule is much clearer'. Hahn and Stroup (1994) refer to 'the phenomenon of "fuzzy group boundaries"—ambiguity about the criteria of group membership' as partially explaining the low reliability in ethnic and racial classification. Callister (2015) has written of the fuzzy boundaries between ethnic groups in New Zealand and Cruise O'Brien (2003) of 'the (fuzzy) boundaries of ethnic self-recognition' in Senegal. Ward-Perkins (2005) declares that 'all ethnic groups have fuzzy edges'. Such fuzziness makes measurement difficult: Butz et al. (1993, p. 15) noted that 'fuzzy definitions and group boundaries, changing terminologies, poor reliability and lack of knowledge of the degree of affiliation with a group make data collection difficult'. In similar terms, Bobo (1993, p. 159) described ethnicity thus: 'it is fuzzy, it's got unclear boundaries, it's got variable measurement and we can't come up with any measure that is in any sense fully standard'. Such descriptions invoke Barth's proposition that identities are to be found and negotiated at their boundaries: 'boundaries persist despite a flow of personnel across them' (Barth 1969).

This fuzziness is a characteristic of the 'Black African' census term which was conceived to capture Black Africans whose origins lie in sub-Saharan Africa. While it is clear that the term is largely successful in doing so, the boundary is fuzzy with respect to some countries of origin and some ethnic groups. Geographically, there is fuzziness with respect to migrants from the Horn of Africa (the region containing the countries of Djibouti, Eritrea, Ethiopia, and Somalia). This is reflected in wider official definitions as well as in how people with origins in Africa assign themselves in standard ethnicity classifications. The definition of 'sub-Saharan Africa' as used in the statistics of UN institutions identifies Mauritania, Mali, Niger, Chad, and Sudan as countries comprising the northern boundary of sub-Saharan Africa. However, Sudan is classified as North Africa by the UN. The ONS National Statistics Country Classification includes Sudan and South Sudan, countries with significant Arab populations, in North Africa. Significantly, ONS does not attempt to map countries of origin to the 'Black African' collectivity: it does this only at the level of 'Black' (aggregating Black African, Black Caribbean, and Other Black) (ONS 2013a).

The terms 'Black African' and 'sub-Saharan Africa' (used as a synonym for Black Africa) are not without their critics in Africa. Ekwe-Ekwe (2012) writes: 'The widespread use of "sub-Sahara Africa" makes no sense and is undoubtedly a racist geopolitical signature' that 'prioritises hackneyed and stereotypical racist labelling'. '"Sub-Saharan Africa" is a pejorative term', writes Onyeani (2009). 'It is an euphemism for contemptuousness employed by the continent's detractors to delineate between the five Arab countries that make up north Africa from the other 42 countries and the islands that make up the rest of Africa' and 'another divisive vestige of colonial domination which balkanized Africa'. Shahadah (2012) argues that 'The very suggestion of a "Black African" implies, without even stating it, that there is also another colour variant on African. Sub-Saharan Africa is another perfect example of this, where the illusion of "two" Africa's is made real only in language; but never in reality.' 'Sub-Saharan Africa', he claims, 'is a linguistic vestige of racist colonialism, nested in the notion of divide and rule, which articulates a perception based on European terms of homogeneity. The notion of some invisible border, which divides the North of Africa from the South, is rooted in racism.' There is less criticism of these constructions in the UK, whether as a regional identifier or as a self-descriptor.

However, some may feel that the term has resonance with the nomen-clature of 'New Commonwealth: Africa', used to stratify ethnic group by country of birth in the 1991 Census. Clearly invoking Britain's colonial past, this term prioritised Britain's former colonies in Africa, leaving a mixed collection of named countries outside this collectivity (Algeria, Egypt, Libya, Morocco, Tunisia, and Republic of South Africa) and a mis-cellaneous collection of 37 other countries encompassed by, yet hidden in, the term 'Other Africa'.

The way people with origins in Africa assign themselves to the 'Black African' and other census categories provides an effective means of defin-ing who is located within this collectivity as allocation to groups in the census is by self-assignment. In the 2011 England and Wales Census, persons born in Somalia tended to identify themselves as 'Black Africans' although significant numbers chose 'Other Black'. Of the 101,370 resi-dents born in Somalia, two-thirds (67,783, 66.9 %) identified as 'Black African' and around a fifth (22,480, 22.2 %) as 'Other Black'. The length of time these residents had lived in the country seems to have had no clear effect on how they identified. While around only a half who had arrived pre-1981 (51.4 %) chose the Black African category, the proportion subsequently stabilised at 68.8 % (1981–2000), 65.5 % (2001–2006), and 66.4 % (2007–2011). The popularity of 'Other Black' has gradually but unevenly increased, from 18.1 % (pre-1981) to 19.8 % (1981–2000), 24.2 % (2001–2006), and 23.4 % (2007–2011).

Eritrean migrants, by contrast, predominantly identify as 'Black African', the 'Other Black' category having little saliency. Of the 17,282 migrants from Eritrea living in England and Wales in 2011, 89.3 % identified as 'Black African' and just 2.0 % as 'Other Black'. Apart from pre-1981 migrants (52.4 %), the proportion identifying as Black African remained consistent with regard to period of migration (89.7 % in 1981–2000, 90.6 % in 2001–2006, and 90.5 % in 2007–2011). Ethiopians show a very similar pattern of identification. Of the 15,209 migrants in 2011, 83.8% identified as 'Black African' and just 3.6% as 'Other Black'. Apart from pre-1981 migrants (39.1 %), the proportions were consistent across periods of migration (86.4 % in 1981–2000, 85.9 % in 2001–2006, and 86.1 % in 2007–2011). Proportions identifying as 'Other Black' varied from 1.0 to 4.2 %.

How Sudanese migrants identify is particularly noteworthy given Sudan's equivocal position as part of sub-Saharan Africa. Of the 17,467 Sudanese migrants, 53.0 % identified as Black African, 18.9 % as Arab, and just 2.2 % as 'Other Black'. Apart from the pre-1981 period of arrival, those choosing a 'Black African' ethnic group increased from 46.1 % for 1981–2000 arrivals to 65.9 % for 2001–2006 arrivals and 60.9 % for 2007–2011 arrivals. Arabs accounted for 23.9 % of those arriving in 1981–2000, falling to 14.8 % in 2001–2006 and 16.7 % in 2007–2011. Thus, on the grounds of being the largest group for arrivals from 1981 to 2011 and exceeding three-fifths since 2001, migrants from Sudan qualify as part of the Black African collectivity. Clearly, the war in Darfur has, since 2003, affected the flows of African Arab and Black African migrants. Different criteria might apply to Sudan's inclusion (or not) as a sub-Saharan African country.

The northern boundary of sub-Saharan Africa (i.e. the countries of origin included in the 'Black African' collectivity) is less fuzzy, besides the case of Sudan already discussed. Western Sahara, Morocco, Algeria, Tunisia, Libya, and Egypt are regarded as part of the Arab world, all but one (Western Sahara) having borders on the Mediterranean Sea. The Transnational Communities Programme describes the area in the following terms: 'North Africa is often treated as part of the Middle East (what the French call the Near East), as part of a common cultural and historical area of the countries bordering the Mediterranean basin (following Braudel) or as *sui generis*, usually under the name "the Maghreb".' However, the Maghreb is usually defined to exclude Egypt but to include Mauritania.

The Arab Maghreb Union's membership comprises the countries Algeria, Libya, Mauritania, Morocco, and Tunisia.

How those living in England and Wales who were born in these North African countries identify in the 2011 Census ethnic group classification shows that these countries of origin are substantially outside the 'Black African' collectivity.[8] Of the 23,929 persons born in Algeria, around a quarter (25.7 %) identified as White,[9] 8.6 % as Black African, 39.0 % as Arab, and 13.9 % as Any other ethnic group. Amongst those born in Egypt (29,821), the proportion identifying as Black African was even smaller (2.6 %), compared with 38.4 % identifying as White, 39.3 % as Arab, and 12.3 % as Any other ethnic group. Moroccan migrants (21,246) identified as Arab (39.3 %), Any other ethnic group (20.2 %), White (17.9 %), and just 5.5 % as Black African. Of the 5,832 persons born in Tunisia, almost half (47.1 %) identified as Arab, 17.6 % as White, 8.8 % as Any other ethnic group, and just 3.9 % as Black African. Finally, over half (57.9 %) of the 15,046 Libyan migrants identified as Arab, around a quarter (24.5 %) as White, just 3.7 % as Black African, and 3.4 % as Any other ethnic group. With respect to the equivocally placed Mauritania, just 218 migrants are recorded in England and Wales in 2011. Black Africans comprised the largest group (36.7 %), substantially larger than the Arab category (3.2 %).

It is more problematic to measure the fuzziness of the *ethnic* boundary for these communities of descent (i.e. the full size of these communities of descent, to include second and subsequent generations) as the 1991, 2001, and 2011 censuses only collected information for the category of 'Black Africans' and not for the more specific communities such as Somalis, Nigerians, and Ghanaians. However, the 2001 and 2011 England and Wales censuses included one free-text field for each of the five major sections of the classification (White, Mixed/multiple ethnic groups, Asian/Asian British, Black/African/Caribbean/Black British, and Other ethnic group being the 2011 labels). The data provide numbers in the different African communities who eschewed the 'Black African' option to give a more specific response, presumably on the grounds that 'Black African' did not provide an adequate description of their ethnic group. However,

---

[8] Data are not available for Western Sahara as it falls within a heterogeneous 'rest of the world' category.

[9] Defined here as 'White English, Welsh, Scottish, Northern Irish, and British' and 'Other White'.

it is not possible to say what proportion these write-ins constituted of the full size of these communities. They simply give us a point of access to those who eschewed the 'Black African' option.

Two African communities are identified in the write-in responses for the 2011 England and Wales Census: Somalis and Nigerians. A total of 44,475 Somalis wrote in their ethnicity (621 in the Other Mixed, 37,708 in the Other Black, and 6,146 in the Any Other open response options). In addition, 5,226 Somalilanders identified in the Other Black and 826 in the Any Other options. If estimates for the Somali population in a selection of towns and cities are taken as guidance, the Somali *ethnic* group may exceed the migrant community fourfold, amounting to around 400,000 Somalis in England and Wales. On these measures, around only one in nine Somalis eschewed the 'Black African' option to give a Somali identity in free text. In addition, just 2,021 respondents wrote in 'Nigerian' in the Other Black free-text field. These same two communities (336 Nigerians and 238 Somalis) self-identified in free text in the Scotland 2011 Census ethnic group question.

Data from the 2001 England and Wales Census and other sources yield similar findings. A total of 8,642 respondents wrote 'Somali' in open response, equating to around 15 % of the estimated 60,000 strong community in Britain (Parekh 2000). In the population profiling project in North Liverpool (School of Health and Human Sciences 2000), over four-fifths of Somalis selected 'Black African' but around 16 % wrote in 'Somali' in the 'Other' free-text field. Other 2001 Census data relate only to the 43,532 born in Somalia migrants in Britain, 39,752 (91 %) of whom selected 'Black African'. These data confirm qualitative findings that 'groups from northern Africa, the Horn of Africa, and some parts of the eastern coastline and islands of Africa may not identify themselves as black African. It was felt that they don't see themselves as black or African and might describe themselves by nationality specifically (for example, Somali or Sudanese), perhaps Afro-Arabs, or Arab-African' (Elam et al. 2001, p. 15). With respect to another subgroup the term 'Black African' probably captured most Nigerians in the England and Wales 2001 Census (though we do not know the origins of the born in Britain 'Black African' and 'Other Black' populations). Only 2,289 eschewed the 'Black African' label to describe themselves as 'Nigerian' in open response.

These findings for Somalis are corroborated by cognitive research. As part of the development programme for the 2011 Census, for example, the Welsh Assembly Government asked the Office of the Chief Social

Research Officer (OCSRO) to explore how Somalis living in Wales interpret, understand, and answer the proposed Census questions that relate to ethnicity, national identity, language, and religion (ONS and Welsh Assembly Government 2007). Fourteen cognitive interviews took place in Cardiff in July/August 2007 with members of the community, exploring their understandings of these questions. The Welsh Assembly Government report that 'there was no "standard way" for Somalis to answer …[the ethnicity] question. Some ticked the "African" response in the British or Black British section. Others wrote in "Somali" in the "Any other black background, write in" section. Others ticked more than one box.' Respondents defined ethnicity as 'individual's background—including where their parents had come from, where they were from "originally" and where their "origins" were'. While all respondents commented that they were Somali, they did not necessarily indicate this in the 'Other' free-text field.

Finally, as noted earlier in the chapter, transitions between categories in LS data and other record linkage studies indicate the permeability and fuzziness of ethnic group boundaries. Those for Black Africans in the ONS LS show very small movements of White British, Mixed White and Black Africans, Indians/Other Asians, and Other Black respondents into and out of this category. In comparing responses in the 2011 English School Census with those in the 2011 England and Wales Census, inconsistent responses were mainly accounted for by the Mixed White and Black African and Other Black responses, but 8 % or less in both cases. These analytical approaches indicate that the membership of the Black African category remains reasonably stable over time and across data sets. In conclusion, then, the 'Black African' collectivity is a fairly stable entity with a core membership and small flows in and out of the group at its boundary.

SOCIAL CATEGORISATION AND GROUP IDENTIFICATION: THE ACCEPTABILITY OF A COLOUR-BASED TERM

There has long been an objection to the use of colour terms like 'Black' and 'White' amongst the community of categorisers and policymakers. In the late 1970s, the Office of Population Censuses and Surveys (OPCS 1980) held that in a compulsory census, terms such as black and white should be avoided as they placed too much emphasis on racial or colour distinctions. Although attitudes changed when the Home Affairs Sub-Committee recommended the use of these terms in 1983, a significant constituency of opinion has continued to resist them. Most recently, Bhopal (2004) has indicated that support for the use of the term 'Black' may be diminishing, Agyemang et al. (2005) further arguing that in an epidemiological context it may be both offensive and inaccurate and should be phased out. However, the use of the term does continue to be actively debated, especially in the US context (Harrison 1994): The view is that the privileging of cultural differences by the use of ethnicity diverts analytical attention from those issues of structural constraint and power that so shape the experiences, socio-economic position, and social relations of the groups thus described. In studies of racism, the use of the term continues to be supported.

The extent to which the use of 'Black' by officialdom accords with the group identifiers used by the 'Black African' community—that is, the extent to which census categories are locally grounded—is likely to be an important factor affecting data quality. While 'Black' competes on coequal terms with 'African American' as the term of choice in the USA (Aspinall 2007a), its acceptability in Britain is difficult to establish as surveys have rarely collected ethnic data on an unprompted open response basis or explored preferences for terminology in representative, population-based samples as in the USA (Tucker et al. 1996). Such evidence as exists is weak (and therefore only indicative).

Some measure of opinion was taken by two African organisations in Britain in 2005. The African Foundation for Development (AFFORD) polled its website visitors on the question: 'Should we adopt the term African British to describe all British nationals with antecedents originating directly from Africa or indirectly via African diasporic communities such as those in the Caribbean and South America?', half responding affirmatively (Ligali Media Network 2005). When Black Net UK asked its online visitors 'How should "Blacks" in the UK be referred to?', two-fifths selected the category 'African British' and the rest terms including 'Black' ('Black', 'Black British', and 'Black African') (Blacknet UK n.d.). AFFORD, the African British IT Association, and Insaka (a movement to promote African culture and values amongst young people in the African diaspora) have all declared their support for 'African British'. The British-based Ligali Organisation that promotes equality for African people also prefers 'African British', arguing that 'the label "Black" disengages African people with their place of cultural and historical origin.' In a letter to the National Statistician (Agbetu 2004), the organisation expressed concern over the terminology used by ONS to define Africans: 'It remains tragic that modern ONS publications continue to perpetuate colour (caste) based definitions to define ethnicity whilst displacing national identity with racially insensitive aberrations such as "non-White" or "Black Africans". We consider this all the more disturbing when more meaningful and less offensive alternatives exist (i.e. not European, Sudanese Fur or African Britons).' The representativeness of this body of opinion that opposes the term 'Black African' is unknown and other community members have argued for the retention of the term (Holloway 2007). However, when added to the concerns expressed by public health practitioners and epidemiologists, there is now a case for questioning the continued routine use of colour-based ethnicity terminology in Britain (Aspinall 2007b).

HOW 'BLACK AFRICANS' IDENTIFY THEMSELVES

Clearly, given the importance of choosing terminology that is acceptable to the communities described by it, there is an argument for exploring salient labels amongst the Black African population, that is, terms that Black Africans would use to describe themselves when unprompted by a census classification. These are the kind of 'top of head' descriptions, albeit summary, that respondents would give in surveys to the question 'how would you describe your ethnic group/cultural background using your own words?' They should provide an important body of evidence to help decide the choice of official label for Black Africans. However, there has been relatively little collection of data on the ethnicity of Black Africans that has not been asked outside the framework of census questions, even though an open response question might yield insights into how people of sub-Saharan African origins prefer to identify themselves.

One of the few sources is a community research intervention amongst Africans in London (Redbridge and Waltham Forest) (Ndofor-Tah 2000). Amongst the 1,008 residents interviewed, more than three-quarters were born in Somalia (48 %), the Congo (13 %), Algeria (10 %), and Ghana (6 %), the remaining being born in around 30 mainly sub-Saharan African countries. Participants were asked how they would describe their 'ethnic group' 'with no set answer'. Almost half the sample described their ethnic group as either 'African' (26 %) or 'Black African' (22 %), confirming the saliency of these terms in unprompted open response. Another quarter (26 %) described their ethnic group as 'Somali'. The remaining quarter used a very wide range of terms to describe their ethnicity. The self-nominated ethnic group terms included national origins ('Algerian', 'Congolese', and 'Nigerian'), regional terms ('North African', 'East African'), and more complex descriptions ('Algerian Berber', 'African Somali', 'North African Arab', 'Bantou-Kongo', 'African Black Congolese', 'Zairean [Congolese] Muslim', 'Akan [Akwapim]' and 'Ugandan [Bantu]'). Self-nominated ethnic group and country of birth did not wholly overlap, several terms being used to describe those born in the same country.

There is no more extensive evidence base on preferred terminology or group identity descriptors of the kind used to inform the 2000 US Census question on race, an example being the use of the Current Population Survey Supplement (Tucker et al. 1996), an interview survey of around 60,000 households from different racial backgrounds, which provided an opportunity for people to express their preferences for specific designations identified in cognitive interviews (in the case of the Black population the terms 'black', 'African American', and 'Afro-American'). The 2001 People, Families and Communities Survey asked respondents to describe their ethnic group and cultural background using the 2001 Census classification. Later in the survey, a question was asked: 'If you were not limited to the descriptions on that card, but could use your own words, how would you describe your ethnic group and cultural background?' While the verbatim descriptions were not released, the responses were coded into 39 subcategories which enable the saliency of certain identity constructions to be established (Table 4.4).

Amongst the 705 respondents selecting the 'Black or Black British: African' category, around only 2.8 % gave a stand-alone 'British' response, and 4.7 % identified as 'British African'. However, over a third (35.9 %) gave a description of 'African/South African/Zimbabwean/Somali/ Nigeria/Zaire/mention of other African country or nationality (*no mention of British/English*)'. Descriptions including the term 'Black' also had saliency: again, over a third (35.7 %) described themselves using the term 'Black', 'Black British/Black English', and 'Black African/Black Nigerian/Black+mention of other African country or nationality'; 7.4 % did not know how to describe themselves. Like the *Capital Assets* survey, these data also show that terms encompassing the word 'Black'—such as 'Black African'—compete on coequal terms with the descriptor 'African'

Table 4.4 Responses to question on how you would describe your ethnic group and cultural background using 'your own words', People, Families and Communities Survey, 2001

Open response answer	Mixed		Black or Black British		
	White and Black Caribbean (n=143)	White and Black African (n=62)	Caribbean (n=1,008)	African (n=705)	Other Black background (n=139)
Same as in ethnicity question	1	0	17	14	1
British	11	3	75	20	11
English	3	1	20	1	4
White	3	1	0	0	0
Welsh/British Welsh/White Welsh	0	0	2	0	1
Scottish/White Scottish	1	0	0	1	0
Irish/White Irish	2	0	0	0	0
Other mentions of UK regions, towns, etc.	2	0	2	0	0
Anglo-Saxon	0	0	0	1	0
French/Italian/Greek/Swedish/Polish/other specific European	1	1	2	1	1
European/White European	0	0	1	2	0
British Asian (or Asian British)/British Indian, etc.	0	0	2	2	2
British West Indian/British Caribbean, British African, etc.	4	3	80	33	11
Asian/Indian, etc. (no mention of British/English)	0	0	4	2	0
Caribbean/Jamaican, etc. (no mention of British/English)	11	0	236	5	5
African/Nigerian/Zaire, etc. (no mention of British/English)	0	13	30	253	6
Other non-European country (no mention of British/English)	1	2	11	6	14
Black	5	0	92	31	13
Black British/Black English	4	4	137	40	23
Black Caribbean/Black Jamaican, etc.	7	1	163	3	9

CATEGORIES AND GROUP IDENTITIES 95

Black African/*Black* Nigerian, etc.	0	10	6	181	2
Mixed race/mixed culture/mixed origin, etc.	70	19	13	7	7
Mention of Muslim/Moslem/Islam/Islamic	0	1	0	13	2
Mention of Christian/Protestant, etc.	0	1	12	14	3
Other mentions of religion	2	0	5	7	0
Reference to class (working-, middle-, etc.)	0	0	5	5	3
Reference to gender	0	1	32	19	6
Reference to other personal characteristics	5	8	62	55	14
Citizen of world/human being, etc.	7	1	28	8	5
Mention of parents' or grandparents' country of origin	5	3	22	5	4
Other coding	3	1	7	10	1
Don't know	11	2	66	52	20
Refused	1	0	7	2	3
Not stated	6	3	31	19	5

Source: Home Office People, Families and Communities Survey (renamed Citizenship Survey), 2001. Dataset SN 4754, accessed via the Economic and Social Data Service (ESDS) and analysed in STATA

or an African country or nationality, that is, 'Africanness' or 'blackness' conjoined with 'Africanness'.

Besides these data, a few studies have pointed to salient terminology for particular African origin communities (notably Somalis). We also have the evidence of the *write-in* responses to the 'Any other Black background' category in the 2001 and 2011 England and Wales Census questions, these being people who felt unable to tick 'Caribbean' or 'African', instead choosing a free-text description in the residual Other Black option.

'AFRICANNESS' VERSUS 'BLACKNESS'

Debates about how the sub-Saharan African population should be categorised lie at the interface between 'blackness' and 'Africanness'. An inclusive 'Africanness' is one that accommodates those who consider themselves African irrespective of ethnic origin. This approach has rarely been used in data collection, a notable exception being Sigma Research's 2008 Bass Line African Health and Sex Survey, commissioned by the African HIV Policy Network (Dodds et al. 2008). This lumps together all those with ancestral origins in Africa, content to define 'Africans' as persons who have origins in any part of the continent, whatever their ethnicity. The survey's ethnicity question offers the categories 'Black African', 'Black African British', 'African Asian', 'African Arab', 'White African', 'African Caribbean', 'Mixed race African', and 'Other' (the two latter being open response). The question instruction adds that 'this survey is for people who consider themselves African'. 'Africanness', here, is defined as an affiliation to the continent of Africa based on one's origins and irrespective of ethnicity, an inclusive 'Africanness' that includes complex histories of migration and non-Black identities and is redolent of Mamdani's (2001) vision of an inclusive African identity in Africa. Such inclusiveness could, potentially, encompass African Indians and 'Black' and 'White' North Africans, for example, depending on their affiliations.

The only similar example was the General Register Office for Scotland's 2006 Census Test questionnaire. The ethnicity question eschewed colour terms ('White', 'Black') for a conceptual base of *ethnic background or culture*, thereby privileging 'Africanness' over 'blackness' but still within an ethnicity context. The set contained seven options ('North African', 'East African', 'Southern African', etc.). However, when the GRO(S) linked responses from the 2001 Census ethnic group question to the same person's response to the 2006 Census Test ethnic group question, the new question demonstrated poor efficacy. There was movement from 'White' in 2001 to 'African' categories in 2006, suggesting that White 'Africans' identified more strongly with the 'African' than 'European' category in the 2006 Census Test, and showing that the public interpreted the options as offering an inclusive 'Africanness' and not one usually mediated by the term 'black'.

'Blackness' invokes the referent 'black', a term that is acceptable to most Black African community members, although some constituencies including academic stakeholders and some African community organisations find the term offensive. Amongst the wide variety of ways in which the term has been used, 'black' in the 1970s and 1980s was employed as a political term to strategically mobilise under a common identity all minority ethnic groups who shared a common experience of discrimination and disadvantage but this usage has all but disappeared. 'Black' also has a long history of use as a colour label to identify those discriminated against on the basis of skin colour. In addition, over the last few decades, the term has been reclaimed by people of African and Caribbean origins as a positive identity label and self-descriptor. While some treat 'blackness' and 'Africanness' as synonymous or interchangeable, the interface between them is complex. 'Africanness' avoids the use of colour as an identity marker and has the potential to be inclusive in a way that 'blackness' cannot. While 'Africanness' does not mean ignoring racism (Pissarra 2004), some argue that the language of colour is needed to set White privilege against Black disadvantage (Krieger et al. 1999).

With respect to 2011 Census categorisation, a notable difference between England and Wales and Scotland is the lack of a 'black' referent in the African categorisation in the Scottish question but the use of a 'black' signalling device (as the first term in the overarching label) in England and Wales. Throughout its 2011 CDP, the Scottish census agency has shown greater concern over the issue of colour categories and considered abandoning them entirely. However, cognitive question testing of a version that did include 'Black' in the overarching label did find that 'in most cases, choice of response option did not stem from any objection to the word "Black" and, indeed, many respondents have spontaneously described themselves as "Black"' (Homes and Murray 2008). The ONS addressed the issue in the England and Wales context in its equality impact assessment of the cultural question set (ONS 2008) with regard to their use in the pan-ethnic labels (the cases of 'White' and 'Black or Black British'). It had indicated that it 'had conducted research into the

acceptability of colour labels amongst majority and minority ethnic communities in England and Wales', suggesting that 'the colour labels are
acceptable to the great majority of people from all communities, but not
to all'. These consultations revealed conflicting views about the acceptability of the colour term 'Black or Black British': 'It is viewed as offensive
to some people of African heritage, setting them apart from others, such
as Asians, who are not defined in the Census by the colour of their skin.
However, other people of African heritage identify with the term "Black",
which they consider to be a term of visibility that draws its meaning from
the civil rights struggle of the 1960s in the USA.'

THE HETEROGENEITY OF THE 'BLACK AFRICAN' GROUP

One of the most intractable problems in undertaking research and policy
work on the 'Black African' group is the substantial diversity or heterogeneity concealed in this label. 'Black African' shares this position with other
broad terms or categories used in censuses and surveys such as 'Other
White background' and 'Any other ethnic group', also difficult to unpack
with the pervasive use of the 2001 and 2011 classifications. Routinely collected data on school pupils (the ASC) are one of the few official sources
that are able to reveal such heterogeneity through a finer granularity of
'extended codes'.

The set of extended codes (Department for Education and Skills
[DfES] 2006a) used for classification by the largest number of local
authorities is, indeed, the 'Other White', followed by the 'Any Other' and
'Black African' categories, the last being the only predesignated or closed
Census category (DfES 2006b) with such codes. The 'Other White'
group encompassed 'Turkish/Turkish Cypriot' (13,814 pupils), 'White
European' (11,515), 'White Western European' (7,779), 'White Eastern
European' (6,563), 'Greek/Greek Cypriot' (4,472), 'Italian' (2,361),
'Kosovan' (2,014), 'Portuguese' (1,580), and 'Albanian', 'Croatian',
'Bosnian-Herzegovinian', and 'Serbian' (each under a thousand). The
constituency of the catch-all 'Any Other' group was, unsurprisingly, most
diverse: 'Arab' ($n = 3,783$), 'Afghani' (2,732), 'Vietnamese' (2,564),
'Latin American' (2,434), 'Yemeni' (1,909), 'Kurdish' (1,748), 'Filipino'
(1,456), 'Iranian' (1,361), and 'Iraqi', 'Korean', 'Moroccan', 'Lebanese',
'Japanese', 'Egyptian', 'Thai', 'Malay', and 'Libyan' (each around a thousand or fewer). Finally, the largest specific groups within 'Black African'
were 'Somali' ($n = 21,077$), 'Nigerian' (15,900), 'Ghanaian' ($n = 6,596$),

and 'Congolese', 'Sierra Leonean', 'Sudanese', and 'Angolan' (each around a thousand or fewer). The diversity concealed within these broad terms is also indicated for adults whose first language is other than English, in the 'Count Me In' national census ranging between one-third and two-fifths (Aspinall 2007a). In the case of the 'Black African' group, it is both the degree of concealed diversity within a geographically specific label and the size and growth rate of the group that calls for action.

As noted in this chapter, the 2001 and 2011 Census socio-cultural question set provides some information on dimensions of ethnicity: country of birth (but not family ethnic origins), religion, and, for 2011, additionally main language and national identity. However, a limiting factor has been the number of countries of birth specified, especially low in the 2001 Census. *Standard* Census tables for the 2001 Census provided a breakdown of the 'Black African' ethnic group by country of birth for just four countries (Nigeria, Kenya, South Africa, and Zimbabwe) and the regions of 'North', 'Central and Western', and 'South and Eastern' Africa. Stand-alone country of birth tables provide additional information on those born in Nigeria, Ghana, Somalia, Zimbabwe, Uganda, Democratic Republic of Congo, Sierra Leone, Kenya, and the rest of Africa in 2001. For some groups, country of birth is a very poor proxy for 'Black African' ethnicity: While in the 2001 Census, 87.7 % of those born in Nigeria were 'Black African', only 37.9 % of those born in Zimbabwe so identified, 10.5 % of those born in Kenya, and just 3.2 % of those born in South Africa.

Other important axes of differentiation are migration channels and migration statuses, including workers, students, migrating spouses and family members, asylum seekers and refugees, and illegal or irregular (undocumented) migrants, although respondent sensitivities with regard to some would make a census question on migration histories impractical. These may be as significant as country of origin, ethnicity, religion, and language in shaping migrants' identities, their group allegiances, and social interactions. How migration impacts on community identity is complex, migrant communities including those who strive to retain their cultural identity and those who endeavour to embrace the culture of the host community, and all the gradations between (Elam et al. 2000).

With respect to country of origin, it is difficult to distinguish the different channels. The Refugee Council has argued that 'Current national ethnicity monitoring categories are too wide and cannot show variations between small ethnic or language groups. For example, within the Black

African group, there is no distinction between Somali refugees and cannot distinguish between Somali refugee and Nigerian expats' (Refugee Council 2004, p. 16). Somalis in Britain may be British citizens, refugees, asylum seekers, persons granted exceptional leave to remain, undocumented migrants, and 'seamen' and their descendants who settled in port areas over 50 years ago. While the Nigerian and Ghanaian communities encompass mainly voluntary, planned migration and students, more recently there has been an asylum-seeker/refugee channel.

Few agencies have addressed this problem of concealed heterogeneity. The Higher Education Statistics Agency's (HESA) guidance indicates that 'any new categories should be introduced only as sub-groups of the core categories... e.g. *Any other Black background* could include Kenyan, Ghanaian and Nigerian' (Higher Education Funding Council for England 2004, p. 13). HESA's requirements do extend beyond ethnicity to include nationality, an optional field, but this is returned with low levels of data. Only 'country of domicile' (the permanent home address immediately prior to entry and a more reliable measure) is useful, data for which indicate that Nigeria has been in the top ten ranking countries, numbers increasing from 5,940 in 2003/2004 to 8,145 in 2004/2005, 9,605 in 2005/2006 (Higher Education Statistics Agency 2007b), and 17,395 in 2012/2013.

In official data collection, some of the country of origin groups are potentially identifiable through the use of 'local'/'extended code lists' when these are used for data collection. In addition to the Census coding frames and ASC, detailed extended ethnicity codes have been developed for the 'Children in Need' collection and Department of Health data sets, amongst others. For example, the DfES (2006a) offers the following extended 'Black African' categories: 'Black Angolan', 'Black Congolese', 'Black Ghanaian', 'Black Nigerian', 'Black Sierra Leonean', 'Black Somali', 'Black Sudanese', and 'Other Black African' (including Black South African, Angolan, Zimbabwean, Ethiopian, Rwandan, and Ugandan). The same codes are used for the National Child and Adolescent Mental Health Service (CAMHS) Dataset (Tingay and Stein 2005).

However, there is no consistency in how local codes map back to the 2001 Census categories. The 'Children in Need' data collection (DfES 2005) uses the following codes for the 'Black or Black British' group: Caribbean, African, Somali, Mixed Black, Nigerian, Black British, and Other Black, Black unspecified. Nigerian, Somali, Kenyan, Black South African, and Other Black African countries are all assigned to 'Black

African', in accord with ONS guidance (Office for National Statistics 2003). However, for the NHS Commissioning Dataset, Hospital Episode Statistics, and Workforce collections, 'Somali', 'Mixed Black', 'Nigerian', 'Black British', and 'Other Black, Black unspecified' all map to 'Any other Black background' (NHS Information Authority 2001). Clearly, this will introduce significant error when such data are used in combination with census denominator data to produce rates and ratios.

This picture is further complicated in the case of some of the maternity databases. The NHS Perinatal Institute's Maternity Core Data Index offers the categories 'North Africa', 'SubSahara', and 'Other' under *Africa* for the Geographical Ethnic Origin of father, mother, and baby, indicating that 'the options do map to ONS requirements for NHS Numbers for Babies submissions' (NHS Perinatal Institute 2004, p. 10). However, the ethnicity mapping given for all three—including 'North Africa'—is to 'Black African'.

Given the pervasiveness of the use of the term 'Black African' in data collections, it is problematic to find disaggregated data, even by country of birth. While some collections relating to educational attainment have been located, examples relating to health status and care are extremely sparse. Educational attainment data routinely reported by DfES utilise nationally agreed ethnic background categories similar to those in the Census, but makes available over 90 'extended codes' for local education authority's (LEA) own management and planning purposes. The rationale for using the extended code set is the variability in educational attainment by geographic origin. Statistics on infectious diseases—notably TB and HIV/AIDS—also reveal that much heterogeneity is concealed by the use of broad categories like 'Black African'. Data recently published by the Health Protection Agency for the South-East (SE) London sector show the number of notifications of TB by country of birth subgroup (Somalia, Nigeria, Ethiopia, Zimbabwe, Ghana, and Uganda), revealing substantial variability in rates.

All the routine HIV/AIDS data collections (such as the Survey of Prevalent HIV Infection Diagnosed or SOPHID, now replaced by the HIV and AIDS Reporting System [HARS]) report on a 'Black African' group. However, country of birth has been used in a number of HIV health surveys and interviews, the study by Chinouya et al. (2003) yielding over 18 countries. The Health Protection Agency uses both regions and countries of birth: South-Eastern and Eastern Africa, Horn of Africa, Southern Africa, Central and South-Western Africa, Western Africa, and Northern

Africa (Sadler et al. 2005). The greatest increase in the number of HIV diagnoses has occurred among heterosexuals born in South-Eastern Africa (a 2.8-fold increase, 452 diagnoses in 2000 to 1,265 diagnoses in 2004), the majority of these individuals being born in Zimbabwe. The African HIV Framework has reported on the diversity of England's African communities in terms of cultural factors, but data collection mechanisms have limited what it has been able to say about the pattern of the epidemic in the UK in terms of the distinctiveness of the communities involved (Department of Health 2005).

CHAPTER 5

Where 'Black Africans' Live

The most reliable data on the residential patterns of Black Africans is the set of three censuses from 1991 to 2011. London has for long been a focal point of settlement for the Black African community. In 1991, a total of 163,622 Black Africans lived in the capital (of whom 108,956, or two-thirds [66.6 %], lived in Inner London). At this time, Black Africans resident in London comprised 78.1 % of the Black African population in England and Wales (209,589). When Daley (1998, p. 1723) examined the spatial concentration and segregation of Black Africans in Britain in the late 1990s, she predicted that 'a pattern of suburbanisation may begin to occur in the manner in which is now evident for the Caribbean community'. London was to maintain its dominance throughout the 1990s to the 2001 Census but then, indeed, came significant change.

In 2001, Greater London contained 378,914 Black Africans, 228,676 (60.4 %) of whom lived in Inner London. Black Africans resident in London comprised 79.0 % of the 479,655 Black Africans in England and Wales, that is, four out of every five. One of the most important changes in the residential patterns of Black Africans between the 2001 and 2011 censuses was the change in the size of the Black African population in London. In the 2011 Census 573,931 Black Africans were enumerated in London, a gain of 195,017. However, Black Africans in Inner London, 276,513, fell to 48.2 % of the London total. Moreover, London's share of the Black African population fell to 58.0 % as a proportion of the England and Wales total (989,628). The Black African population became substantially less

© The Editor(s) (if applicable) and The Author(s) 2016
P.J. Aspinall, M.J. Chinouya, *The African Diaspora Population in Britain*, DOI 10.1057/978-1-137-45654-0_5

concentrated in the capital as a result of a dramatic spreading out from London.

This chapter focuses on this dispersal or spreading out from the capital, the different patterns of residence according to communities of descent or country of birth, the decrease in segregation of the Black African group, and the extent to which Black Africans live in deprived neighbourhoods.

THE SPREADING OUT OF THE BLACK AFRICAN POPULATION

There has been a dramatic spreading out of the Black African population that has accompanied its increase in size during the decade 2001–2011, from an adjusted 494,669 (0.9 % of the population in England and Wales) to 989,628 (1.8 %). However, caution is needed in interpreting the percentage changes over this intercensal decade as 29.1 % of the 2001 Census count for Black Africans was imputed (i.e. estimated data to replace a combination of non-response and invalid data). Moreover, Sabater and Simpson (2009) have reported that the full estimated size of the Black African population in 2001 was 494,669 after taking into account 'Census undercount', compared with the England and Wales 2001 Census count of 479,665. However, the figures for changes at a local authority level given in this chapter do not take into account this undercount in 2001. Nearly every local authority in England and Wales experienced an increase in numbers over the decade. Only Camden (–8.4 %), City of London (–9.3 %), Kensington and Chelsea (–7.9 %), Cornwall UA (–0.7 %), West Somerset (–50.0 %), and Teignbridge (–32.4 %), Torridge (–38.9 %), and West Devon (–50.9 %), all in Devon, experienced decreases, along with Powys (–19.2 %) in Wales.

In Inner London of the 11 boroughs that experienced increases, there were those with modest increases of 15–25 % (Hackney, Haringey, Islington, Lambeth, Newham, and Southwark) and several with increases of >25–50 % (Hammersmith and Fulham, Lewisham, Tower Hamlets, Wandsworth, and Westminster), all well below the 100 % increase nationally. In Outer London, several boroughs exceeded the national percentage increase: Barking and Dagenham (293.8 %), Bexley (290.2 %), Bromley (191.0 %), Enfield (137.5 %), Greenwich (129.8 %), Havering (452.6 %), Hillingdon (166.7 %), and Sutton (147.8 %). It can be recalled that around 80 % of the Black African population lived in London in 2001.

However, the most dramatic changes have taken place outside London. A total of 267 local authorities experienced increases in excess of the national average, though as noted no adjustment is made for the

2001 undercount. While many of these were local authorities with small Black African populations in 2001 (Fig. 5.1), they also included large towns and cities. For example, in the north of England, the Black African population grew from 742 to 4,664 in Newcastle upon Tyne; from 6,651 to 25,718 in Manchester; from 3,077 to 8,490 in Liverpool; from 640 to 2,472 in Kingston upon Hull; from 3,297 to 11,543 in Sheffield; and from 2,437 to 14,894 in Leeds. In the East Midlands, the Black African population in Nottingham increased from 1,278 to 9,877; from 3,428 to 12,480 in Leicester; and from 1,363 to 6,473 in Northampton. In the West Midlands, Birmingham's Black African population increased from 6,205 to 29,991, and even larger percentage increases were seen in Coventry, Dudley, Sandwell, Walsall, and Wolverhampton. Many small towns around the West Midlands Metropolitan County with small African populations in 2001 experienced dramatic increases, including Stoke-on-Trent (872 %), Litchfield (842 %), Nuneaton and Bedworth (650 %), and Rugby (1,093 %), perhaps suggesting a movement away from inner-city areas.

The ring of small towns in the home counties also experienced substantial growth: from 365 to 2,054 in Central Bedfordshire UA; from 970 to 9,742 in Thurrock UA; from 479 to 3,339 in Basildon; from 357 to

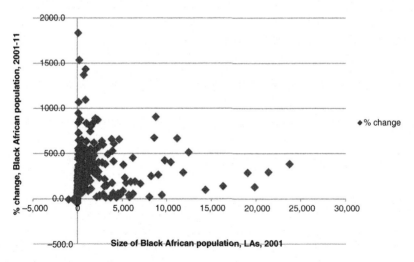

Fig. 5.1 Percentage change in the size of the Black African population, 2001–2011, local authorities in England and Wales.
Source: 2001 and 2011 Censuses, England and Wales

2,256 in Harlow; from 388 to 1,915 in Stevenage; from 265 to 1,727 in Norwich; from 668 to 4,742 in Medway UA; and from 225 to 2,226 in Gravesham. Increases were smaller in Surrey, West Sussex, and East Sussex towns, possibly because of high property prices and a lack of affordable housing. However, in the South-West, 6 of the 12 Unitary Authorities experienced increases of over 300 %, including Bristol. Increases above the national average were experienced in most Welsh local authorities, including in particular Swansea (808 %) and Newport (500 %).

What might have caused this dramatic spreading out from London in particular? Many Black Africans and their families may have chosen to move out of the Inner London boroughs—that is, out of the inner city—to better-class housing areas. The increase in the Black African population across nearly all local authorities, including those with a very small Black African population in 2001, does suggest a more general move out of Inner London to provincial cities and to suburban and even relatively rural areas. Moreover, while new Black African migrants arriving in the decade 2001–2011 might have chosen locales in the traditional areas of settlement in Inner and Outer London, replacing those Black Africans who had decided to move out, others might have sought locations in the rest of England or been allocated to those areas through the asylum-seeker dispersal programme. The concentration of the Black African population in the private rented housing sector may have facilitated the spreading out process.

Indeed, a striking finding of the Understanding Population Trends and Processes (UPTAP) research programme (Mitton and Aspinall 2011) was how frequently Black Africans move. Over 20 % had moved in the 12-month period before the 2001 Census. It can be recalled from Chap. 3 that the Black African group had the highest proportion (25.6 %) of any ethnic group with a different address 1 year before the 1991 Census, almost three times the proportion compared to the Black Caribbean group.

VARIATIONS IN PATTERNS OF RESIDENCE BY
COMMUNITIES OF DESCENT

The heterogeneity concealed in the 'Black African' Census group or category clearly has implications for policy as linguistic and national origin subgroups vary in terms of disadvantage, and these subgroups frequently have different geographical distributions (including how they compare to the Black African group as a whole). The dilemma is articulated by Mateos (2014, p. v): 'Because Bangladeshis comprises an ethnic group on their own in the census form, they get all the good and bad attention in academia and public policy. Meanwhile in Camden an equally sized group, the Somalis, complained of not getting the same level of resources because they were "statistically hidden" under the all-encompassing "Black African" group.'

While a pattern of concentration of Black Africans in London was a consistent picture across the 1991 and 2001 censuses, a spreading out of the Black African population was notable in the 2011 Census. The distinctive patterns of residence for Black African subgroups have been more difficult to establish over recent decades as the Census ethnic group question does not break down the 'Black African' collectivity into its specific communities of descent. A number of sources of evidence can be used to investigate these more finely grained distributions. Firstly, the decennial censuses offer the scope to explore patterns by country of birth, though the number of country origins is quite limited at a small spatial scale. Similarly, information on religion subgroups (notably, Black African Muslims and Christians) is available for more detailed geographical areas. In the 2011 Census, information was collected for the first time on 'main language' (with a write-in space for languages other than English) and how well the person speaks English, though the number of African languages reported is limited.

In addition to the decennial censuses, two other sources have been used to investigate residential patterns of Black African subgroups. Firstly, Mateos (2014) has used distinctive Black African first names and surnames to map the residential patterns of a number of communities of descent in London. This work has been pioneering in its use of names and in its robust statistical techniques. However, the deletion of this resource—Onomap Subgroups—from the University College London website represents a substantial loss to the scholarly community, though some distribution maps survive in publications (e.g. Nigerian and Somalian). Secondly, the Annual School Census offers local authorities the use of 'extended' ethnicity codes for some of the census ethnic categories. Such codes are widely used by London boroughs, so they offer scope to map Black Africans for selected national origin groups but for school pupils only. Further, information has been collected on the language spoken at home by school pupils since 2007, offering a further dimension or subgroup that is amenable to mapping. The data have been exploited by a number of scholars (Mitton 2011; Eversley et al. 2010) to delineate specific residential patterns of Black African subgroups by language. Thus, while 10 years ago relatively little was known about where various Black African subgroups lived, recent exploitation of these sources has added significantly to our understanding of these residential patterns. They enable the distribution of several large African communities—including Somalis, Nigerians, and Ghanaians—to be determined.

Most of these sources have drawbacks. Country of birth data yields information for migrants rather than the full sizes of different communities of descent, including the second generation. Census language data are limited with respect to main language as it only includes speakers of African languages whose main language is not English. Moreover, the number of African languages that are separately distinguished is very limited. Data on language from the Annual School Census are clearly limited to the school cohorts, though the concept used, 'first language'[1] provides a useful measure with respect to diversity. The data provide a more comprehensive picture of the diversity of languages spoken by Black African families than other sources, though routine data at small-scale geographies are very limited. Published analyses are largely confined to London. Data on Black African names are limited to Mateos's (2014) analysis for London which is now a decade out of date, being based on data for 2004. Moreover, patterns are discerned for only a very small number of (Onomap) African subgroups.

Data on Somali speakers provide one of the most comprehensive sources of information on the distribution of the Somali population as the group was not captured in the census's ethnicity question. However, there are drawbacks, notably, that speakers of Somali are mainly located in Somalia but there are also speakers in the adjacent regions of Ethiopia, Kenya, and Djibouti. The 2011 Census records persons who identified their main language as Somali, a total of 85,918 persons with this main language being enumerated in England and Wales, 54,852 (63.8 %) of whom were resident in London, a larger proportion than all Black Africans. Outside London significant numbers were found in the North-West (4,982), East Midlands (4,327), West Midlands (9,544), and South-West (5,131) regions. The largest London communities were in Brent (6,079) and Ealing (5,611), though around a dozen boroughs had Somali-speaking communities of between 2,000 and 3,500 (Camden, Enfield, Hammersmith and Fulham, Haringey, Hillingdon, Hounslow, Islington, Lambeth, Newham, Tower Hamlets, and Wandsworth).

---

[1] 'First Language' is the language to which a child was initially exposed during early development and continues to be exposed to this language in the home or in the community. This is a compulsory data item for all pupils aged 5 and over.

Distribution maps of pupils in London whose first language was Somali (the count of resident pupils per Middle Layer Super Output Area [MSOA], a geographical unit with a population range of 5,000–15,000), based on the Annual School Census, show a similar pattern.[2] Though the community is more dispersed than for some other language groups—such as Bengali speakers, concentrated in Tower Hamlets, and Urdu speakers in the neighbouring boroughs of Newham, Redbridge, Waltham Forest, Ealing/Hounslow, and Merton/Wandsworth—there are, nevertheless, noted concentrations of Somali-speaking pupils in the eastern part of Hillingdon and the abutting part of Ealing, in Brent and the northern part of Hammersmith and Fulham, and in the eastern part of Enfield (Eversley et al. 2010; Von Ahn et al. 2010a, b). There is an almost complete absence of this community in the eastern and southern boroughs (Havering, Bexley, Bromley, Croydon, Sutton, Merton, Kingston upon Thames, and Richmond upon Thames). The 2008 Annual School Census records 27,126 Somali speakers, the boroughs with the highest numbers being Ealing (3,531), Brent (2,034), Newham (1,582), Hillingdon (1,525), Enfield (1,483), Camden (1,331), and Harrow (1,316). However, both borough- and MSOA-level data show that Somali speakers were spread out across London north of the Thames. There were 33 MSOAs with 117–525 Somali-speaking pupils, 59 with 74–117 pupils, 95 with 48–74 pupils, 151 with 29–48 pupils, and 645 MSOAs with 0–29 pupils.

The residential patterns of some other Black African communities of origin can also be captured by language. Yoruba is a language of south-west Nigeria and Benin and reveals a very different pattern to that of Somali speakers. In the 2008 Annual School Census there were 13,961 speakers in London (Eversley et al. 2010). The boroughs with the largest numbers were Southwark (2,130), Greenwich (1,936), Hackney (1,512), Lambeth (1,223), Lewisham (1,042), and Newham (1,018). The map of Yoruba speakers at MSOA level[3] shows this concentration in boroughs in South and East London abutting the Thames. A total of 22 MSOAs had 99–278 speakers, 34 MSOAs with 62–99 speakers, 59 MSOAs with 34–62 speakers, 142 MSOAs with 14–34 speakers, and 726 MSOAs 0–14 speakers. The Onomap Subgroup for Nigerian shows clustering similar to that of the map of Yoruba speakers.

---

[2] See Eversley et al. (2010), p. 53: Individual language maps: Somali.
[3] See Eversley et al. (2010), p. 57: Individual language maps: Yoruba.

This pattern is confirmed by another analysis at ward level of Yoruba speakers from the 2008 Annual School Census (Mitton 2011, Fig. 2), with high concentrations in Greenwich, Bexley, Hackney, and Southwark. Yoruba pupils were most concentrated in Thamesmead Moorings in Greenwich (which has been dubbed 'Little Lagos'), where an estimated 16 % of pupils were Yoruba speakers. There was also a high concentration of Yoruba speakers in Thamesmead East Ward in neighbouring Bexley. While Yoruba speakers were overwhelmingly concentrated in London, there were clusters outside London in Thurrock, Gravesham, and Croydon.

Speakers of other West African languages show a similar distribution in London (Eversley et al. 2010). Igbo is a language with over 18 million speakers in south-east Nigeria where it has regional status. In 2008 there were 2,837 pupil speakers of this language in London. The boroughs with the largest numbers were Hackney (305), Greenwich (284), Enfield (254), and Southwark (247). Akan/Twi/Fante is a language spoken in southern Ghana by 8–9 million people, about 35 % of the population. Akan/Twi/Fante speakers in London numbered 8,117 according to the 2008 Annual School Census. The boroughs with the largest numbers were Lambeth (837), Newham (830), Haringey (807), Hackney (733), Enfield (729), that is, including areas of traditional Black African settlement. If all these West African languages are summed (Yoruba, Akan/Twi/Fante, Igbo, and other West African languages), the largest numbers were to be found in Southwark (3,475), Hackney (2,831), Greenwich (2,710), Lambeth (2,620), Newham (2,290), and Lewisham (1,940).

Pupil speakers of East, Central and South African languages (Lingala, Swahili, Luganda, Shona, and other East, Central, and South African languages) numbered 11,161 in 2008, including Lingala (3,135), Swahili (2,895), Luganda (1,689), and Shona (1,098). The boroughs with the largest number of these languages were Newham (1,180), Barking and Dagenham (819), Enfield (780), Haringey (752), and Southwark (752). Amongst other languages in this group, there is a concentration of Acholi speakers in Southwark (242 out of 361 in London as a whole) (Eversley et al. 2010), while four boroughs in North-East London (Haringey, Waltham Forest, Newham, and Redbridge) account for about half of all speakers of Mauritian/Seychelles Creole (142 out of 286).

Shona is the language of Zimbabwe where it is spoken by over 10 million people or nearly 80 % of the population and Shona dialects are also spoken in Mozambique. There is a cluster of Shona speakers in Lewisham and Greenwich which jointly account for 20 % of the total Shona-speaking pupil population in London. An analysis at ward level (Mitton 2011, Fig. 3) confirms that Shona-speaking pupils were dispersed across the whole of London, with a partial clustering effect in North Greenwich (especially Thamesmead) and north Bexley. Outside London (Mitton 2011, Fig. 4), Shona speakers were found in relatively large numbers in several regions of England, notably, Yorkshire and Humberside and the South-East, including the ring of small towns around the capital. Small clusters were discernible within parts of Harlow, Luton, Slough, Leicester, Southend-on-Sea, and Stevenage, though concentrations were low. For example, in the ward with the highest concentration of Shona-speaking pupils (Milton in Southend-on-Sea) they comprised only 2.5 % of the pupil population.

With respect to country of birth, Nigeria and Ghana have tradition-ally been the largest migrant communities in London, the latter now overtaken by Somalia (65,333 residents in London). The 2011 Census enumerated 191,183 persons in England and Wales who were born in Nigeria, 114,718 (60.0 %) of whom lived in London. There were 93,846 persons born in Ghana, of whom 62,896 (67.0 %) lived in London. The Zimbabwean migrant community in London was smaller (21,309). Smaller communities of origin in London included persons born in the Democratic Republic of Congo (19,193 of whom 10,388 or 51.1 % lived in London) and persons born in Sierra Leone (23,118, of whom 17,245 or 74.6 % lived in London). Thus, apart from the Congolese, these three migrant communities had higher proportions living in London than Black Africans as a whole. This may reflect the fact that recent migrants still grav-itate towards the locale of London—a traditional settlement area for Black Africans—while others including Black African families start to move away.

These larger country of birth groups (Nigeria, Ghana, Zimbabwe, and Somalia) and others to which asylum seekers have contributed significantly (Sierra Leone, Democratic Republic of Congo, Eritrea, and Ethiopia) all show distinctive patterns of residence in 2011 (Fig. 5.2).

In 2011 the average per ward of Nigerian migrants in London was 183.5 persons. The main concentrations of Nigerians clustered in East London, Greenwich (Thamesmead Moorings, Abbey Wood, Glydon, and Woolwich Common), Bexley (Thamesmead East), and Southwark (Peckham), all these wards having counts of over 1,500. The average per ward of Ghanaian migrants was 100.6. The main areas of residence were more

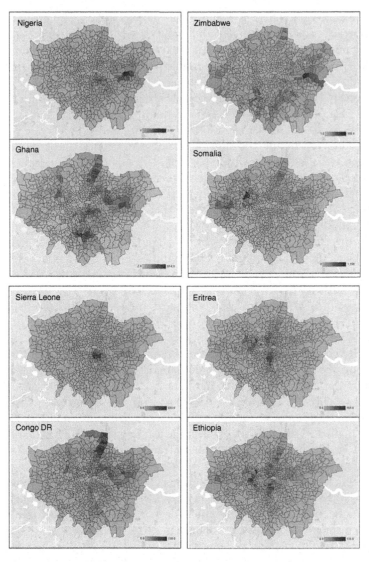

Fig. 5.2   Where African migrants lived in London in 2011: Nigeria, Ghana, Zimbabwe, Somalia, Sierra Leone, Congo DR, Eritrea, and Ethiopia country of birth groups.
Source: Data taken from 2011 Census Commissioned Table CT0226.
Notes: The mapping tool is from the Greater London Authority London Datastore (© OpenStreetMap contributors). Key shows counts

dispersed than for Nigerians: Merton (Pollards Hill), Enfield (Edmonton Green), Croydon (Bensham Manor and Thornton Heath), and Haringey (Northumberland Park), all wards with counts of over 540. The average per ward of Somali migrants was 104.5, the highest concentrations of this dispersed community being in Brent (Stonebridge, 1,158, and Harlesden, 947, wards), but with significant concentrations in wards in Ealing, Hammersmith and Fulham, and Enfield. The average per ward of Zimbabwean migrants was 34.09, the main concentrations (again dispersed) being in Greenwich (Thamesmead Moorings), Wandsworth (Earlsfield), Bexley (Thamesmead East and Erith wards), and Merton (Dundonald), all wards with counts of over 100. These counts, of course, may include ethnically White Zimbabwean migrants.

The smaller migrant communities with significant numbers of refugees showed more concentrated patterns of residence in London. The average per ward of the Sierra Leonean migrant community (17,245 in London) was 27.59. The community was highly concentrated in Southwark: all of the top ranking 11 wards (each with a count of over 200) were in Southwark. The average per ward of Democratic Republic of Congo migrants was 16.62. The main area of concentration was in Enfield wards, 5 of the 6 wards with a count of over 100 being in this borough. The average per ward of the Eritrean migrant community (10,198) was 16.32. The main concentration was in wards in Lambeth: 6 of the 7 top ranking wards, each with a count of more than 100, were in the borough, the first ranking ward (with 164 Eritrean migrants) being in Brent. Finally, average per ward of the Ethiopian migrant community in London (numbering 10,517) was 16.83. This community was more dispersed with a total of 5 wards in the boroughs of Brent, Hammersmith and Fulham, and Lambeth having counts of over 100.

SEGREGATION AND MIXING

Residential segregation based on ethnicity has been high on the political agenda in Britain for some 15 years. It became a policy issue following the disturbances in Bradford, Burnley, and Oldham in 2001. From this time a policy of informal multiculturalism was increasingly abandoned for one focusing on integration, community cohesion, national identity ('Britishness'), and citizenship, as was evident in the White papers *Secure Borders, Safe Haven* (2002) and *Our Shared Future* (2007). Concepts like 'self-segregation' and 'parallel lives' were used to justify policies of community cohesion advanced by the Commission on Integration and Cohesion. Following the July 2005 bombings in London, Trevor Phillips's 'Sleepwalking to Segregation' speech warned of 'marooned communities' and 'no-go areas'. Once again, in July 2015, the headlines in the quality press have been 'war on segregation is rife with pitfalls' and 'No. 10 demands ethnic mix' following the Prime Minister's speech in Birmingham, in which he claimed that there were areas where young people could 'hardly ever come into meaningful contact with people from other backgrounds and faiths'. Segregated social housing estates and schools were particularly condemned.

Many of these myths—that 'so many minorities cannot be integrated', that 'minorities do not want to be integrated', that 'minorities want to live in segregated neighbourhoods', and 'Britain is becoming a country of ghettos'—have been challenged and countered by Finney and Simpson (2009) through a careful analysis of census and other statistics. Moreover, analyses based on the 2011 Census show that residential segregation has been decreasing and neighbourhood residential mixing increasing. The Black African group has more strongly demonstrated these trends than most other ethnic groups.

MEASURES OF SEGREGATION

There has been extensive debate about the optimal measures of residential segregation and mixing. Much of the pioneering work was undertaken by Massey and Denton (1988) who identified 'five dimensions of residential segregation': evenness, exposure, concentration, clustering, and centralisation. The last was derived for US cities where ethnic minority groups typically occupy well-defined core inner-city areas. This dimension is less applicable to European cities, for example, London has a multiplicity of historic town centres, and generally deemed less relevant.

Evenness is measured through the Index of Dissimilarity (ID) (Duncan and Duncan 1955) which has now become the standard segregation index in academic studies. The ID represents the proportion of the group's population that would have to move between areas in order for the group to become distributed in the same way as the rest of the population (i.e. evenly distributed).[4] *Exposure* measures the degree of potential contact, or physical interaction, between two groups within geographical areas of a

[4] Definitions have been taken from Mateos (2014). The formula is given as (9.1) in Mateos (2014), p. 225.

city, by virtue of sharing a common area of residence (Massey and Denton 1988). The index of exposure most widely used is the index of isolation P* proposed by Shevky and Williams (1949) and modified by others. As used by Mateos (2014),[5] the isolation index measures the probability of a member of ethnic group x entering into contact with a member of the same group within an area of residence. *Concentration* refers to the relative amount of physical space occupied by a group in a city. The Absolute Concentration Index (ACO) was proposed by Massey and Denton (1988) and calculates the total area inhabited by a group and compares this figure with the minimum and maximum spatial concentration that could be inhabited by the group in a given city or an area.[6] The maximum spatial concentration is achieved when all members of the group live in the smallest space possible. Finally, the *clustering* dimension measures the degree to which members of a group inhabit areas which are contiguous and closely packed (i.e. presenting a clustered pattern). The Absolute Clustering Index (ACL) (Massey and Denton 1988) expresses the average number of members of a group in neighbouring spatial units as a proportion of the total population in those neighbouring units.

Several studies have provided an analysis of residential segregation, using different data sources and with different focuses. Simpson (2012) and Catney (2015) use the census's ethnicity categories to analyse segregation using ID. The main benefit of using the census is that national and local change in residential change over time can be measured. Mateos (2014) has undertaken a more extensive exploratory analysis of a wider range of residential segregation indices at a more finely granulated level than the census categories, including the four main indices reviewed by Massey and Denton (1988), spatial indices (which include spatial features) proposed by Wong (2003, 2004), and segregation classifications based on thresholds (Brimicombe 2007; Johnson et al. 2003). As some, such as those proposed by Wong, yielded very similar results he focuses on just the four indices (outlined in the measures of segregation above), and an additional measure of clustering. These measures are calculated for only one point in time (2004), which is more than a decade out of date. However, the Onomap Subgroups uncover the substantial variability in the residential patterns of disaggregate ethnic groups which are concealed in the aggregate 'Black African' census category.

[5] The formula is given as (9.2) in Mateos (2014), p. 229.
[6] The formula is given as (9.2) in Mateos (2014), p. 231.

NEIGHBOURHOOD ETHNIC RESIDENTIAL SEGREGATION
USING CENSUS CATEGORIES

Catney (2015) has analysed residential segregation, across the three most recent censuses which have all included an ethnic group question (1991–2001–2011) for the whole of England and Wales. All ethnic groups (the 'Other' ethnic groups are excluded from the analysis) have become more dispersed over time. One of the most notable changes has been in the Black African group. Segregation changed little between 1991 and 2001 but fell by around 10 percentage points between 1991 and 2011, nearly all of this taking place in 2001–2011. By contrast the fall between 1991 and 2011 was 8, 6, and 5 percentage points for the Indian, Bangladeshi, and Pakistani groups, respectively. The Mixed White and Black African and Mixed White and Black Caribbean groups experienced a decrease of around or under 3 percentage points.

Percentage point *local* change in neighbourhood segregation between 2001 and 2011 is also calculated by Catney (2015) using the ID. This is calculated for Output Areas within each local authority district in England and Wales. In most districts segregation decreased for all minority ethnic groups. The Black African group saw a decrease in neighbourhood segregation in 69 % of districts and an increase in 31 %. Several other ethnic groups saw decreases of more than two-thirds of districts: Black Caribbean (decrease 72 %, increase 28 %), Indian (decrease 71 %, increase 29 %), and Mixed (decrease 71 %, increase 29 %) ethnic groups. The Black African and Mixed groups saw the largest median change in segregation (–7 and –6 percentage points, respectively) and larger than the Black Caribbean group (–4 %).

Clearly, dynamic processes of demographic change (Chaps. 2 and 3) are taking place in areas between censuses that affect the level of segregation: growth or decline may be affected by natural change (births and deaths), immigration and emigration, and by internal migration (migration into or out of the area from/to other parts of the country). The main mechanisms with respect to decreasing segregation are likely to be what Catney (2015) calls 'the spreading out of diversity (migration away from co-ethnic clusters) and natural change'. While movement out from urban clusters is common to all ethnic groups, researchers have shown that the process is differentiated by socio-economic position (Simpson and Finney 2009; Catney and Simpson 2010). Moreover, there remain some increases in segregation that reflect minority ethnic disadvantage, such as inequalities in the housing and labour markets or, as Catney (2015) suggests marginalised populations seeking protection from racism in areas with more dense populations of their ethnic group and where support networks may be more extensive.

When changes in segregation are calculated for districts in different types of area (Inner London, Outer London, Metropolitan districts, and other large city districts), the change in the ID for Output Areas within local authority districts is dramatic for some of these area types and for some ethnic groups (Catney 2015). Inner London saw a very small increase in segregation (of less than 1 percentage point) for the Black African group and increases of under 5 percentage points for the White British and Black Caribbean groups. Outer London's decrease in segregation was around 4 percentage points for the Black African group but much larger for the Bangladeshi (–12 percentage points) and Chinese (–11 percentage points) groups. For metropolitan districts (such as Birmingham, Bradford, Leeds, and Manchester) segregation decreased for all minority ethnic groups, the Black African group having a decrease of almost 15 percentage points, the largest of any ethnic group. For Black Africans in Bradford, for example, reduced segregation amounted to 16 percentage points. In other large cities (like Cardiff and Nottingham) decreasing segregation was, again, most notable for the Black African group with a decrease of 20 percentage points. The overall picture, then, is of increasing residential mixing in urban areas.

Other census indicators support this picture of increasing mixing. The size of the mixed group increased from 1.3 % of the population of England and Wales in 2001 to 2.2 % in 2011. Moreover, the Mixed White and Black African group increased from 80,705 (0.2 %) to 165,974 (0.3 %) over this period. These figures underestimate the size of the mixed population as measured by parentage or more distant ancestry, as many of the latter identify with a single group. Further, Simpson (2012) notes that the proportion of mixed households has grown in 346 out of 348 local authorities, 1 in 8 households (excluding one-person households) now having more than one ethnic group. In 2011, the number of households with multiple ethnic groups was 2.0 million or 12 %, a figure which has increased from 1.4 million in 2001. The percentage of households with multiple ethnic groups varies between geographical areas, being at its highest (39 %) in Inner London. Clearly, mixing also takes place in work settings and in schools though such socialisation is not captured in the census.

ANALYSIS OF RESIDENTIAL SEGREGATION AT SUBCENSUS CATEGORY LEVEL: ONOMAP SUBGROUPS

Mateos (2014) identified 66 Onomap Subgroups in London, 12 of which relate specifically to African communities (Table 5.1). These subgroups have been defined using the 2004 electoral registers for Greater London, which contained 5 million electors, and the 2001 Census. This classification clearly has much more utility than the Census classification (which offers only 'Black African') in capturing the diversity of the Black African collectivity. Indeed, amongst the 2001 Census's ethnic group categories, Mateos (2014) identified as 'poorly studied' groups the five write-in 'Other' categories (Other White, Other Mixed, Other Black, Any Other Asian background, and Any other ethnic group), but also the Black African category. However, most of the analyses take into account only the most frequent Onomap Subgroups with a total population size in London greater than 3,000 people (i.e. the six top ranking African subgroups in Table 5.1). These analyses demonstrate the advantage of using a name-based classification in segregation studies.

Table 5.1 African Onomap Subgroups and their total and relative population sizes in London (2004)

Onomap Subgroup	Total population	% in London
Nigerian	68,596	1.37
Ghanaian	35,255	0.70
Somalian	20,376	0.41
African	4,879	0.10
Sierra Leonean	3,854	0.08
Afrikaans	3,036	0.06
Black South African	2,161	0.04
Muslim North African	2,044	0.04
Eritrean	1,053	0.02
Ethiopian	918	0.02
Ugandan	812	0.02
Congolese	598	0.01

Source: Extracted from Table 9.2 in: Mateos P. *Names, Ethnicity and Populations. Tracing Identity in Space*. Heidelberg: Springer, 2014, p. 222.
Note: The table is ordered by decreasing population size

Evenness

The most segregated Onomap Subgroups in London according to the ID were Afrikaans (South Africa has a long history of migration to the UK, having established communities living there) (rank 1), Sierra Leone (rank 2), African[7] (rank 3), and Ghanaian, Somalian, and Nigerian (ranks 25, 26, and 27). English, Welsh, Scottish, and Irish were the least segregated (ranks 43–46, respectively). There is some indication of a negative relationship between the ID and population size, but is probably explained by the very high number of areas in which the city is divided. Another factor that appears to account for the difference in the ID is the length of time since migration (ethnic groups longer established in the UK are likely to have lower residential density). Indeed, the scatter plot shows that Nigerians and Ghanaians, both long-established communities, have middling ID ranks and scores.

Exposure

A high value of this index indicates a high probability of finding a member of the same ethnic group living in the same area (that is, being 'highly exposed'). Nigerians and Ghanaians were in the top half of the rank order, ranking tenth and 15th, respectively. Somalians (rank 28), Sierra Leoneans (rank 34), Africans (rank 40), and Afrikaans (rank 45) were in the lower half. The exposure measure is quite strongly positively correlated with the size of the group (but more weakly than the ID). Ghanaian was amongst the Onomap Subgroups which were less exposed than might be expected given their population size.

Concentration

The ACO (where a score of 1 indicates that the group experiences the maximum spatial concentration possible and a score of 0 indicates the minimum spatial concentration possible) is not reported for the Onomap Subgroups as all these obtain very similar and high values, an artefact of applying the ACO to a large number of finely grained ethnic groups over a large number of small areas.

---

[7] A category encompassing other Black African names not included in the rest of the Onomap Subgroups.

Clustering

The ACL varies from a minimum of 0 (low clustering) to a maximum that approaches but never equals 1 (high clustering). Two African Onomap Subgroups in London fall within the top half of the rank order: Nigerian (rank 8) is the most clustered (most neighbours of its own subgroup), followed by Ghanaian (rank 14). In the bottom half of the hierarchy—the less clustered—Somalian ranked 28, Sierra Leonean 32, African 39, and Afrikaans 43. The relationship between ACL and group population size while positive was very weak and only held for Onomap Subgroups with a population above 60,000.

Mateos (2014) also applies a geographical approach to spatial clustering using spatial autocorrelation statistics which measures the tendency of similar values to cluster together in space.[8] This approach enables the areas within London of highest and lowest clustering of each Onomap Subgroup to be identified. In a five-group classification of adjacency types, the *high–high* category (Output Areas with high proportions of people from the Onomap Subgroup next to areas with similar values) is particularly relevant. Mateos (2014) selects 22 out of the total of 66 Onomap Subgroups which have a larger number of highly clustered Output Areas in London and presents maps of the five types of local clustering for each of the Onomap Subgroups. Two of these maps are for African subgroups: Nigerian and Somalian. The Nigerian Onomap Subgroup is mainly clustered in the East of London on both sides of the River Thames, an area traditionally settled by Black Africans in London. The pattern for the Somali subgroup is quite different, with the most clustered areas being found in several parts of the city. Mateos (2014, p. 241) suggests that the pattern is probably attributable to 'the sparse availability of public housing into which this community was originally accommodated following the refugee arrivals from the Horn of Africa in the early 1990s'. However, there is also a much larger cluster in Haringey and Enfield.

Finally, Mateos (2014) provides an average composite index based on the four dimensions (Evenness ID, Isolation P, Concentration ACO, and Clustering ACL). Most segregated of the African groups across the 46 ranked Onomap Subgroups are Sierra Leoneans (0.479, rank 2), Afrikaans (0.478, rank 4), and Africans (0.468, rank 8). Much less segregated are Nigerian (0.409, rank 26), Ghanaian (0.408, rank 27), and Somalian (0.397, rank 29).

---

[8] For a technical description of this method, see Mateos (2014), pp. 235–236.

Mateos (2014) draws attention to the spatial inequalities in the most segregated groups, noting that Afrikaans represents the more affluent or highly educated groups seeking exclusive areas of residence, and Sierra Leonean and African being amongst the more socio-economically constrained groups.

Mateos's (2014) study is the only example of the application of names analysis to the dimensions of residential segregation, though limited to London and one point in time. However, this much finer analysis than is achievable using census categories has revealed a number of highly segregated small groups and different structuring processes based on socio-economic factors. Given the marked decrease in residential segregation amongst Black Africans that took place during the decade 2001–2011, more up-to-date analyses are needed to reveal how these more finely grained categories are changing with respect to residential segregation.

Living in Deprived Neighbourhoods

There is debate in the academic literature about the consequences of living in deprived neighbourhoods, so-called 'neighbourhood effects', with respect to labour and housing market prospects and other areas. Jivraj and Khan (2015, p. 211) conclude that most research suggests that 'there is some residual influence of the area where a person lives on individual outcomes over and above their own circumstances and their history that led them to live there'. They suggest that effect of neighbourhoods on individual outcomes may operate through a number of processes, including stigma attached to deprived neighbourhoods, negative socialisations with others out of work, institutional underinvestment, overdemand for public services, and a lack of networks to better opportunities.

It is clear that many Black Africans are forced to live in deprived neighbourhoods when they arrive as migrants and subsequently find that they cannot afford to move away. Having to remain in such areas, they experience greater disadvantage the longer they live in these deprived neighbourhoods. Jivraj and Khan (2015) exploit the English Index of Multiple Deprivation (IMD) and the 2011 Census to look at clustering in deprived neighbourhoods by ethnic group, how clustering has changed since 2001, and how it varies by type of neighbourhood deprivation and regions of England.

The English IMD has appeared as three releases (2004, 2007, and 2010) using broadly the same methodology. The IMD has now become the standard for measuring area-based deprivation and has been widely used by government, for example, with respect to strategies for neighbourhood renewal. It comprises seven dimensions or 'domains' (see Table 5.2), which are combined using a weighting scheme to create an overall deprivation score, though income and employment carry the most importance. The overall score and the domain scores are calculated for each lower layer super output area (LSOA) in England using the 2001 Census boundaries. LSOAs have a similar population size (containing an average of 1,500 people) and are referred to by Jivraj and Khan (2015) as 'neighbourhoods'. The standardised scores for the overall IMD provide a *relative* measure of deprivation (whether it is more deprived than other areas as determined by its ranking among all neighbourhoods).

Jivraj and Khan's (2015) analysis of the IMD 2010 distribution by ethnic group (Table 5.3) shows the cumulative percentage of the population living in neighbourhoods at selected percentiles on the IMD 2010 distribution. The most deprived neighbourhoods (0–3 % of the IMD score) were dominated by the South Asian (Pakistani and Bangladeshi) and Black

Table 5.2   The seven domains of the IMD 2010

IMD domain	What it measures
Income	The proportion of people in receipt of at least one of the following: Income Support, Income-Based Jobseeker's Allowance, Pension Credit, Child Tax Credit, or asylum-seeker subsistence support
Employment	The proportion of the working-age population who are involuntarily excluded from the labour market. The indicators comprise claimants of Jobseeker's Allowance, Incapacity Benefit, Severe Disablement Allowance, Employment and Support Allowance, and participants in New Deal
Health	Premature death and poor health using the following indicators: years of potential life lost; illness and disability ratio; acute morbidity rate; and adult mood and anxiety disorder rates
Education	Uses average point scores of pupils at key stages 2–4; secondary school absence rates; the proportion of 16-year-olds not staying on in education; the proportion of people aged under 21 not entering higher education; and the proportion of adults aged 25–54 with no or low qualifications
Barriers to housing and services	Household overcrowding; homelessness, housing affordability; and road distance to a GP, food shop, primary school, and post office
Crime	Uses rates of violence; burglary; theft; and criminal damage
Living environment	Combines indicators of housing in poor condition; houses without central heating; poor air quality; and road traffic accidents

Table 5.3   Cumulative percentage of population living in neighbourhoods at selected percentiles on the IMD 2010 distribution, by ethnic group, 2011 (%)

	Most deprived				Least deprived	
	0–3 %	3–10 %	10–20 %	20–50 %	50–80 %	80–100 %
Pakistani	10	32	52	84	95	100
Bangladeshi	9	35	60	87	96	100
Arab	7	20	37	73	92	100
Other Black	6	24	49	86	96	100
Black African	6	23	48	84	95	100
Mixed White and Black Caribbean	6	19	37	72	91	100
Mixed White and Black African	5	18	36	71	90	100
Black Caribbean	5	21	44	83	95	100
Other	4	17	35	71	91	100
White Gypsy or Irish Traveller	4	12	25	57	86	100
Chinese	4	11	25	58	84	100
Other mixed	4	13	29	64	87	100
Other Asian	4	13	27	6	89	100
Mixed White and Asian	3	11	23	55	81	100
Other White	3	11	25	61	87	100
White British	3	8	17	46	78	100
White Irish	3	10	21	55	83	100
Indian	2	10	24	63	87	100
England average	3	10	20	50	80	100

Source: Jivraj and Khan (2015), Table 13.1.
Notes: Ethnic groups rank-ordered by % living in 3 % most deprived neighbourhoods

(including Mixed Black) groups. Black Africans ranked fifth with 6 % of the population living in these neighbourhoods, the same as Other Black and Mixed White and Black Caribbean and higher than Mixed White and Black African (5 %) and Black Caribbean (5 %). These proportions compare with White British (3 %). If the most deprived fifth of neighbourhoods is taken, Black Africans ranked fourth, with almost half (48 %) of their population living in these neighbourhoods, similar to Other Black (49 %) and above the Mixed Black groups (36–37 %) and Black Caribbeans (44 %). With respect to the 50 % most deprived neighbourhoods, Black Africans rise to joint third with 84 % of their population living in these neighbourhoods.

There was little penetration by Black Africans of the least deprived quintile of the IMD scores, just 5 % compared with 22 % of White British and 20 % for the England average. Thus, Black Africans are overrepresented in the most deprived neighbourhoods and have not been able to relocate to the least deprived neighbourhoods.

This analysis is extended by Jivraj and Khan (2015) to changes in the proportion of each ethnic group living in the 10 % most deprived neighbourhoods in 2001 and 2011.[9] While for most ethnic groups the proportion living in the most deprived neighbourhoods decreased over the decade, the proportion remained the same for Black Africans (23 %). The Chinese, Indian, and White British groups also showed little change.

The IMD's multiple deprivation refers to seven dimensions or 'domains' that measure separate dimensions of neighbourhood deprivation: income, employment, health, education, barriers to housing and services, crime, and living environment (Table 5.3). Jivraj and Khan (2015) report the proportion of each ethnic group that live in the 10 % most deprived neighbourhoods on each domain.

On the income domain, Black Africans ranked fourth (after Bangladeshis, Pakistanis, and Other Black) with around 31 % living in the 10 % most deprived neighbourhoods, below Other Black (32 %) but higher than Black Caribbean (27 %). This compares with just 8 % for the White British group. With respect to employment-deprived neighbourhoods, again Black Africans (15 %) are in the top four groups, though there is much less variation on this domain than income. The Black African group had around 15 % of its population living in health-deprived neighbourhoods, lower than the Pakistani (23 %), Bangladeshi (20 %), and Arab (17 %) groups. It can be recalled that Black Africans had good generic health, with this measure only indicating that more people have health problems in the neighbourhoods where the group is concentrated. The Black African group had around 10 % of its population living in education-deprived neighbourhoods, the same as White British and the England average. The range on this domain was 24 % (Pakistani group) to 6 % (Irish group).

The Bangladeshi group (33 %) had the highest proportion of its population living in neighbourhoods with barriers to housing and that are service-deprived. Other groups concentrated in London, including Other Black, Black African, Black Caribbean, and Arab, have a quarter of their population living in these neighbourhoods, compared with just 9 % in the White British group. The Black African group (26 %) has the highest percentage living in neighbourhoods with high crime rates,

---

[9] See Jivraj and Khan (2015), p. 202 for technical information on comparing deprivation over time.

reflecting the group's concentration in London and other large cities. Proportions were also high (with proportions exceeding a fifth of their population in these neighbourhoods) for the Other Black, Pakistani, Black Caribbean, and Bangladeshi groups, compared with just 9 % in the White British group. Finally, the Pakistani group had 39 % of its population living in living environment-deprived neighbourhoods, while the proportion was more than a quarter for the Bangladeshi, Other Black, Arab, and Black Caribbean groups. The proportion was around 23 % for Black Africans and just 8 % for the White British group.

Jivraj and Khan (2015) calculate for each ethnic group the proportion of people living in a neighbourhood in the 10 % most deprived nationally on the overall IMD 2010, separately for each of the nine regions. For the South East and East of England, the proportions of the different ethnic groups living in the 10 % most deprived neighbourhoods were very low (under 10 %). In the South-West (SW) region, only two groups exceeded the 10 % threshold (the Other Black and Black African groups) and in London only the Bangladeshi group. In the East Midlands, the Black African and Other Black groups had the highest (around 15 %) proportion of their populations living in the 10 % most deprived neighbourhoods. In the West Midlands, proportions were high (25–30 %) in the Bangladeshi, Pakistani, Other Black, Black African, and Arab groups. The Black African group had the highest proportion in these deprived neighbourhoods in the North-West and North-East regions and the second highest in Yorkshire and Humberside (within the range of 20–30 %). Inequalities between ethnic groups were greatest in the West Midlands and Yorkshire and the Humber regions.

In their final analysis, Jivraj and Khan (2015) compare the unemployment rate and economic inactivity, both for people aged 25–49 excluding students, relative to the White British group, in 2011, in deprived neighbourhoods (the 10 % most deprived neighbourhoods) and all other neighbourhoods (not the 10 % most deprived). The White British unemployment rate was 12.5 % in deprived neighbourhoods and 4.6 % in all other neighbourhoods. The Black African rate was actually higher relative to the White British rate in all other neighbourhoods than deprived neighbourhoods (+8 % vs +7 %). The Black Caribbean group also experienced higher rates in all other neighbourhoods than in deprived neighbourhoods, relative to the White British group, while in the Other Black group rates were +10 % higher than the White British group in both deprived and all other neighbourhoods. With respect to economic inactivity, the proportions in the Black African group, relative to the White British group, were +5 % higher in other neighbourhoods and around 2 % lower in deprived neighbourhoods. Thus, on both labour market measures inequalities for Black Africans were greater in less deprived neighbourhoods.

There is one additional measure that is added to the National Pupil Database. The Income Deprivation Affecting Children Index (IDACI) is derived from the Communities and Local Government Indices of deprivation. It measures the proportion of children under the age of 16 who are income deprived in an area.[10] It has a range from 0 to 1, 0 being the least deprived. Given the relatively large size of Black African families, the measure is particularly important. Across 21 first languages spoken at home by Black African school pupils, the IDACI was lowest for Shona and English speakers (between 0.3 and 0.4) who were substantially less likely to be living in a disadvantaged locality than Black Africans in general (Mitton 2011). The most disadvantaged on this measure were first language at home Lingali and Somali speakers, whose index value exceeded 0.5. Akan (Twi/Asante), Tigrinya, Krio, French, and Akan/Twi/Fante were also substantially disadvantaged. Yoruba and Igbo speakers had values around the mid-point of the range 0.4–0.5.

ETHNIC DENSITY EFFECTS

Generally, living in a poorer or more deprived area is associated with worse health. Members of ethnic minorities who live in areas where there is a low density of their own ethnic group are likely to be better off materially and living in better neighbourhoods, than those who live in areas with a higher concentration of their own group. However, some of these disadvantages of living in areas with high levels of ethnic minority concentration may be offset by positive effects associated with ethnic density, providing ethnic minority residents with health-promoting and protective effects on health and thereby moderating the impacts of racism and deprivation. As place is the context of everyday encounters, including the site of collective consumption requiring high levels of social interaction,

---

[10] These are described as children in households receiving Income Support or Income-Based Jobseekers Allowance; children in families receiving Working Families Tax Credit or Disabled Persons Tax Credit whose equivalised income (excluding housing benefits) is below 60 % of the median income before housing costs; and National Asylum Support Service (NASS) supported asylum seekers in receipt of subsistence only and accommodation support.

one might also expect place in this context to have an important effect on identity development processes.

While first recognised in studies of mental illness, 'ethnic density' or 'group density' effects have been reported for a wide range of outcomes, including psychological well-being, physical health, alcohol consumption, educational attainment, fluency in English, and social cohesion and civic participation. Some studies show a difference in strength of effects across ethnic groups. Explanatory or mediating effects (often partial) have been reported to include reduced exposure to racism, discrimination, and intimidation in everyday encounters and the protective effects from within one's community, including improved social support, improved social networks, and improved access to culturally specific facilities and services.

While some of the early studies of ethnic density effects were based on surveys that excluded Black Africans, some of these effects have been reported more recently for Black Africans. Protective ethnic density effects were found for sensible drinking among Black African people living in areas of high own ethnic density (Bécares et al. 2011). Though not statistically significant, ethnic density was found to be related to less depression among Black African mothers (but more depression among Black Caribbean mothers) (Pickett et al. 2009). Boydell and colleagues found a higher incidence of schizophrenia among ethnic minorities (Caribbean, African, and all minorities) in electoral wards where they comprised the smallest proportion of the population (Boydell et al. 2001). With respect to social cohesion and civic participation, African and Bangladeshi people tended to report greater participation in informal volunteering as their own ethnic density increased (Stafford et al. 2010).

CHAPTER 6

Socio-economic Position

Housing Circumstances

Decennial censuses have included a number of questions on household housing circumstances. The 2011 England and Wales Census asked about the type of accommodation (detached, semi-detached, terraced, flat, maisonette, or apartment, and mobile or temporary structure), whether the accommodation is self-contained; rooms available for use by the household and number that are bedrooms; type of central heating; and housing tenure. The 1991 Census asked a question about household amenities (a bath or shower, an inside flush toilet, and central heating in living rooms and bedrooms), but this was shortened in the 2001 England and Wales Census (to a bath/shower *and* toilet and separate question on central heating).

In the 2011 England and Wales Census, Black Africans (as defined by the ethnic group of the Household Reference Person [HRP]) had the lowest rates of owner-occupation across all 18 ethnic groups, with just 24 % owning their houses (Fig. 6.1). Rates were also low amongst Mixed White and Black Africans (28 %), and the Other Black category (28 %), but higher for Black Caribbeans (45 %). These proportions compare with 69 % for Indians and 68 % for White British. Significant proportions of Black Africans lived in each of private rented and social rented housing. Just over a third (34 %) lived in private rented accommodation, substantially lower than the Other White (51 %) and Arab (49 %) ethnic

© The Editor(s) (if applicable) and The Author(s) 2016
P.J. Aspinall, M.J. Chinouya, *The African Diaspora Population in Britain*, DOI 10.1057/978-1-137-45654-0_6

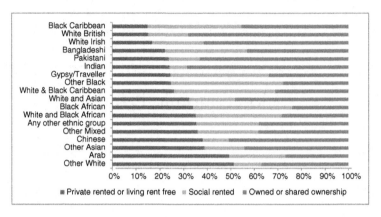

Fig. 6.1   Proportion of ethnic groups in owned or shared ownership, private rented or living rent-free, and social rented accommodation, 2011, England and Wales.

Source: ONS 2011 Census. Table DC4202EW. Tenure by ethnic group of household reference person (HRP)

groups but higher than the White British (15 %) and Black Caribbean (15 %) groups. However, Black Africans (42 %) had one of the highest proportions in social rented housing, only exceeded by Mixed White and Black Caribbeans (43 %) and Other Black (48 %). The low proportion of the Black African group in home ownership probably reflects their disadvantage in the labour market and consequent difficulties in securing a mortgage.

There have been important changes in housing tenure across the three censuses (1991, 2001, and 2011). The percentage of Black African HRPs who owned their own home declined from 27.9 % in 1991 to 25.9 % in 2001 and 24.0 % in 2011. Indeed, there were declines for all ethnic groups (African, Bangladeshi, Caribbean, Chinese, Indian Pakistani, and White) between 1991 and 2011, with only the Chinese and White groups increasing their proportions between 1991 and 2001. In contrast, Black Africans substantially increased their occupation of privately rented accommodation from 19.9 % in 1991 to 23.4 % in 2001 and 34.0 % in 2011, as did all ethnic groups. Only the Chinese had higher rates across the 3 census years (21.5 %, 24.8 %, and 38.0 %, respectively). Black African HRPs saw diminished proportions in social rented housing between 1991 and 2011, in common with all other ethnic groups, the 52.2 % in 1991 falling to

50.7 in 2001 and 42.0 % in 2011. However, the decline was steepest for Black Africans.

The decennial census asked respondents about their dwelling type, notably whether their accommodation was a whole house or bungalow (detached, semi-detached, or terraced, including end terrace); a flat, maisonette, or apartment (in a purpose-built block of flats or tenement, part of a converted or shared house, or in a commercial building); or a caravan or other mobile or temporary structure. Across England and Wales, 84.1 % of the population lived in a whole house or bungalow. In the case of Black Africans, this proportion fell to 52.6 % of Black African HRPs, the lowest of any ethnic group (including Gypsies or Irish Travellers, 60.7 %). Proportions were also low amongst Other Black HRPs (54.7 %) and Arabs (55.6 %). Terraced houses comprised 30.8 % of all occupied whole houses or bungalows across England and Wales but 43.5 % in the case of Black African HRPs, though proportions for Black Caribbeans (49.7 %) and Bangladeshis (54.5 %) were substantially higher.

The 2011 England and Wales Census asked the respondent if the household's accommodation is self-contained (where all rooms, including the kitchen, bathroom, and toilet, are behind a door that only the household can use) or not. This yielded data by the ethnic group of the HRP on unshared and shared dwellings.[1] In the population as a whole, only 0.34 % of all dwellings were shared. The proportion was highest for Black African HRPs (1.65 %), probably reflecting their concentration in the rented sector. Proportions were also high (over 1 %) for Other White (1.33 %), Mixed White and Black African (1.35 %), Other Mixed (1.14 %), Chinese (1.42 %), Other Black (1.40 %), Arab (1.34 %), and Any Other ethnic group (1.21 %).

The decennial census also asked if households had central heating (a central system that generates heat for multiple rooms) and the type of such heating (gas, electric, oil, solid fuel, or other types). Across England and Wales, very few dwelling types (2.67 %) lacked central heating. The proportion was lower amongst Black African (2.48 %), Black Caribbean (2.03 %), and Other Black (2.43 %) HRPs. The low proportion in the Black African group may be partially explained by the high concentration (42 %) of Black Africans in social rented housing.

---

[1] Table DC4206EW. Dwelling type by type of central heating in household by occupancy rating (bedrooms) by ethnic group of Household Reference Person (HRP) (from Nomis).

The 2011 England and Wales Census asked: 'How many rooms are available for use only by this household?' (with details of which rooms to count and not count), and a supplementary question: 'How many of these rooms are bedrooms?' These findings have been converted into measures of underoccupied housing, housing that meets the standard and statutory requirements, and overcrowded housing for both rooms and bedrooms. Based on the number of bedrooms, Black Africans had one of the highest levels of overcrowding (22 %) along with Pakistanis, only Bangladeshis having a higher proportion (30 %) (Finney and Harries 2015). Only 31 % of Black Africans underoccupied their accommodation, that is, at least one spare bedroom, only Bangladeshis having a lower proportion (30 %). By contrast, more than two-thirds of the White British and White Irish ethnic groups underoccupied their accommodation. Moreover, four times as many White British (36 %) as Black African (9 %) and Bangladeshi (10 %) groups lived in accommodation with two or more spare bedrooms. Further, Black Africans had the highest proportion with required bedrooms (47 %).

If a measure of overcrowding is based on rooms rather than bedrooms, this gives higher levels of overcrowding for each ethnic group but with similar relative positions as the bedroom-based measure. Thirty-five per cent of Black African accommodation (and the same proportion for Bangladeshis) was overcrowded, the highest proportion across all ethnic groups (Finney and Harries 2015). These investigators suggest that 'the switch to a bedroom-based measure of overcrowding hides the experience of these ethnic groups (Black African, Arab, and Chinese) having fewer than the required number of rooms for daily living activities other than sleeping' (p. 154). Overcrowding amongst Black Africans was particularly concentrated in London, with one in five households in Inner and North London being overcrowded.

Finally, Finney and Harries (2015) compare change over time in overcrowding and underoccupancy using the room-based measure in the 2001 and 2011 censuses. Levels of overcrowding decreased for most ethnic groups but particularly so for Black Africans and Bangladeshis, resulting in a reduction in ethnic inequalities on this measure.

Housing Circumstances in Black African Subgroups

These census measures show that Black Africans were amongst the most disadvantaged in the housing market. However, these aggregate figures conceal substantial heterogeneity in the Black African group. In the 2011 England and Wales Census, the proportion of people living in social rented housing was highest for the Nigerian-born (24 %) and this proportion remained high irrespective of the length of residence (ONS 2014c). Households with a Somali-born HRP had the highest levels with more than 1.5 persons per room (10.6 %), although proportions were also high in the Nigeria (5.2 %) and Ghana (4.2 %) country of birth groups (Table 6.1).

Karlsen and Nazroo (2008) found substantial differences in housing tenure between Black African Christians and Muslims. Owner-occupation accounted for 30 % of Black African Christian households but just 12 % of Muslim households, while the respective percentages for renting were 65 and 87 %, and for other tenures 4 and 1 %.

These statistics may reflect differing economic pressures, families with a Somali-born family reference person having both the highest proportion with three or more dependent children, and the highest proportion of lone parent families (see Chap. 2).

Of Somali migrants identified in the 2005/2006 Labour Force Survey (LFS) data who had been resident in the UK since before 2000 (IPPR 2007), just 4 % owned their home outright or were buying with a mortgage or loan. The proportions for the other 24 migrant groups lay in the range of 35–86 %. Nigerians (50 %) and Ghanaians (38 %) substantially

Table 6.1 Persons per room in households by selected country of birth of household reference person, England and Wales, 2011

	Up to 0.5 persons per room	Over 0.5 and up to 1.0 persons per room	Over 1.0 and up to 1.5 persons per room	Over 1.5 persons per room
Bangladesh	21.2	53.5	19.4	6.0
Somalia	28.9	42.9	17.6	10.6
Ghana	39.6	47.5	8.7	4.2
Nigeria	39.4	46.1	9.3	5.2
Kenya	55.8	40.3	3.1	0.8
Zimbabwe	52.0	43.7	3.2	1.1
Ireland	80.0	18.9	0.7	0.4
Non-UK-born	52.6	39.6	5.4	2.4
UK-born	74.5	24.4	0.9	0.2

Source: 2011 Census, ONS, using Table CT0151 (Bangladesh and Ireland are ONS-selected comparators); also Table CT0153: no. of persons per room in household by country of birth of Household Reference Person (HRP) (national)

exceeded the Somali proportion. Eighty per cent of Somali migrants were living in local authority or housing association housing, the highest of any of the migrant groups and substantially higher than migrant Nigerians (29 %) and Ghanaians (39 %).

Other research portrays Somalis as having the worst housing circumstances. Cole and Robinson (2003) describe a community living in extremely overcrowded housing whose condition is extremely poor, with damp and condensation problems, insufficient heating, and inadequate security measures. Incidents of harassment and racial discrimination were common but often went unreported because of the language barrier and inadequate interpretation and translation services. Homelessness (especially the 'statutory homeless' and 'homeless and living with family and friends') has been reported as a problem in the Somali community (ICAR 2007), though not appearing in homelessness statistics as they do not approach local authorities for help and are not aware of their role (Cole and Robinson 2003).

EDUCATION

The educational experiences and attainment of minority ethnic groups have focused on a number of key themes: how educational attainment in minority ethnic groups differs across groups and has changed over time; access to education in countries of origin and in the UK; factors affecting educational attainment, such as gender, patterns of union and family formation, and cultural practices; heterogeneity in educational attainment in census categories based on national origins, language, and other factors; the transferability of foreign qualifications to the UK; and the relationship between the holding of educational qualifications and employment outcomes.

There are a number of key sources of evidence that enable us to investigate the educational experiences and attainments of Black Africans compared with other ethnic groups and of differences within the Black African group. Firstly, the decennial census has asked questions about ethnic group and educational attainment across three censuses (1991, 2001, and 2011). In the 2011 England and Wales Census, people aged 16 or over were asked: 'Which of these qualifications do you have?', the list comprising 13 options which ranged from no qualifications to degree-level qualifications. Those with qualifications gained outside the UK were asked to tick the 'Foreign qualifications' box and the nearest UK equivalents.

The ONS combined responses into five categories for the highest level of qualification held, plus one category for no qualifications, and one for other qualifications (including foreign qualifications where an equivalent qualification was not given). The 2001 Census question was generally comparable, though only asked of people aged 16–74. In 1991, the Census asked if the person has obtained any qualifications after reaching the age of 18 and to indicate 'no such qualifications' or to write in the name of any degrees or vocational qualifications obtained excluding school-level qualifications. The responses to this question were processed only for a 10 % sample of households and people in communal establishments.

A number of generic measures of educational attainment have been derived from the decennial census that enable Black Africans to be compared with other ethnic groups (Lymperopoulou and Parameshwaran 2014): degree-level or equivalent qualifications (a completed education at Level 4 or above, including first and higher degree, vocational and professional qualifications) compared across the 3 census years, and no academic or professional qualifications compared across 2001 and 2011. In the 2011 England and Wales Census, the Black African group had the lowest proportion (just 11 %) of people aged 16 and over with no qualifications, compared with 13 % (ranked fourth) for the 'White and Black African' group, 20 % for 'Black Caribbeans' (ranked 11th equal), and 24 % for 'White British' (ranked 14th). On the measure of people with degree-level qualifications, Black Africans had the third highest percentage (40 %), after the Chinese (43 %) and Indians (42 %), and substantially higher than 'White and Black Africans' (29 %, 11th), Black Caribbeans (26 %, 13th), and White British (26 %, 13th equal). The educational advantage of Black Africans on these measures may be due to the significant contribution of migration—including international students—to the group's growth over the last 10 years (Lymperopoulou and Parameshwaran 2014).

The two generic measures of educational attainment can be used to obtain a measure of change across the three censuses (1991, 2001, and 2011). The proportion of Black Africans with degree-level qualifications increased from 26.31 % in 1991 to 38.78 % in 2001, an increase of 12.5 percentage points. However, this increase fell to just 1.2 % (39.99 % in 2011) during 2001–2011. While the 1991–2001 increase was one of the highest, the 2001–2011 increase was the lowest (amongst the White, Indian, Pakistani, Bangladeshi, Chinese, and Black Caribbean groups).

Variation in Educational Attainment by Census Subgroups

The census offers only limited information on concealed heterogeneity in educational attainment in the Black African group. The 2011 Census tables do not provide a breakdown of qualifications by gender. Qualifications by age (16–24, 25–49, 50–64, and 65+) are only available for broad ethnic groups (White British, White Irish, Other White, Mixed, Asian, and Black), 'black' combining the very different experiences of Black Africans and Black Caribbeans. Countries of birth tabulations are limited to the country or broad region: ONS grouped African countries of birth into the categories 'Nigeria', 'South Africa', and 'Other Africa', which have limited utility as 'South Africa' includes Black and White migrants, and 'Other Africa' includes North African and East African Asian migrants. Published data on qualifications are unavailable by main language.

Amongst persons born in Nigeria, the proportion with no qualifications was consistent across age groups: 4 % of 16–24-year-olds, 3 % of 25–49-year-olds, and 4 % of 50–64-year-olds. The more heterogeneous categories of 'South Africa' (7 %, 3 %, and 6 %, respectively) and 'Other Africa' (10 %, 12 %, and 17 %) also show clustering and an absence of high proportions found in the older age groups amongst persons born in Bangladesh and Pakistan. With respect to degree-level qualifications, persons born in Nigeria have higher proportions in the older age groups (26 %, 62 %, and 62 %, respectively), as do those born in South Africa (16 %, 51 %, and 50 %, respectively) and Other Africa (16 %, 39 %, and 35 %). With respect to degree-level qualifications, Nigerian migrants had the fifth highest proportion in the 16–24 age group (26 %) amongst the 23 countries of birth groups (after India, Ireland, China, and Canada). In the 25–49 age group it ranked joint third (62 %) with other EU states in 2001, after Canada and the USA. In the oldest age group (50–64), Nigeria and the USA had the joint highest proportions (62 %) with degree-level qualifications.

Variations in Educational Attainment by Linguistic, National Origin, and Religion Subgroups

In addition to these large differentials in educational attainment across the different census ethnic and migrant categories, research studies have also shown substantial variations within the Black African category, based on national origins and linguistic subgroups, reaffirming concerns about the heterogeneity concealed in the broad census label. Until around half a dozen years ago or so, there were only fragmentary sources that could be used to explore this concealed heterogeneity (Aspinall and Chinouya 2008). However, an increasing focus on language in censuses and surveys and the more extensive use of 'extended codes' in the Annual School Census have enabled a more comprehensive picture to emerge. Two types of subgroup data are now available: language and national origin.

With respect to language, Von Ahn et al. (2010a, b) used a linked data set (Annual School Census and pupil educational attainment) to show significant variation by linguistic group within the Black African category (Table 6.2). The Black African group comprises substantial concealed heterogeneity in language use as well as national origins, and this is reflected in the wide spread in attainment measures. The Black African Lingala, French, and Somali language groups have low attainment, even below the lowest attaining ethnic group category (Black Caribbean). The Black African English, Yoruba, and Igbo groups all have higher attainments than the Black Caribbean and Black African averages, and Black African Igbo speakers have scores similar to White British students. The London Borough of Lambeth (Demie 2006) published differentials in educational attainment (% of pupils achieving 5+A*–C passes at GCSE) amongst selected Black African language heritage groups—Ibo, 73 %, Yoruba, 65 %, and Twi/Fante, 58 %—that are consistent with these wider findings. These data have clear policy implications with regard to addressing underattainment.

Table 6.2 Lowest and highest attaining linguistic groups within the Black African category, compared with other selected ethnic groups, London, 2008

Language/ethnic group (by median score)	25th percentile	Median	75th percentile
Black African—Lingala	10.56	12.58	13.78
Black African—French	11.18	13.01	14.27
Black African—Somali	11.40	13.02	14.31
Black Caribbean (average)	12.23	13.55	14.62
Black African (average)	12.25	13.73	14.85
Black African—English	12.84	14.13	15.21
Black African—Yoruba	13.02	14.19	15.13
Black African Igbo	13.04	14.36	15.48
White British (average)	13.03	14.38	15.52

Source: Table 2 in: Von Ahn M, Lupton R, Greenwood C, & Wiggins D. *Languages, Ethnicity and Education in London. Research Findings.* UPTAP, ESRC, 2010 (July)

However, it is likely that socio-economic position underlies some of the differentials in educational attainment across language groups. Von Ahn et al. (2010a, b) have added to the relevant Annual School Census indicators—whether or not a pupil receives free school meals and an index of deprivation describing the pupil's residential neighbourhood—using record linkage, yielding additional variables for three or more children and single parent.

Table 6.3 shows marked differences in socio-economic circumstances across language and ethnic groups in Newham which may account for differences in educational attainment. Black African Somalis are substantially the most disadvantaged group on the poverty indicators and have the highest proportion of single parent and 3+ children families. By contrast, the Yoruba group—the highest attaining language/ethnic group—is relatively advantaged.

An analysis by Strand et al. (2015) provides a robust analysis of attainment by language subgroup amongst Black Africans, adjusted for potential confounders. They identified the top ten languages spoken other than English and compared their attainment with English speakers for both KS2 average point scores and KS4 Best 8-point score. Results were adjusted for socio-economic deprivation and other student background variables. At KS2, Black African Igbo and Yoruba speakers achieved as well as English speakers. However, French and Arabic speakers were 4 National Curriculum (NC) months behind, Lingala speakers 6 NC months behind,

Table 6.3 Socio-economic characteristics of largest ethno-linguistic groups in Newham (KS2 only)

Language/ethnic group	Pupils	3 or more children (%)	Single parent (%)	Free school meals (%)	Council Tax Benefit (%)
Black African English/ believed to be English	85	58	21	32	38
Black Africa Somali	88	89	41	91	97
Black African Yoruba	65	72	15	25	26
Black African Akan	47	68	19	30	36
Black African other than English/unknown	118	80	32	59	63
Black Caribbean English	175	45	39	27	44
White British English	366	50	39	45	61

Source: Table 3 (modified) in: Von Ahn M, Lupton R, Greenwood C, & Wiggins D. *Languages, Ethnicity and Education in London. Research Findings*. UPTAP, ESRC, 2010 (July)

and Portuguese speakers 8 NC months behind Black African English speakers: indeed, the Black African Lingala and Portuguese speakers achieve at a lower level than Black Caribbean students. Similar differentials are seen at KS4. Igbo and Yoruba speakers did as well or better than English speakers. However, Somali and Lingala speakers were 16 Best 8 points behind and Portuguese speakers 24 points behind the Black African English speakers and lower than Black Caribbean students. All these differences were robust once socio-economic deprivation and other student background variables are controlled for. This analysis thus shows that first language can be an important factor in identifying subgroups within the Black African category at risk of low educational attainment.

National Origins

With respect to national origin subgroups, the Annual School Census uses a range of 'extended ethnicity codes' more detailed than the decennial census: these are available for nine of the 2001 Census ethnic groups, including 'Black African'. The Black African extended codes include 'Angolan', 'Congolese', 'Other Black African', 'Ghanaian', 'Nigerian', 'Sierra Leonean', 'Somali', and 'Sudanese'. However, these are available for optional use so not all local authorities use them. The Department for Education and Skills published data on use of extended codes in 2005 (Department for Education and Skills 2006b), where the code set was used by local authorities to classify 90 % or more of their pupils from that specific main ethnic group. 'Black African' was the set of codes used by the largest number of local authorities (19 %, $n = 28$), after 'White Other' (33 %, $n = 49$) and Any Other ethnic group (25 %, $n = 37$). The proportion of local authorities using the 'Black African' set of codes in London was even higher (52 %, $n = 17$), making it second equal across the census code sets, these percentages suggesting that local authorities find the heterogeneity concealed in the 'Black African' category problematic, especially where the local authorities contain above average size populations within these groups. A total of 76,724 pupils were classified in the 'Black African' extended code set,[2] of whom, however, 40 % ($n = 30,481$) were categorised as 'Other Black African'. Apart from the latter, the two largest Black African groups within those local authorities included in the

---

[2] In those local authorities where 90 % or more of pupils from the Black African group are categorised using the extended codes.

analysis were Somali ($n = 21,077$) and Nigerian ($n = 15,900$), followed by Ghanaian ($n = 6,596$), Congolese (1,098), Sierra Leonean (1,057), Sudanese (297), and Angolan (218).

Some of these larger subgroups provide a point of access to differences in educational attainment[3]: findings are available for Ghanaian, Nigerian, and Somali pupils (the extended Black African categories with 4,000 or more pupils) achieving 5+A*–C at GCSE in 2003 and 2005. While all groups increased their attainment between 2003 and 2005, Black Nigerians achieved at a higher level (54 % and 56 %, respectively) than all Black African pupils (41 and 48 %) and all pupils (51 and 55 %). Black Ghanaian pupils also achieved (46 and 53 %) above the overall Black African level. Black Somali pupils achieved (22 and 29 %) well below the average for all Black African pupils. These data also show that between 2003 and 2005, the increase in the percentage of Somali and Black African pupils achieving at this level was consistent with that for all Black African pupils and above that for all pupils nationally. A few LEAs have reported disaggregated counts for non-Somali Black Africans, Somalis, and Congolese, these data showing a marked (but diminishing) differential between standard measures for Black Africans and Somalis with around a 1.5- to twofold difference remaining (see Aspinall and Chinouya 2008, Table 2).

More recent data confirm these differentials. The 2008 National Pupil Database showed that 60 % or more of Black Ghanaians, Mixed White and Black Africans, and Black Nigerians achieved 5+ GCSE passes at grades A*–C, but was much lower for Black Somali (34 %) and Black Congolese (28 %) pupils (Mitton and Aspinall 2011). The London Mayor's 2011 report on education reported that Black Nigerian and Ghanaian children were almost three times as likely to reach the national benchmark (of 5 GCSE's grade A*–C including English and Maths) as those from Black Congolese or Black Angolan backgrounds (Mayor of London 2012) (Fig. 6.2).

The concealment of these differentials by language and national origins in much standardised reporting has been a concern for agencies. The London Health Commission has recommended that these new educational statistics 'have demonstrated the inadequacy of broad categories like "Black"...further refinement is needed at local level, to establish the needs, for example, of...Somali communities in London' (London

---

[3] Amongst the 25 LEAs who classified 90 % or more of their pupils using the Black African extended codes, data are available for the proportion of pupils achieving 5+A*–C GCSEs in 2003 and 2005 (Department for Education and Skills 2006b).

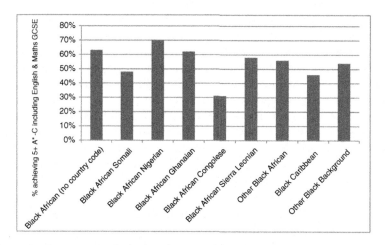

Fig. 6.2   Percentage of pupils achieving the national benchmark of 5 grades A*–C including English and Maths by ethnicity, 2011.

Source: Department for Education, as cited by *The Mayor's Education Inquiry First Report*.

Health Commission 2004, p. 20). The Education Commission has also argued that 'The picture for Black African pupils is difficult to fully assess since there was considerable variation in attainment for the children from diverse African backgrounds. The category "Black African" will need to be broken down further at LEA, London-wide and national levels to achieve a more detailed picture' (London Development Agency 2004, p. 8).

With respect to variations by religion, Burgess et al. (2009) report the number of GCSE/GNVQs at grades A*–C by religious affiliation within ethnic group for England, 2003–2004. Black African girls with no religion reported 9.77, Christians 7.12, and Muslims 4.39. The differential between Black African Christian and Muslim boys was smaller, 5.68 and 4.83, respectively, while Black African boys with no religion reported 6.57. These findings are indicative as the differences were not statistically significant. Black African Christians outperformed Muslims with respect to highest educational qualification (higher, 54 % vs 25 %; A-level, 15 % vs 18 %; compulsory, 16 % vs 20 %; none, 14 % vs 27 %; and foreign/other, 2 % vs 9 %) (Karlsen and Nazroo 2008).

Reasons for Variations in Educational Attainment

There is a variety of evidence that indicates that Black Africans may be treated unfairly at all levels in the educational system. Studies in schools have shown that some teachers have substantially lower expectations for ethnic minority students. Business in the Community (2010) stated that Black African British students (as well as students of Black Caribbean, Pakistani, and Bangladeshi ethnic backgrounds) continue to be strikingly underrepresented in the UK's most prestigious universities. In 2010, David Lammy, MP, deplored the fact that 'Just one British black Caribbean student was admitted to Oxford last year [in 2009].' A number of investigators have claimed that when university applicants from Black and other ethnic minority backgrounds do apply to Russell Group universities, they are substantially less likely to be offered places than comparable White applicants. Further, ethnic minority students have been shown to receive poorer marks at degree level than White students with the same level of prior attainment. Some organisations (such as Equality Challenge Unit, 2011) have found racism to be commonplace.

Boliver (2015a) has explored ethnic inequalities to Russell Group universities using a database of 68,632 UCAS candidates who submitted 151,281 applications in all. The mean offer rate for Black Africans was the lowest of all ethnic groups. She calculated comparative odds of an offer of admission using a variety of models (controlling for year of application, plus controls for other applicant characteristics, plus controls for prior attainment, plus controls for numerical competitiveness, plus interaction with percentage of ethnic minority applicants). For all but one of these models, Black Africans had the poorest odds of an offer of admission across minority ethnic groups where the White group was the reference. Boliver concludes that 'ethnic minority applicants are less likely than comparably qualified white applicants to receive offers from Russell Group universities, especially in relation to degree programmes that attract disproportionately high numbers of ethnic minority applicants'. Ethnic disparities in offer rates have been shown to exist (but of smaller magnitude) at other Old (pre-1992) and New (post-1992) universities too (Boliver 2015b).

Labour Market

Trends in Labour Market Participation by Ethnic Group

Trends in employment and economic activity rates for ethnic groups have shown variations. Data from the LFS—the main source for current aggregate data on labour market statistics—provide an overall picture of the broad ethnic group categories. ONS analysis shows that employment rates for people aged 16–64 in England and Wales from 2001 to 2014 are lower for the broad (pan-ethnic) ethnic minority groups than the White group. In 2014, the employment rate was 74.7 % for the White ethnic group. The Mixed/Multiple group (63.4 %) had the highest employment rate of the minority groups, and the Other ethnic group (56.7 %) had the lowest employment rate. The Black African/Caribbean/Black British group occupied an intermediate position (60.6 %). Indeed, this rate had been fairly stable over the period 2001–2014, ranging from 57.5 %, 2009, to 63.7 %, 2006.

Similarly, the overall trend in inactivity rates for people aged 16–64 in England and Wales from 2001 to 2014 show that these are higher for the broad ethnic minority group categories than for the White ethnic group. In 2014, the inactivity rate for the White group was at 21 %, compared to 36 % for the Other ethnic group, the highest inactivity rate of the ethnic minority groups, followed by Asian/Asian British at 32 %. Again, the Black African/Caribbean/Black British rate occupied an intermediate position at 28 %. While the White inactivity rate was fairly stable during 2001–2014, that for the Black group increased from 30 to 32 % during 2001–2005, fell to 27 % in 2006, and has mainly oscillated around 27/28 % since then.

Economic Activity by Ethnic Group

While the LFS provides labour market trend data for broad ethnic groups, the 2011 Census offers a snapshot in time (albeit across three censuses) for the full census ethnicity classification, including the Black African category.

Black Africans (and Mixed White/Black Africans) had a relatively low employment rate (59 %), 14 percentage points below the White British group and 8 percentage points below Black Caribbeans (Table 6.4). Black Africans (13 %) also had one of the highest unemployment rates, 8 percentage points higher than the White British group and only exceeded by the Mixed White/Black Caribbean and Other Black (14 %) groups. Twenty-eight per cent of Black Africans were economically inactive, compared with 22 % in the White British group.

However, there were important regional variations in labour market participation for Black Africans (Table 6.5). The proportions in employment varied from 50 % in the North East to 66 % or over in the East of England and South East. Groups with the highest proportion of

Table 6.4   Economic activity of people aged 16–64, by ethnic group, England and Wales, 2011 (percentages)

Ethnic group	In employment	Unemployed	Inactive	Total (000s)
All	71	6	23	36,274
White	73	5	22	31,055
E/W/S/NI/B[a]	73	5	22	28,732
Irish	73	5	22	338
Gypsy/Irish Traveller	40	10	50	36
Other White	77	5	19	1,949
Mixed/Multiple	60	11	30	638
White/Black Caribbean	56	14	30	225
White/Black African	59	11	29	81
White/Asian	62	8	31	171
Other Mixed	63	9	29	161
Asian/Asian British	60	7	33	2,937
Indian	70	6	24	1,026
Pakistani	49	9	42	705
Bangladeshi	48	10	41	275
Chinese	53	5	43	323
Other Asian	63	6	31	608
Black/African/Caribbean/ Black British	61	13	26	1,241
African	59	13	28	667
Caribbean	67	12	22	408
Other Black	56	14	29	165
Other ethnic group	53	9	39	403
Arab	42	8	50	157
Any Other ethnic group	59	9	32	246

Source: Office for National Statistics. *Ethnicity and the Labour Market, 2011 Census, England and Wales.* London: ONS, 2014 (13 November)

[a]English/Welsh/Scottish/Northern Irish/British

the population aged 16–64 who were unemployed (White and Black Caribbean, Other Black, and Black African) had higher than average proportions across all regions. The highest proportions for Black Africans were in the North East (17 %), West Midlands (16 %), and Wales (16 %). The proportion economically inactive was lowest in the East of England and South East.

Differences in Labour Market Participation by Gender

A slightly higher proportion of Black African men (than all Black African persons) were in employment (62 %), lower than Black Caribbean men

Table 6.5 Economic activity of Black Africans by regions, England and Wales, 2011 Census: proportion of the population 16–64 in employment, unemployed, and economically inactive

	In employment	Unemployed	Economically inactive
North East	50	17	33
North West	55	15	30
Yorkshire and The Humber	55	15	30
East Midlands	56	13	30
West Midlands	51	16	33
East of England	67	10	23
London	58	13	29
South East	66	10	24
South West	60	11	29
England	59	13	28
Wales	51	16	33
England and Wales	**59**	**13**	**28**

Source: ONS (2014) (linked table).

Notes: All usual residents aged 16 and over in employment the week before the census

(65 %) but higher than the Other Black group (58 %) (Fig. 6.3). The unemployment rate was 14 % but exceeded by the Black Caribbean and Other Black groups, the latter being amongst the highest. Inactivity amongst Black African men was 24 %, higher than amongst Black Caribbeans (20 %). Reasons for inactivity vary markedly across ethnic groups. Sixty-two per cent of Black African men were students (including full-time students), substantially higher than amongst Black Caribbean men (36 %), Other Black men (49 %), and White British men (31 %). By comparison, rates of retired and long-term sick or disabled, 2 % and 10 %, respectively, were much lower than in the White British group (23 % and 30 %, respectively).

With respect to Black African women (Fig. 6.4), 55 % were in employment, the differential between men and women being much less than in the Arab and South Asian groups. For women, unemployment was highest in the Black African (12 %), White and Black Caribbean (11 %), and Other Black (11 %) groups. The inactivity rate amongst Black African women was 32 %, 10 percentage points higher than in the Black African group. An even higher proportion of Black African women (46 %) (compared with men) were inactive for the reason of being a student (including full-time student), exactly twice the rate for the general population and higher than the rate for Black Caribbeans

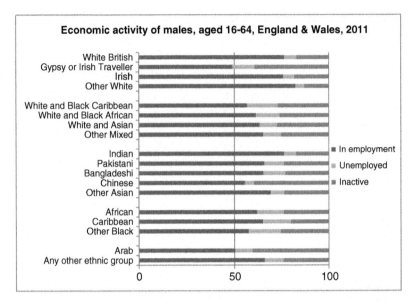

Fig. 6.3 Economic activity of males, by ethnic group, aged 16–64, England and Wales, 2011.

Source: 2011 Census

(32 %) and Other Black (39 %) group. Twenty-seven per cent of Black African women were inactive because they were looking after the home or family. Again, rates of retired and long-term sick or disabled (3 % and 8 %, respectively) were much lower than in the White British group (27 % and 17 %, respectively).

Though the census does not provide a detailed breakdown of the Black African subgroup for economic activity data, some findings are available from the LFS. Pooled data from the Labour Force Survey for 2005–2009 reveal substantial heterogeneity in economic activity across Black African country of birth groups (Table 6.6). Amongst males, the proportion in employment was higher amongst Ghanaians than Nigerians but lower for Zimbabweans. Somalians had an exceptionally low rate at 34 %. Amongst females, Zimbabweans had the highest rate amongst Black Africans but only 14 % of Somalis were in employment.

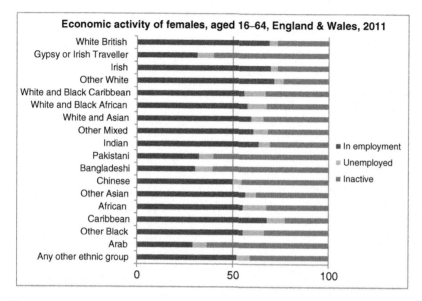

Fig. 6.4   Economic activity of females by ethnic group, aged 16–64, England and Wales, 2011.

Source: 2011 Census

Occupation and Industry

The 2011 Census collected two sets of information about the jobs people held: the type of work undertaken and the industry in which they worked. The information was classified by occupation and industry for those who were employed in the week before the census was completed and reported for the population aged 16 and over in employment.

Low-Skilled Jobs

In the 2011 Census, occupation was derived from a person's main job title and details of the activities involved in their job. Nine major occupations were reported,[4] but ONS has split these into low-skilled (administrative and secretarial occupations; caring, leisure and other service occupations; sales and customers service occupations; process plant and

[4] 2011 Census table DC6216EW.

Table 6.6   Economic activity of Black Africans and White British People aged 16–59 in the UK, by country of birth

Country of birth	% In employment	% ILO unemployed	% Inactive	Total %
Male				
Black African, UK-born	69	6	25	100
Ghana	82	7	11	100
Nigeria	72	12	17	100
Somalia	34	32	34	100
Zimbabwe	64	14	22	100
White British	82	6	12	100
Female				
Black African, UK-born	49	14	37	100
Ghana	60	10	30	100
Nigeria	60	12	28	100
Somalia	14	12	74	100
Zimbabwe	69	10	21	100
White British	72	4	24	100

Source: Mitton L, Aspinall PJ. *Black Africans in the UK: Integration or Segregation*. Research Findings. ESRC UPTAP, January 2011. Data from Labour Force Survey, 2005–2009.

Notes: The White British category refers to all those stating their ethnicity to be White British irrespective of their country of birth

machine operatives; and elementary occupations) and high-skilled occupations (managers, directors, and senior officials; professional occupations, associate professional, and technical occupations; and skilled trade occupations). The Black African group had one of the highest proportions (54 %) of men in low-skilled occupations, along with Pakistanis (57 %) and Bangladeshis (53 %) (Fig. 6.5). These proportions compared with 37 % of men in employment in the general population who worked in low-skilled occupations in the 2011 Census.

In all ethnic groups, women were more likely than men to be in low-skilled occupations. In the population as a whole, 59 % of women were in low-skilled occupations. However, the proportion of Black African women (58 %) was only slightly higher than for men, the 4 percentage point difference being the smallest across all ethnic groups. Black African women occupied an intermediate position across all ethnic groups, the proportion being similar to Black Caribbean and Other Black women.

Industry

In the 2011 Census, industry data were derived from information provided on the main activity of a respondent's employer or business. The broad

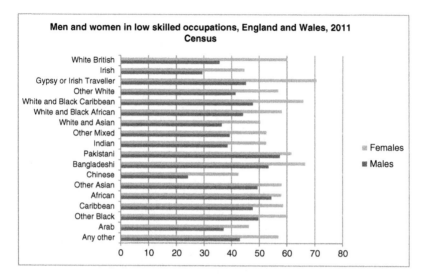

Fig. 6.5 Men and women in low-skilled occupations by ethnic group, England and Wales, 2011 Census.

Source: 2011 Census

categorisation is of only limited utility for analysing the main industries in which Black African men and women are concentrated. Black African men were distributed across all categories of industry but concentrated in wholesale and retail trade (13.4 %), administrative and support service activities (11.6 %), and human health and social work activities (15.2 %) (Table 6.7). Black African women showed a more concentrated pattern, 38.5 % being in the human health and social work activities category and smaller proportions in wholesale and retail trade (11.1 %) and education (9.1 %).

Nurses

Industry data from the 2011 England and Wales Census are derived from information provided on the main activity of a respondent's employer or business.[5] Traditionally, certain ethnic groups have been concentrated in particular industries. Table 6.8 shows the industries that had the highest proportions of women in ethnic groups working in a particular industry.

---

[5] Question 37 on the 2011 Census England Household Questionnaire asked: At your workplace, what is (was) the main activity of your employer or business?

Table 6.7 Industry: Black African men and women, England and Wales, 2011 Census

All industry categories:	Agricul-ture, energy, and water	Manu-facturing	Constr-uction	Wholesale and retail trade; repair of motor vehicles and motor cycles	Transport and storage	Accommo-dation and food service activities	Informa-tion and commu-nication	Financial and insurance activities	Real estate activities	Professional, scientific and technical activities	Adminis-trative and support service activities	Public adminis-tration and defence; compul-sory social security	Educa-tion	Human health and social work activities	Other activities
Men															
200,198	2,558	9,885	9,342	26,832	19,571	12,342	9,868	8,049	3,864	11,877	23,264	10,909	11,787	30,333	9,717
	1.3	4.9	4.7	13.4	9.8	6.2	4.9	4.0	1.9	5.9	11.6	5.4	5.9	15.2	4.9
Women															
194,466	866	3,272	2,143	21,671	4,630	11,590	4,091	6,459	3,862	9,325	14,791	10,890	17,631	74,810	8,435
	0.4	1.7	1.1	11.1	2.4	6.0	2.1	3.3	2.0	4.8	7.6	5.6	9.1	38.5	4.3

Source: 2011 Census. Table DC6216EW. Industry by ethnic group by sex.

Notes: All residents aged 16 and over in employment the week before the census. ONS Crown Copyright reserved

Table 6.8 Top five industries for women with highest proportion of ethnic group, England and Wales, 2011 Census

Ethnicity	Industry	Proportion (%)
Black African	Human health and social work activities	39
Other Asian	Human health and social work activities	31
Black Caribbean	Human health and social work activities	29
Other Black	Human health and social work activities	27
White Irish	Human health and social work activities	25

Source: ONS. *Ethnicity and the Labour Market, 2011 Census, England and Wales.* ONS: London, 2014 (13 November): Table 3

Women from Black ethnic minorities and Other Asians were highly concentrated within the 'Human health and social work activities'. Nearly four in ten (38 %) of Black African women were working in this sector. However, the census provides only limited information at one point in time.

The National Health Service (NHS) annual workforce censuses for medical and non-medical staff incorporate the Black African count into an aggregate Black African/Black Caribbean/Other Black group. However, data have been abstracted from the Electronic Staff Record (Table 6.9) to yield data for qualified Black African Nurses in England as at the end of September for each year for the period 2008–2014. This shows that the headcount for Black African nurses increases from 16,263 to 18,354 over 2008–2010, then stabilises at around 18,500 until 2014.

HCHS data for 30 September 2014 indicate that there were 353,359 qualified nursing, midwifery, and health visiting staff in NHS Hospital and Community Health Services in England (i.e. in contracted positions within English NHS organisations). These included 273,297 White staff, 4,154 Mixed, 25,125 Asian or Asian British, 26,486 Black or Black British, 1,445 Chinese, 9,387 Other, and 13,465 Unknown ethnicity, total minority ethnic groups (whose ethnic group is known) comprising 17.1 % in this staff group. The Black or Black British group contributes more nurses, midwives, and health visiting staff than any other minority ethnic group and around 70 % of these Black staff are likely to be Black Africans, a group that therefore makes a key contribution to the NHS.

More detailed information on the source countries of newly registered nurses is available from the Nursing and Midwifery Council Register, and

Table 6.9   Qualified Black African nursing, midwifery, and health visiting staff in England as on September 30 for each specified year: headcount

	2008	2009	2010	2011	2012	2013	2014
Black African (OEC)[a]	270	265	219	193	179	160	141
Black or Black British— African (NEC)[a]	15,993	17,519	18,135	18,392	18,233	18,443	18,300
	16,263	17,784	18,354	18,585	18,412	18,603	18,441

Source: Commissioned table, NHS Hospital and Community Services (HCHS)

[a]The list of categories used was changed in 2001, to reflect those used in the 2001 Population Census. Since 2001, HCHS has allowed a mixture of Old Ethnic Codes and New Ethnic Codes to be returned. For this analysis, figures for 'Black Somali' and 'Black Nigerian' have been included in the total, although they appear under 'Any Other Black Background' in the ONS ethnicity classification. The monthly workforce data are for those staff on the electronic staff record (ESR) and do not include primary care staff or bank staff

the research undertaken by Gloria Likupe provides a rich source of data on the motivations and experiences of Black African nurses in the UK.

During the late 1990s and early 2000s, there was a very high level of recruitment of nurses from overseas, to work in the NHS and in private health care. Such recruitment took place in spite of the Department of Health's 2001 (advisory) Code of Recruitment Practice advising against recruitment of nurses from countries with nurse shortages of their own, most of which were sub-Saharan African countries. Over the years 1998/1999 to 2007/2008, the largest African source countries were South Africa (9,810), followed by Nigeria (3,460), Zimbabwe (2,232), and Zambia (1,006) (Table 6.10).

Numbers increased gradually from these African countries, reaching a peak in 2001–2002 (3,789) and remaining high in 2002–2003 (3,195) and 2003–2004 (3,118). Thereafter numbers gradually declined. Data on initial registrations on the NMC register show that non-EEA source countries have in aggregate contributed very low numbers since 2008/2009 (though initial registrations from EEA countries have risen sharply from 2010/2011 to 2014/2015).

The NHS has relied on Black African and other overseas nurses for decades, bringing increased diversity to the workforce. Largely as a result of overseas recruitment, Black Africans now comprise a significant

Table 6.10 Newly registered overseas nurses[a]: African Source Countries, 1998–2008

Country	1998–1999	1999–2000	2000–2001	2001–2002	2002–2003	2003–2004	2004–2005	2005–2006	2006–2007	2007–2008
South Africa	599	1,460	1,086	2,114	1,480	1,689	933	378	39	32
Nigeria	179	208	347	432	524	511	466	381	258	154
Zimbabwe	52	221	382	473	493	nd	311	161	90	49
Ghana	40	74	140	195	255	354	272	154	66	38
Kenya	19	29	50	155	152	146	99	41	37	19
Zambia	15	40	88	183	135	169	162	110	53	51
Mauritius	6	15	41	62	60	95	102	71	27	19
Malawi	1	15	45	75	57	64	52	41	0	3
Botswana	4	0	87	100	39	90	91	44	0	2
Non-EU total[b]	3,621	5,945	8,403	15,064	12,947	14,122	13,608	10,985	8,673	2,309

Source: NMC 2008

[a]Counts of newly registered trained nurses and midwives provided by the Nursing and Midwifery Council based on their register of qualified nurses and midwives. Based on the top 25 non-EU foreign source countries

[b]Includes counts of all non-EU newly registered nurses

proportion of all staff and the nursing staff in major NHS trusts, as reported in recent equality and diversity reports. For example, in Homerton NHS Trust, Black Africans comprised 15.0 % of all staff and 29.2 % of nursing staff (the highest proportion of any ethnic group in 2013). Black Africans comprised almost 20 % of the workforce of Barnet, Enfield, and Haringey Mental Health Trust in 2014, the largest minority ethnic group. Black Africans comprised 23 % of the staff of Newham University Hospitals NHS Trust in 2012.

However, there is robust evidence of racism, discrimination, and lack of equal opportunity for Black Africans in the NHS. Likupe (2015) uses a qualitative approach—focus group discussions and semi-structured interviews amongst participants in the north-east of England—to obtain an insight into Black African nurses' experiences and those of their managers in the NHS. She reveals that many internationally recruited nurses have negative experiences in the NHS, including racism, harassment, bullying, discrimination, and lack of equal opportunities. She reports that racism was perceived as emanating from White colleagues and other overseas nurses, managers, and patients and their relatives. Discrimination was largely concerned with equal opportunities and the daily work of nursing on the hospital wards. Black African nurses felt that their experience and knowledge in nursing were not respected. Managers displayed stereotyping between different groups of overseas nurses, treating Black African nurses less favourably and confirming Black African nurses' suspicion that they were regarded as being of low motivation compared with others. They also labelled these nurses as confrontational when they voiced concerns. Ward managers did not trust Black African nurses' ability to perform certain duties and so applied excessive scrutiny when working with and supervising these nurses.

Racism went hand in hand with discrimination in terms of promotion, professional development, supervision of duty rotas, and the way mistakes were dealt with. Black African nurses described being passed over for promotion and having to prove themselves beyond the usual requirement by getting extra qualifications. Even then, they found it difficult to move up the career ladder, indicating a glass ceiling inhibiting upward mobility. Black African nurses also reported that they were often not given information on equal opportunity policies, in addition to not putting these policies in practice. Moreover, professional skills of overseas nurses were constantly questioned. In summary, there was a nursing hierarchy with Black African nurses at the bottom. Likupe's findings clearly have implications with respect to the Equality Act (2010), and these will be examined in Chap. 8.

Doctors

The GMC provides statistical information about doctors on the List of Registered Medical Practitioners (LRMP).[6] Current statistics as at 8 May 2015 show that a total of 266,841 doctors were registered on the LRMP. Amongst the top 20 countries of qualification were South Africa (5,207, 2.0 %, fourth in rank), Nigeria (4,245, 1.6 %, fifth in rank), and Sudan (1,687, 0.6 %, 17th in rank). By ethnic origin, 7,102 (2.7 %) were Black Africans, substantially higher than Black Caribbeans (624, 0.2 %), and Other Black (571, 0.2 %).[7] Mixed White and Black African doctors (871, 0.3 %) also exceeded Mixed White and Black Caribbean (291, 0.1 %) doctors. No breakdown is available by gender.

The Nationality of NHS Hospital and Community Health Service Workforce: Doctors, Nurses, and Support Staff

Nationality is a poor proxy for ethnic group or communities of descent as members of the African workforce in the NHS may have acquired British nationality. Moreover, the numbers from different African countries who have obtained British nationality may be affected by the length of time they have lived in the country. Also, nationality is unknown for 121,784 staff. However, as no data are available by ethnic group below the broad category of Black African, the nationality data do provide a proxy measure of diversity across the main staff groups (Table 6.11).

These data show that in September 2014, while 970,000 British staff comprise 80 % of the NHS workforce, 34 African countries also contribute 20,075 staff with African nationality, or 1.7 % of the total. The African nationalities contributing the largest proportions are Ghanaian (11.6 %), Mauritian (6.7 %), Nigerian (25.0 %), South African (9.4 %), and Zimbabwean (21.5 %). Clearly, some of the South African and Zimbabwean nationals may have been of White ethnicity.

The largest staff group of African nationals was qualified nursing, midwifery, and health visiting staff (8,537 or 42.5 %). The largest nationality

[6] General Medical Council. List of Registered Medical Practitioners: Statistics. http://www.gmc-uk.org/doctors/register/search_stats.asp
[7] In addition, there were 19 Black or Black British doctors whose detailed ethnic group was not specified.

Table 6.11   NHS Hospital and Community Health Service monthly workforce statistics, September 2014

	All HCHS staff	Professionally qualified clinical staff[a]	All HCHS doctors (incl. locums)	Total HCHS non-medical staff	Qualified nursing, midwifery, and health visiting staff	Qualified scientific, therapeutic and technical staff	Qualified ambulance staff	Support to clinical staff	NHS infrastructure support
All nationalities	1,210,760	640,678	112,911	1,097,965	353,359	155,960	18,673	360,402	212,123
British	970,027	499,393	78,921	891,175	276,298	130,181	14,170	299,024	173,585
Algerian	64	25	12	52	7	6	–	20	19
Angolan	27	8	–	27	4	2	2	9	10
Burundi	28	11	1	27	10	–	–	13	4
Cameroonian	246	122	16	230	92	14	–	93	31
Central African	141	81	9	132	64	8	–	27	33
Congolese	129	40	4	125	27	9	–	49	40
Eritrean	125	32	3	122	15	14	–	22	71
Ethiopian	76	28	4	72	17	7	–	25	23
Gambian	173	47	5	168	36	6	–	62	64
Ghanaian	2,330	1,200	101	2,229	982	117	–	763	373
Guinean	23	5	–	23	4	1	–	6	12
Ivorian	50	11	–	50	7	4	–	26	13
Kenyan	780	505	82	698	347	76	–	194	83
Libyan	158	146	141	17	2	3	–	8	4
Malawian	220	137	23	197	105	9	–	53	31
Mauritanian	247	149	19	228	123	7	–	74	24
Mauritian	1,355	808	104	1,251	658	46	–	465	83
Moroccan	47	6	1	46	4	1	–	21	20

Motswana	46	41	6	40	27	8	–	5	–
Namibian	25	8	–	25	5	3	–	11	6
Nigerian	5,025	2,443	671	4,355	1,525	247	–	1,933	658
Nigerien	91	40	17	74	20	3	–	36	15
Rwandan	57	33	1	56	31	1	–	16	9
Senegalese	20	4	–	20	4	–	–	7	9
Sierra Leonean	545	311	8	537	288	15	–	179	56
Somali	234	68	2	232	56	10	–	86	81
South African	1,891	1,358	324	1,567	550	477	7	323	215
Sudanese	393	365	350	43	7	8	–	17	11
Swazi	37	29	1	36	28	–	–	6	2
Tanzanian	140	78	17	123	50	11	–	40	22
Tunisian	23	6	5	18	–	1	–	7	10
Ugandan	478	227	29	449	178	20	–	197	54
Zambian	525	391	25	500	324	43	–	93	41
Zimbabwean	4,326	3,361	72	4,254	2,940	349	–	752	216
Unknown	121,784	60,228	7,603	114,187	33,936	14,408	4,299	36,305	25,449

Source: NHS Hospital & Community Health Service (HCHS) monthly workforce statistics—Provisional Statistics, September 2014

^aCounts are full-time equivalents

group was Zimbabweans (2,940), though Nigerians (1,525), Ghanaians (982), Mauritians (658), and South Africans (550) were also important. There were 2,053 doctors (including locums) of African nationalities working in the NHS, with large representation of Nigerians (671), Sudanese (350), and South Africans (324). There were also 5,638 staff (28.1 %) with African nationalities in the support to clinical staff group and 2,343 (11.7 %) in the NHS infrastructure support group.

Social Work Staff
The same drawback of concealed heterogeneity that applies to nurses, midwives, and health visiting staff also applies to the staff of Social Services Departments. The majority (86 %)[8] of the 130,100 adult social services jobs in 2014 were carried out by White workers (Health and Social Care Information Centre 2015). Around 7 % of all employees were Black or Black British but no breakdown is available by the census categories (so 'Black Africans' yet again remain invisible in the published data). This proportion varied from 1 % in the SW region to 10 % in the West Midlands and 31 % in London. While White employees accounted for 86 % of the 116,845 job roles and Black and minority ethnic groups 14 %, the White group was overrepresented in manager/supervisor roles (89 %) and underrepresented in professional roles (81 %). Black and minority ethnic groups were underrepresented in manager/supervisor roles (11 %) and overrepresented in professional roles (19 %).

Self-Employment

The proportion in self-employment amongst those in employment aged 16 and over was low amongst men in the Black groups: 15 % amongst Black Africans (the lowest rate, along with Mixed White and Black Caribbeans) and 16 % amongst Black Caribbeans and Other Black men. By contrast, 20 % of White British men were self-employed. Rates of self-employment were substantially lower amongst women in all ethnic groups. Only 7 % of Black African women were self-employed, with only Bangladeshis and Black Caribbeans (6 %) having a lower rate. Nine per cent of White British women were self-employed, though rates were higher, for example, amongst Other White (14 %) and Chinese women (15 %).

---

[8] The percentage of male and female workers is based on 152 councils but with less than 100 % employee completion rate and so can be treated as an estimate for England.

Nevertheless, there is evidence of an emerging entrepreneurship amongst Black Africans with the diaspora playing a key role in Africa's development (remittances accounting for 2 % of the continent's gross domestic product in 2010, the second largest source of foreign direct investment) (Ojo 2012). According to Ojo (2012, p. 146), these transnational Black African entrepreneurial activities are 'conducted by individuals who are rooted in two different social and economic arenas' with such individuals maintaining business relationships with their 'home' country and their area of residence in the diaspora. Such businesses tend to utilise family and personal knowledge about market opportunities in Britain and their countries of origin, this knowledge being used as a resource to import goods and services for these diaspora communities and to create employment opportunities.

Categorising African entrepreneurships is problematic because of their diversity. African businesses tend to follow the residential pattern of African migrants (Ekwulugo 2006), and some are informal. Excluding informal traders Nwankwo (2005) identifies a range of African entrepreneurship enterprises: professional services (accountancy, legal/solicitors, financial advice, and training/consultancy); food (restaurants/catering, public houses, and food retail); general merchandising/international trading; fashion and beauty (hairdressing, barber saloons); and general services (auto mechanics, electric/electronics, logistics/freight forwarding, and cab offices). African business enterprises tend to be gendered with women specialising in fashion and beauty whilst men focus on professional and general services. The viability and success of these enterprises are largely unknown, though they rarely get business support. Ojo (2012) notes that London is the epicentre of Nigerian entrepreneurship in the UK, and that competition contributes to difficulties in securing funding. Some businesses may have been set up as an escape from the ethnic penalty in employment markets.

Hours Worked

Overall 16 % of men in the general population worked part-time (up to 30 hours a week) at the time of the 2011 census.[9] Part-time working amongst men is higher in ethnic groups that are not White (apart from

---

[9] The number of hours that a person aged 16 and over in employment in the week before the census, worked in their main job (including paid and unpaid overtime).

Gypsies/Irish Travellers). Black African men occupied an intermediate position with 26 % working part-time and 9 % worked for 15 hours or less. Just 12 % of Black African men worked full-time for 49 or more hours, only Pakistanis (10 %) and Bangladeshis (6 %) having lower proportions. Forty per cent of Black African women worked part-time, and 12 % worked part-time for 15 hours or less. This was a lower proportion than that for White British women (45 % and 14 %, respectively). Substantially higher proportions of Pakistani women (52 %) and Bangladeshi women (56 %) worked part-time. Low proportions of Black African and Black Caribbean women worked full-time for 49 or more hours.

Young People (Aged 16–24) in the Labour Market

The 2011 Census recorded over 6.6 million people young people (aged 16–24) in England and Wales, nearly a quarter (23 %) of whom were from an ethnic minority group, a population generally with a younger age profile compared with the White British group. The participation in the labour market of young people (aged 16–24) from minority ethnic groups (see Table 6.12) is dominated by the high proportions who were full-time students. Amongst Black African young people, 73 % were full-time students, a proportion only exceeded by the Chinese and Arab groups. Moreover, the Black African proportion was distinctive in the Black group, being substantially higher than for Black Caribbean young people (55 %) and the Other Black group (63 %). Only 44 % of White British young people were students.

In consequence, a relatively low proportion of young Black Africans were in employment or self-employed (15 %), though this proportion will exclude full-time students who were also in work. Similarly, the proportion who were unemployed (7 %) was low and similar to the White British proportion.

Black African Subgroup Variations in Labour Market Participation

Only limited information is available on labour market participation by African subgroups. This includes 2011 Census data for economic activity by year of arrival in the UK by country of birth for residents aged 16 and over in England and Wales. However, counts are only reported for the total of African born and persons born in Nigeria, South Africa, and Other

Table 6.12 Labour market participation of young people (aged 16–24) by ethnic group, England and Wales, 2011 Census

		Employed and self-employed	Unemployed (excluding full-time students)	Inactive excluding students	All full-time students[a]
	All	38	8	7	48
White	British	42	8	7	44
	Irish	37	5	4	54
	Gypsy or Irish Traveller	26	14	31	30
	Other White	43	4	6	47
Mixed/ multiple ethnic groups	White and Black Caribbean	30	13	10	47
	White and Black African	24	8	6	61
	White and Asian	26	7	5	62
	Other Mixed	28	7	7	57
Asian/Asian British	Indian	26	5	4	65
	Pakistani	21	9	11	60
	Bangladeshi	22	9	10	59
	Chinese	9	2	2	87
	Other Asian	19	4	6	71
Black/ African/ Caribbean/ Black British	African	15	7	6	73
	Caribbean	26	12	8	55
	Other Black	20	10	7	63
Other ethnic groups	Arab	11	5	8	76
	Any Other ethnic group	22	7	8	63

Source: 2011 Census

[a]Students are reported as a separate group in order to give a clearer picture of youth employment and unemployment and the groups that are particularly affected. Students here are defined as full-time students who were economically active or inactive and part-time students who were economically inactive

(Africa). ONS's own Census Analysis includes economic characteristics (ONS 2014). The highest proportions in employment were observed for residents born in South Africa (78 %), only Poles having a higher proportion in the subset of 11 countries. Amongst those who had lived in the UK for 5–10 years, the Census shows that residents born in South

Africa had an employment rate of 80 %. Based on estimates from the 2011 Labour Force Survey, the South African-born had an employment rate of 82 % (the same as those born in EU8 countries). South African-born recent arrivals had the lowest proportion of students (11 %). UK-born Nigerians had an employment rate of 58.6 %. However, this proportion fell amongst recent arrivals (resident less than 5 years) to 40.4 % and those who had been in the country 5–10 years to almost the rate of the UK-born (58.3 %). Longer lengths of residence had higher employment rates: 69.2 % for those resident 11–30 years and 74.7 % for those resident more than 30 years.

Two sources were exploited for the UPTAP project (Mitton and Aspinall 2010, 2011): pooled LFS data for 2005–2009 and the Controlled Access Microdata Sample. The latter showed markedly varying employee rates by country of birth. Amongst males, 50.2 % of Black Africans were employees and a slightly higher proportion of UK-born Black Africans (51.8 %). The Ghana country of birth group (64.0 %), Nigeria country of birth group (53.2 %), and Zimbabwe country of birth group (51.4 %) all had high proportions. However, the employee rates for the Democratic Republic of Congo-born (23.5 %) and Somalia-born (20.3 %) were much lower. Self-employment rates were highest in the longer established Nigerian-born (14.0 %) and Ghana-born (7.5 %) groups but <5 % in the other country of birth groups. Similar differentials were found amongst women. The Black African employee rate was 46.5 % amongst Black Africans but 57.0 % in UK-born Black Africans. Again, rates were high for the Nigerian-born (53.4 %), Ghana-born (56.2 %), and Zimbabwe-born (55.5 %) but very low for the Democratic Republic of Congo-born (15.0 %) and Somalia-born (6.4 %). The self-employment rate was 3.8 % amongst the Nigerian-born and 2.0 % for the Ghana-born but negligible in the other groups.

CHAPTER 7

Generic Health Status

LIMITING LONG-TERM ILLNESS

Two measures of generic health status are available in the decennial census: limiting long-term illness (LLTI) and general health. In 2011, the former asked: Are your day-to-day activities limited because of a health problem or disability which has lasted, or is expected to last, at least 12 months? The question instruction stated 'include problems related to old age' with response options of 'yes, limited a lot', 'yes, limited a little', and 'no'. An LLTI question was first asked in the 1991 Census and the general health question was introduced in 2001, though there have been minor changes in wording. Analyses of these data (Bécares 2013, 2015) show important variations across ethnic groups and by gender.

Age-standardised ratios of LLTI for men, comparing minority ethnic groups with the White British group, show that in 2011 Black African males were one of the most healthy ethnic groups. Their age-standardised illness ratio of 0.59 was only bettered by the Other White (0.55) and Chinese (0.42) categories. By comparison, the age-standardised rate (ASR) for Black Caribbeans was 1.02 (i.e., worse than White British), similar to the Mixed White and Black Caribbean category (1.01) (Mixed White and Black Africans had a lower rate at 0.88). Black African females also occupied a favourable position on this measure. Their age-standardised LLTI ratio was 0.69, with only Other White (0.61) and Chinese (0.44) being better. However, female Black Caribbeans had a ratio of 1.04 and Mixed

White and Black Caribbeans 1.04 (worse than the 0.88 for Mixed White and Black Africans).

Moreover, Black African males and females had amongst the lowest rates of LLTI across age groups (0–15, 16–64, and 65 and over). In 2011 amongst 0–15-year-old males, 3.55 % of Black Africans had LLTI, ranking the fifth lowest rate after Other White (2.75 %), Indians (2.59 %), Chinese (2.37 %), and Other Asian (2.33 %). Amongst 16–64-year-olds, Black Africans (6.92 %) had the third lowest rate, after Chinese (4.34 %) and Other White (5.89 %). Even amongst the elderly (65 and over), Black Africans had the second lowest rate (42.61 %), after the Chinese (39.45 %). Similarly, Black African females report low proportions of LLTI across all three age groups. Amongst 0–15-year-old Black Africans the proportion was 2.45 %, only Other White (1.97 %), Indians (1.96 %), and Chinese (1.72 %) had lower rates. Only 8.67 % of 16–64-year-olds had LLTI, with only the Other White (6.67 %) and Chinese (4.72 %) having lower proportions. Finally, amongst the 65 and over population, Black Africans (54.24 %) had the sixth lowest proportion with LLTI after Chinese, Mixed White and Asian, Other White, White Irish, and Mixed White and Black African.

Analyses of LLTI by region showed that Black Africans had less advantage in London (with the health advantages being larger outside London). The advantage for Black African men in 2011 resident outside London was more than double that for those within London. The health advantage for Black African women resident outside London was around threefold.

Relative rankings in the age-standardised ratios of LLTI have changed little since 1991, though changes in wording may have affected how people interpreted the question, requiring caution in drawing comparisons.[1] The 2001 Census findings showed that amongst Black African men, age-standardised ratios were the second lowest (after the Chinese category) and Black African women had the third lowest (after Chinese and Other White). In 1991 (when the range of categories was much reduced), Black African males had the third lowest age-standardised ratio of LLTI (after

---

[1] In the 2001 England and Wales Census the question asked: Do you have any long-term illness, health problem or disability which limits your daily activities or the work you can do?, accompanied by the instruction 'include problems which are due to old age'. The response options were 'yes' and 'no'. In the 1991 Great Britain Census, the question asked: 'Do you have any long-term illness, health problem or handicap which limits your daily activities or the work you can do? Include problems which are due to old age'. The response options were: 'Yes, I have a health problem which limits activities' and 'I have no such health problem'.

Chinese and Other Asians). Only Black African women had a somewhat different ranking of illness ratios, being the fifth-ranking ethnic group in 1991 (with a ratio of 1.05 and therefore slightly worse than White British and also Chinese, Other Asian, Other, and Other Black).

One major drawback of these data is that they yield findings for the highly heterogeneous Black African group as a whole and not for national origin or other subgroups. Only limited information on generic health is available at this finer level of granularity. In the 2011 Census, only one table was released for LLTI and general health by detailed country of birth. Fortunately, it was for the London Borough of Greenwich which had experienced a substantial increase (130 %) in its Black African population between the 2001 and 2011 censuses. Numbers are large enough to estimate persons who were limited a lot in day-to-day activities, aged 16–64 (as a percentage of total day-to-day activities for this age group) and persons with bad/very bad health, not broken down by age (as a percentage of total general health). For LLTI, only data for the age group 16–64 were released, thus ruling out age standardisation. However, the exclusion of the 65+ age group should substantially eliminate the effect of the old age group on the derived rates (Table 7.1).

Amongst African countries of birth, rates were high for Mozambique, some North African countries (Morocco, Tunisia, Egypt), Somalia, Ethiopia, countries that were predominantly Asian in migrant flows (Tanzania, Kenya, and Uganda), Liberia, Malawi, and Sierra Leone. By contrast, rates were low in Ghana and Nigeria, representing the long-settled communities of migrants, and also in the Zimbabwe country of birth group. In many countries of birth, the proportions for limited a lot and with bad/very bad health were very similar.

Data to construct ASRs of LLTI (and general health) by country of birth for African countries was only available for the 2001 Census. It shows that the collective term 'African' conceals substantial variability (though the data are not cross-tabulated by ethnic group) (Piggott 2006). Figure 7.1 presents ASRs for migrants from different African countries, both sub-Saharan and North African, resident in London.

Not surprisingly, migrants with the highest rates of LLTI were those from countries with known high flows of refugees and asylum seekers to Britain, notably, Burundi, Somalia, Sudan, Eritrea, Algeria, Ethiopia, and Rwanda. The rates were much lower for the two largest and long-established migrant groups: Nigeria and Ghana. Clearly, care is needed in interpreting these data from the 2011 and 2001 censuses as a high

Table 7.1 % limited a lot, aged 16–64, and % with bad/very bad health, by African countries of birth: London Borough of Greenwich, 2011

Country of birth[a]	% Limited a lot, aged 16–64[b]	% Bad/very bad health[c]	Country of birth	% Limited a lot, aged 16–64	% Bad/very bad health
Mozambique (46)	10.9	7.3	Congo (132)	3.8	4.0
Morocco (130)	10.8	9.9	Botswana (26)	3.8	0.0
Tunisia (48)	10.4	5.9	Ghana (2,131)	2.6	1.8
Tanzania (240)	10.0	7.5	Eritrea (174)	2.3	5.5
Africa (not elsewhere specified) (130)	10.0	9.3	Ivory Coast (305)	2.3	2.6
Somalia(1,465)	9.4	9.8	South Africa (1,213)	2.2	2.2
Ethiopia (78)	9.0	6.3	Zimbabwe (850)	1.8	1.6
Egypt (154)	8.4	2.8	The Gambia (274)	1.8	1.4
Liberia (72)	8.3	4.1	Burundi (57)	1.8	1.5
Malawi (41)	7.3	9.1	Zambia (292)	1.7	1.9
Kenya (894)	7.0	6.4	Nigeria (11,565)	1.6	1.1
Uganda (912)	6.1	5.8	Cameroon (392)	1.5	1.2
Sierra Leone (723)	5.1	3.4	Rwanda (138)	0.7	0.7
Guinea (20)	5.0	5.0	Sudan (53)	0.0	1.8
Angola (178)	4.9	5.0	Senegal (32)	0.0	2.5
Algeria (283)	4.9	5.5	Libya (31)	0.0	0.0
Mauritius (413)	3.9	5.2	Swaziland (13)	0.0	9.1
Congo (Democratic Republic) (272)	3.8	3.2	Namibia (24)	0.0	0.0

Source: 2011 England and Wales Census. Commissioned Table CT0268

[a]Figures in brackets are TOTAL: day-to-day activities, aged 16–64. Percentages where count of total day-to-day activities is <30 may be inaccurate estimates
[b]Day-to-day activities, limited a lot: aged 16–64 as % of total day-to-day activities aged 16–64
[c]Bad and very bad health as % of total general health (no age breakdown)

proportion of migrants from some countries (Zimbabwe and South Africa) are 'White' and from others (Kenya, Tanzania, and Uganda) primarily 'Asian'. Further, some of the variation may be due to cross-cultural differences in the interpretation of the LLTI question.

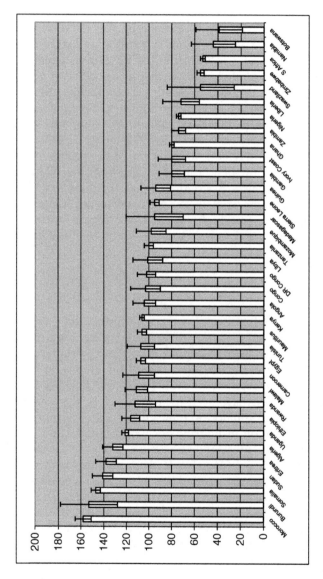

Fig. 7.1 Age-standardised rates of LLTI by African countries of birth, London, 2001.
Source: Extracted from: Piggott (2006), *DMAG Briefing 2006-3* [Table A10], citing 2001 Census, Commissioned Table C0116, as the source. Error bars show 95 % confidence intervals (*Note:* countries of birth may conceal considerable ethnic heterogeneity so caution is required in interpreting these rates, for example, only 37.9 % of those born in Zimbabwe identified as 'Black African')

GENERAL HEALTH

The general health question in the England and Wales 2011 Census asked: 'How is your health in general?', with response options of 'very good', 'good', 'fair', 'bad', and 'very bad'. A similar question was asked in the England and Wales 2001 Census: 'Over the last 12 months would you say your health has on the whole been: Good? Fairly good? Not good?'. Bécares' analysis using this measure of health yields a similar pattern of inequalities as LLTI, though across ethnic groups in general inequalities in general health are larger than inequalities in LLTI as minority ethnic groups tend to under-report the latter (Nazroo 1997). In the 2011 Census, age-standardised illness ratios, relative to the White British group, showed that Black African men had the best health, followed by Other White and Chinese men. Amongst women, Black Africans had the third best health after Other White and Chinese women. The pattern of inequalities was the same when inequalities in general health in 2011 are compared with those in 2001. Black African men and women had the second best health, after the Chinese group.

MORTALITY

A large number of studies based on American, Danish, Dutch, Finnish, and Swedish data show that self-reported health is a very good predictor of subsequent mortality. Such studies are carried out using data from large-scale population surveys which ask a range of questions on health and link them to national registers of deaths for the individuals in the survey. While such methods have been used for the UK, there are few direct sources of mortality for minority ethnic groups. Ethnic group is not recorded at death registration in England and Wales, the data on country of birth only providing information on migrants. However, in 2012 Scotland introduced ethnic origin on its death certificates, the first UK country to do so, though the provision of this information is voluntary.

Mortality data by country of birth are limited, the most recent data available being that for 2001–2003 (Wild et al. 2007) and, amongst the thirteen countries and regions, three regions in Africa (East Africa, North Africa, and West Africa). Persons born in East Africa will include African Asians as well as Black Africans. Men aged 20 years and over born in West Africa had an all-cause Standardised Mortality Ratio (SMR) of 117 (95 % confidence interval [CI] 111–124), only the born in Ireland (128, 95 % CI 126–129) and born in Bangladesh (120, 95 % CI 114–127) groups having a higher SMR. Women aged 20 years and over born in West Africa had an SMR of 121 (95 % CI 112–130), the highest of the thirteen countries/regions of birth. The next highest rate amongst women was the born in Ireland group (113, 95 % CI, 111–115). Thus, SMRs for men and women born in West Africa were statistically significantly higher than for England and Wales as a whole.

When narrower age bands are used (20–44 years, 45–59 years, 60–69 years, 70+ years), similar patterns are found with some important exceptions. Amongst Black African men born in West Africa, the SMR was 129 (115–144) in the 20–44 age group, the fifth highest; 106 (94–120) in the 45–59 age group, the seventh highest); 118 (105–132) in the 60–69 age group, fourth highest; and 116 (104–130) in the 70+ age group, second highest. Women born in West Africa had a significantly elevated SMR for the broad age group ≥20 years but a statistically significantly lower SMR for all-cause mortality amongst the oldest age group. For example, the SMR was 175 (154–199) in the 20–44 age group, substantially the highest, the second highest ratio being 130 (113–150) in the born in East Africa group. Amongst women aged 45–59, the West African ratio was again the highest (121, 106–139). It is unclear to what extent deaths from AIDS might have influenced these rates (based on 1,238 deaths of men from all causes and 807 of women of West African birth during the years 2001–2003), especially the substantially raised ratio for younger women, as the disease has affected women more than men. HIV-diagnosed Black African men seen for HIV care in the UK numbered 8,682 in 2013, compared with 16,627 women. However, all-cause mortality among people in the general population with HIV aged 15–59 years in England and Wales between 2002 and 2012 declined from 15 per 1,000 in 2002 to 4.5 per 1,000 in 2012.

Cause-specific mortality—circulatory disease, ischaemic heart disease, cerebrovascular disease, all cancers, and lung, colorectal, breast, and prostate cancers—for the population born in West Africa is considered in Chap. 8. However, maternal morbidity and mortality is addressed here as it reflects broader issues such as access to services. Many different theories have been advanced for why generic health status should vary across ethnic groups. The determinants of health and health inequalities (such as socio-economic position, security of housing tenure, education, labour participation, income, neighbourhood of residence, deprivation, social support, and experiences of racism and discrimination: see Chap. 6) are key. In addition, a substantial body of literature describes the 'healthy migrant' effect: the fact that on a range of measures, the first generation (migrants) are often healthier than residents in the host country who share similar ethnic or racial backgrounds. Over time, however, there is a literature that reports that migrant health advantage diminishes, the so-called 'paradox of assimilation'. The change from health advantage to disadvantage of migrants has been described as a function of circumstances in the host country, including limited access to labour market participation, education, and healthcare and the effects of racism. While the predominantly migrant Black African population has very good generic health, it is difficult in practice to measure the contribution of the 'healthy migrant' effect to this health status.

MATERNAL MORBIDITY, MORTALITY, AND INITIATION OF ANTENATAL CARE

Maternal morbidity and mortality has long been raised amongst Black Africans. However, the latest data on maternal deaths (2006–2008) indicate a significant reduction in the death rate amongst Black African mothers, a statistically significant downward trend over the 3 years (Centre for Maternal and Child Enquiries 2011). Estimated Black African rates of direct and indirect maternal deaths per 100,000 maternities declined from 72.1 (95 % CI 48.6–102.9) in 2000–2002 to 62.4 (43.7–89.0) in 2003–2005, and 32.8 (22.2–48.6) in 2006–2008. Although the rate for Black Africans was the highest among all ethnic groups (White, Black Caribbean, Black African, Indian, Pakistani, and Bangladeshi), the size of the gap between Black Africans and Black Caribbeans had narrowed very substantially by 2006–2008 (32.8 and 31.9, respectively). However, these rates were still substantially higher than in the White (8.5), Indian (12.5), Pakistani (14.3), and Bangladeshi (6.1) groups.

Of the twenty-eight Black African women who died during 2006–2008, nine were known to be UK citizens. Most of the remainder, citizens of other countries, were recently arrived new migrants, refugees, and asylum seekers. Around a quarter of Black Caribbean and Pakistani mothers were poor (after 22 weeks of gestation) or non-attenders for maternity care, there being no difference for women of Black African origin. Access to maternity care appears to have improved over recent years.

A similar picture emerges for severe maternal morbidity (Nair et al. 2014). The risk of severe maternal morbidity by ethnic group can be examined in a national cohort using data collected by the UK Obstetric

Surveillance System (UKOSS). Compared with White European women, the odds of severe maternal morbidity were 83 % higher among Black African women (adjusted odds ratio [aOR] = 1.83; 95 % CI 1.39–2.40), 80 % higher amongst Black Caribbean (aOR = 1.80; 95 % CI 1.14–2.82), 74 % higher in Bangladeshi, and 43 % higher amongst Pakistani women. This increased risk could not be explained by known risk factors for maternal morbidity and the odds of severe maternal morbidity did not differ by socio-economic status, between smokers and non-smokers, or by body mass index (BMI).

The UK standards of maternity care recommend that women engage with maternity services and establish a plan of care prior to the twelfth completed week of pregnancy. A number of studies have found that the late initiation of antenatal care is associated with an ethnicity other than White and particularly amongst women who identify themselves as Black. The 2011 Confidential Enquiries into Maternal Deaths in the UK identified pregnant migrants who may not be familiar with British language or culture as potentially vulnerable. Cresswell et al. (2013) undertook a cross-sectional analysis of routinely collected patient record data from Newham University Hospital NHS Trust for all women who attended their antenatal booking appointment between 2008 and 2011. Adjusted odds ratios for the effects of different ethnicities on late booking (after 12 weeks) showed that, compared with White British women, Somalis were at greatest risk (OR 1.58, 95 % CI 1.28, 1.96) but little different from Black Africans except Somalis (OR 1.56, 95 % CI 1.38, 1.77). Black Caribbeans ranked third (OR 1.33, 95 % CI 1.09, 1.61). Amongst Black Africans (except Somali) 55.2 % booked at a gestational age of up to 12 (+6 days), 29.5 % at 13–19 (+6 days), and 15.2 % at 20 or more days. Amongst Somalis, the proportions were 44.6 %, 35.2 %, and 20.2 %, respectively. Being an African or Caribbean, speaking English and born in the UK yielded an OR of 1.40 (95 % CI 1.11, 1.76), though this increased to 1.85 (95 % CI 1.62, 2.12) for those who speak English and are not born in the UK, and 2.20 (95 % CI 1.82, 2.66) for those who do not speak English and are not born in the UK.

Thus, Black African women may be at greater risk because of their ethnic group but that excess of risk may be further enhanced by being a migrant and not being able to speak English. An earlier report of the CEMACH (2004) reported that Black African women, especially including asylum seekers and newly arrived refugees, had a mortality rate seven times higher than White women. It found that they had major problems in accessing services.

CHAPTER 8

Long-Term Conditions and Infectious Diseases

The 'Black African' population is primarily youthful so currently little affected by diseases of ageing. However, mental illness can affect all age groups and there is evidence of elevated admission rates for diagnoses of anxiety, depression, and psychoses. Asylum seekers from sub-Saharan African countries suffer from post-traumatic stress disorder (PTSD), anxiety, and depression as a result of their pre-migration experiences and flight. Amongst older 'Black Africans', there is evidence of elevated burdens of disease for long-term conditions such as stroke, hypertension, and diabetes (though not of coronary heart disease). Other conditions that are examined include sickle cell disease. An attempt is made to describe the impact of HIV (now a chronic condition) and other infectious diseases on the Black African population. Finally, issues related to social and community care are discussed.

Long-Term Conditions

The 2004 Health Survey for England is the key source of evidence on the health of minority ethnic groups (National Statistics and Health and Social Care Information Centre 2005). The 2004 survey's main sample was augmented by an additional boost sample from the largest minority ethnic groups in England (which in 2004, unlike the previous such survey in 1999, included Black Africans). The 2004 Survey provided an emphasis on cardiovascular disease (CVD) and also focused on the behavioural risk

© The Editor(s) (if applicable) and The Author(s) 2016   173
P.J. Aspinall, M.J. Chinouya, *The African Diaspora Population in Britain*, DOI 10.1057/978-1-137-45654-0_8

factors associated with CVD such as drinking, smoking, and eating habits, and health status risk factors such as blood pressure and diabetes. With respect to children, the emphasis was on respiratory health. It remains the most comprehensive source of information on the health of the Black African population. The findings are based on unweighted bases of around 390 Black African men and 468 Black African women.

Cardiovascular Disease and Diabetes

The prevalence of angina was lowest in Black African (0.7 % and 0.5 %, respectively, amongst men and women) and Chinese informants, and highest in Pakistani men (6.9 %) and Indian men and women (4.9 % and 3.2 %, respectively). People from minority ethnic groups reported lower rates compared with the general population of heart murmur, abnormal heart rhythm (except for Irish women), and 'other' heart trouble (except for Black Caribbean women). The prevalence of stroke was highest among informants aged 55 and over. In this age band, Black Caribbean men had the highest prevalence (11.5 %) as did Bangladeshi (11.9 %) and Pakistani (10.1 %) women. This compared with just 1.5 % of Black African women (numbers were too small to report a male rate).

With respect to any CVD condition, women from the general population had the highest prevalence (13.0 %) and Chinese women had the lowest (5.3 %), Black African women being not far behind (5.5 %). Irish men had the highest prevalence of any CVD (14.5 %) while Black African men (2.3 %) had the lowest. With respect to IHD (angina or heart attack), among men aged 55 and over, Pakistani males had the highest prevalence (35.1 %) and Chinese (7.2 %) and Black African (5.2 %) males had the lowest. For women aged 55 and over, the prevalence was highest in the Indian group (14.7 %) and lowest in the Black Caribbean (6.3 %) and Irish (6.6 %) groups (figures being too small to report a rate for Black African women). With regard to IHD or stroke, the prevalence of IHD or stroke amongst those aged 55 and over was highest in Indian women (18.9 %) and Pakistani men (41.1 %) and lowest in the Chinese group (8.7 % men, 9.0 % women). In Black Africans, it was around 5.2 % in men and 1.5 % in women (though estimates were based on small numbers).

Data on mortality by country of birth for circulatory disease also reveal important differences. Circulatory disease mortality was high among men born in West Africa (Standardised Mortality Ratio (SMR) 128 [116–141]) and also for women (SMR 126 [110–145]) (Wild et al. 2007). These figures mask differences in IHD and cerebrovascular disease. IHD SMRs were relatively low for the West Africa country of birth group: 61 (51–73) for men and 81 (62–103) for women. Cerebrovascular disease mortality was particularly elevated for men born in West Africa (SMR 234 [197–278]) but was also significantly elevated for women (SMR 131 [102–166]).

The prevalence of doctor-diagnosed diabetes (type 1 and 2) was amongst the lowest in the Black African group. The rate in men was 5.0 %, only the Chinese (3.8 %) and Irish (3.6 %) having lower rates. Amongst women, the rate was 2.1 %, the lowest of all groups. However, type 2 diabetes accounted for the majority of cases. Black African, Black Caribbean, Indian, Pakistani, and Bangladeshi men had higher prevalence of type 2 diabetes at aged 35–54 to ages 35–54 and (except Black African men) aged 55+ than the general population. Among women, type 2 diabetes was more common in participants from Indian, Pakistani, and Bangladeshi groups (aged 35+) and Black Caribbean women (aged 55+).

Cancers

Amongst women, Shirley et al. (2014) compare the incidence of breast, ovarian, cervical, and endometrial cancer in British Indians, Pakistanis, Bangladeshis, Black Africans, Black Caribbeans, Chinese, and Whites between 2001 and 2007. Incidence rates were calculated from 357,476 cancer registrations using mid-year population estimates from 2001 to 2007, ethnicity being obtained through linkage to the Hospital Episodes Statistics database. Incidence rate ratios (IRR) were calculated, comparing the six minority ethnic groups to Whites and adjusted for age and income. Evidence of differences in incidence was found by ethnic group for all four types of cancers. For breast cancer, the age standardised rate (ASR)/100,000 person-years for Black Africans was 62.8 and incident rate ratio (IRR) 0.89 (0.81 to 0.96) (for all ages). For ovarian cancer, the ASR was 8.9 with an IRR of 0.74 (0.59–0.94). The ASR for cervical cancer was 10.1 and the reported IRR 0.82 (0.66–1.01). For endometrial cancer, the ASR was 6.2 and the IRR 1.15 (0.92–1.45). Thus, relative to the White population, Black Africans had lower rates of breast, ovarian, and cervical cancer but higher rate of endometrial cancer (but not significantly so).

Amongst male cancers, the UK studies of prostate cancer incidence rates/ratios across ethnic groups consistently show that these are higher in the Black group compared with the White group but lower in the South Asian group. Some of these estimates are measured with imprecision because of the small number of cases or limited by the high proportion of cases with unknown ethnicity (37–41 %). However, robust evidence (Ben-Shlomo et al. 2008) indicates that ASRs per 100,000 were 56.4 (95 % confidence interval [CI], 53.3–59.5) for the White group and 139.3 (95 % CI, 110–168) for the Black African group, a 2.5-fold difference.

With respect to other cancers, Black African men have incidence rates for lung cancer around half that of White men (IRR 0.4), based on Thames Cancer Registry data for 1998–2003.[1] Compared with White women, women from the other ethnic groups studied have much lower lung cancer incidence rates (an IRR of 0.3 in the case of Black African women).

The above findings are broadly consistent with mortality data. Wild et al. (2006) reported mortality from all cancers and lung, colorectal, breast, and prostate cancer by country of birth in England and Wales for the period 2001–2003. The sub-Saharan population is only adequately captured in the West Africa country of birth group, as a large proportion of people born in East Africa who live in England and Wales are of South Asian ethnicity. For all cancers combined, cancer mortality was higher for men born in West Africa (SMR 115) but not significantly so in the case of women (SMR 109). Lung cancer mortality was low in West African men (SMR 68, 95 % CI, 50–89) and women (40, 23–65). Breast cancer mortality was high among women born in West Africa (SMR 132, 95 % CI, 105–163). The investigators report that the high breast cancer mortality among women born in West Africa was unexpected, and a French study that adjusted for confounding factors did not find an excess of breast cancer mortality in migrants from sub-Saharan Africa compared to French natives (Bouchardy et al. 1995). Mortality from prostate cancer was around two or three times higher for men born in West Africa (SMR 271, 95 % CI, 207–349) (and the West Indies). The SMR for colorectal cancer amongst the West African-born was not significantly different from the national average for men (82, 53–120) and women (125, 80–186).

Mental Health

The Mental Health Minimum Dataset provides the most comprehensive information on the number of people in contact with adult and older adult mental health services (Health and Social Care Information Centre

---

[1] National Cancer Intelligence Network. Ethnicity and lung cancer. Accessed at: http://www.ncin.org.uk/publications/data_briefings/ethnicity_and_lung_cancer

2014). It shows that while Black Africans had a relatively low contact rate with services, but those who were in contact with services had a very high admission rate to hospital (Health and Social Care Information Centre 2014). In 2013–2014 (the most recent data), a total of 13,817 Black Africans were in contact with such services. This represented a population-based standardised rate of 3,005.0 per 100,000, the lowest in the Black group (Black Caribbeans had a rate of 4,535.7 and Other Black 9,914.7) and lower than for the White British group (3,514.4) and the Mixed White and Black African group (3,238.8).

Of those in contact with services, 81.8 % (11,301, comprising 11,232 NHS and 69 independent patients) were not admitted to hospital,[2] that is, people who were only in contact with community mental health services. This was the lowest percentage of any of the census ethnic groups, and compares with 86.1 % of the Black Caribbean group and 93.7 % of the White British group. Conversely, the Black African group had the highest proportion admitted to hospital (18.2 %), that is, people who spent time in hospital in that year, more than three times higher than for all people (6 %) and higher than both Black Caribbeans (13.9 %) and Other Black (16.2 %) patients. The age- and sex-standardised rate for those who spent some time in hospital of all those in contact with services was 12.9 per 100 (CI 0.6), again the highest of any ethnic group and almost twice the rate for the White British group (6.5 %). These figures could be indicative of a greater need for mental health services within these ethnic groups, or more complicated needs, once they are in contact with mental health services.

Similar findings were reported for the 1-day census, Count Me In, a survey carried out on 31 March each year for all of Britain's psychiatric patients. The census for 2006 showed that of the 32,000 people in hospital, those who described themselves as Black Caribbean and Black African were overrepresented by three- or fourfold, while Black British (mainly young, British-born Black people) were 18 times more likely to be in hospital than the general population.

Amongst those Black Africans with a hospital stay during the year (2,532), 50.6 % (1,281) were subject to the Mental Health Act 1983, the highest of any of the Census ethnic group categories and just above the Chinese (50.0 %). Of these hospital stays subject to the Mental Health Act

[2] Data source: Health and Social Care Information Centre, Mental Health Minimum Dataset (MHMD), 2013/14.

1983, 60 (4.7 %) were court and prison disposals, 1,154 (90.1 %) were civil detentions, and 67 (5.2 %) were subject to holding powers compared with 2.6 %, 86.2 %, and 11.3 %, respectively, in the White British group. Of hospital stays, 47.1 % in the Black Caribbean group were subject to the Mental Health Act 1983, 48.8 % in the Other Black group, and 32.5 % in the White British group.

The Care Programme Approach (CPA) is a national system which sets out how mental health services should help people with mental illnesses and complex needs. National guidance exists, though each provider of mental health services has their own CPA policy. According to NHS Choices, it is recommended that the person who needs CPA support is involved in the assessment of their own needs and in the development of the plan to meet those needs. The person should be informed about their different choices for care and support available to them, and they should be treated with dignity and respect. Of the 13,847 Black Africans in contact with services, 41.3 % had CPA status, in common with other Black/Black British sub-groups (Black Caribbean, 39.9 %; Other Black, 40.2 %). This compared with 20.5 % amongst all people and 22.3 % in the White British group. Rates were also lower in the pan-ethnic Mixed (31.3 %) and Asian or Asian British group (26.8 %). This suggests that people from the Black/Black British ethnic groups are presenting with more complex needs.

Mental healthcare clusters (or *care clusters*) are the nationally mandated currency model for mental health. The model covers most mental health services for working-age adults and older people. The care clusters were mandated for use from April 2012 by the Department of Health (DH). The 'care clusters' approach allows mental health services to group people together, based on their needs. There are currently 21 care clusters, further grouped into three 'super classes'—non-psychotic, psychotic, and organic—based on much broader similarities in need. There is substantial variation in the super class of care clusters assigned across ethnic groups. At the end of the year, the number of 'super class' care clusters assigned for the Black African group were 2,016 non-psychotic, 6,380 psychotic, and 464 organic. This compares with 245,630 non-psychotic, 162,636 psychotic, and 212,744 organic in the White British group. Thus, care clusters in the non-psychotic super class were more frequently assigned to people in the White than in the Black African and Other Black groups. More care clusters were assigned from the psychotic super class to people in both the Asian/Asian British (20,338, 52.9 %) and Black/Black British (21,102, 68.3 %) ethic groups than in the White group.

However, within the Black/Black British groups, Black Africans had lower median lengths of stay overall and for ward security levels. With respect to all discharges of Black Africans in 2013/2014 (2,733), the mean length of stay was 29 days, similar to the Asian/Asian British and Chinese groups but lower than that for Black Caribbeans (40 days). The White British median length of stay was 22 days. On low secure wards (112 discharges), it rose to 38 days (much lower than for Black Caribbeans, 76 days, and Other Black, 55 days). On medium secure wards, the median length of stay for Black Africans was 135 days, substantially below the 335.5 days for Black Caribbeans and 191.0 days for the Other Black group. However, on high secure wards, Black Africans (2,185.5 days) had a much longer median length of stay than Black Caribbeans (1,596.5 days) and Other Black (15.0 days) and the 77.5 days for the White British group.

The elevated risks for psychosis revealed by the Mental Health Minimum Data Set (MHMDS) are confirmed by many research studies and other mental health data sets. McKenzie (2008) has spoken of 'an epidemic of psychotic illness in those of African and Caribbean origin'. This has been reported with striking consistency, over 20 studies over the last 30 years, which show that people of Caribbean and African origin have an increased risk of being treated for serious mental illness such as schizophrenia and mania. The increased risk is of the order of 5–12 times greater than for White people and is said to be getting worse. Several sources have enabled researchers to assess the risks.

A longitudinal study undertaken amongst the general population in SE London, Nottingham, and Bristol during 1997–1999—the AESOP (Aetiology and Ethnicity of Schizophrenia and Other Psychoses)—provides some of the most robust evidence. This was the largest population-based incidence study of psychosis at the time of reporting and incorporated a number of methodological improvements over previous studies. Amongst a study population of 1,029,802, people aged 16–64 years living in the three study areas (all with well-established, heterogeneous minority populations) 568 people were diagnosed with psychotic illness during the 1.6 million person-years of follow-up. The incidence of psychosis was higher in all British ethnic minority groups than in the White British group (Table 8.1).

Table 8.1 shows that the age-standardised incidence rate of psychosis in the UK was highest in the African-Caribbean group (140.8 per 100,000 persons/year), followed by Black Africans (80.6). These rates were substantially above the White British rate (20.2). Moreover, incidence rates were

Table 8.1   Incidence of psychosis in British ethnic groups

Ethnic group	Age-standardised incidence rate (per 100,000 persons/year)	Incidence rate ratio (95 % CI)
African-Caribbean	140.8	6.7 (5.4–8.3)
Black African	80.6	4.1 (3.2–5.3)
Other	55.0	2.6 (1.7–3.9)
Mixed	45.9	2.7 (1.8–4.2)
Other White	33.1	1.6 (1.1–2.2)
Asian	31.6	1.5 (0.9–2.4)
White British	20.2	1 (reference group)

Source: Fearon et al. (2006)

markedly raised for all psychoses in *both* men and women amongst African-Caribbeans and Black Africans and across all three study sites. Schizophrenia and mania were highest in African-Caribbeans (schizophrenia incidence per 100,000 persons/year: 70.7 in African-Caribbeans vs 7.2 in White British; IRR 9.1, 95 % CI 6.6–12.6; mania incidence per 100,000 persons/year: 15.5 in African-Caribbeans vs 2.2 in White British; IRR 8.0, 95 % CI 4.3–14.8), and second highest in Black Africans (schizophrenia incidence per 100,000 persons/year: 40.3; IRR vs White British: 5.8, 95 % CI 3.9–8.4; mania incidence per 100,000 persons/year: 12.3; IRR vs White British: 6.2, 95 % CI 3.1–12.1). These rates were amongst the highest ever reported for migrant groups.

In a longitudinal record linkage study in Scotland (Scottish Health and Ethnicity Linkage Study [SHELS]) (Bansal et al. 2014), African women had higher risk of any psychiatric disorder (139.4, 95 % CI 119.0–163.2). African men and women had the highest risk for psychotic disorders (230.8, 95 % CI 177.8–299.5 and 240.7, 95 % CI 163.8–353.9) and were also overrepresented in Short-Term Detentions (214.3, 95 % CI 122.4–375.0) and Compulsory Treatment Orders (486.6, 95 % CI 231.9–1,021.1). However, due to small numbers, the investigators amalgamated the ethnic categories of African, Caribbean and Black Scottish, and Other Black groups as 'African Origin' group, referred to as 'African' for short.

While the causes for the increased amount of serious mental illness remain largely unexplained and are widely contested, migrants appear more likely to develop mental illness, especially Black migrants to White countries, and in the children of such migrants. By comparison, the rate of mental illness in the Caribbean and African countries is not high. Cantor-Graae and Selten (2005) and Cantor-Graae (2007) have noted that studies from the European continent have reported similar findings for other migrant groups but conclude that 'the extent to which the migrant "effect" in African-Caribbeans may be extended to all ethnic minority groups in the UK and to other types of psychoses remains unclear'. However, findings of more modestly raised incidence rates for all psychoses in the other minority ethnic groups do seem to implicate migration as a factor contributing to increased risk for psychosis. These findings indicate an urgent need for adequate prevention and treatment services that target these high-risk groups, especially Black Caribbeans and Black Africans.

PTSD and depression are amongst the most frequently reported health problems among asylum seekers. Some studies have yielded estimates as high as a half with PTSD and a fifth with major depressive disorders amongst refugees settled in the UK. Both pre-migration experiences of violence and post-migration social difficulties appear to determine the severity of PTSD and depression. Vulnerable groups of asylum seekers and refugees, such as children from war zones, are particularly likely to experience mental health problems, including high rates of PTSD.

Only a few studies report the prevalence of PTSD in Black African samples. Frissa et al. (2013) sought to estimate the prevalence of PTSD in a representative sample of an inner city, SE London population. A community sample of 1,698 adults aged 16 years and over were interviewed face to face with structured survey questionnaires. Amongst the sample of Black Africans (234, 13.8 %), the prevalence of PTSD symptoms was 5.8 % (95 % CI 2.7–8.8). This yielded an adjusted (age and gender) odds ratio of 1.1 (0.6–2.1). Prevalence of PTSD among asylum seekers is substantially higher. Bhui et al. (2006) found a prevalence of current major depression of 26.6 % and a prevalence of PTSD of 14 % amongst recent migrants to the UK from Somalia for resettlement, with a duration of residence in the UK of 0–5.5 years.

Sickle Cell Disease

Every year 300–400 children are born with the disease and currently there are 12,000–15,000 affected individuals in the UK. With respect to risks for haemoglobinopathies prior to screening, the chance that the couple are both carriers and require risk assessment is greatest when the family (ethnic) origins of both partners (mother and baby's father) are both Black

African (1 in 14) and risks remain high (risks higher than 1 in 100) when one parent is Black African (Aspinall 2013; Aspinall et al. 2003). However, other ethnic, including mixed, groups are also at risk. While universal antenatal screening takes places in Britain in areas of high prevalence, the Family Origin Question (FOQ) is used as a decision-making tool primarily to identify partners of high-risk status in 'low prevalence' areas (a fetal prevalence of 1.5 cases per 10,000 pregnancies or below, where universal screening is not regarded as cost-effective) in antenatal screening for haemoglobin variants. The purpose of the early (pre-10 weeks gestation) antenatal screening programme and preconception counselling is to enable women/couples to make informed choices and decisions for their pregnancy, and to provide appropriate referral and care for prenatal diagnosis with either continuation or termination of pregnancy according to these choices.

BEHAVIOURAL AND HEALTH STATUS RISK FACTORS

A range of health and behavioural risk factors for chronic illnesses are reported in the 2004 Health Survey for England (National Statistics and Health and Social Care Information Centre 2005).

Self-Reported Cigarette Smoking

According to the 2004 Health Survey for England's self-reported cigarette smoking statistics, Black African men (21 %) had one of the lowest rates of current cigarette smoking, along with Indians (20 %) and Chinese (21 %), and below the general population (24 %). Black African men also had the highest level of having never been a regular cigarette smoker (71 %). By contrast, the highest rates of current cigarette smoking were amongst Pakistani (29 %) and Bangladeshi (40 %) men. Moreover, with respect to estimated daily consumption of cigarettes, Black African men were the least heavy smokers, with 5 % smoking 20 or more cigarettes per day, compared with 31 % of male smokers in the general population smoking 20 or more cigarettes per day.

Amongst Black African women, only 10 % were current cigarette smokers. Only the Asian groups (Indian, Pakistani, Bangladeshi, and Chinese) had lower rates. By contrast, 24 % of Black Caribbean women, 26 % of Irish women, and 23 % of women in the general population were current cigarette smokers. Moreover, an estimated 2 % of Black African women smoked 20 or more cigarettes a day, compared with 27 % in the general population. These figures are in broad accord with those estimated from General Household Survey pooled data for 2001–2005 for Great Britain, in which rates for Black African men and women were reported as 18 % and 5 %, respectively.

However, such data are now more than a decade out of date. A recent analysis (Aspinall and Mitton 2014) uses the GP Patient Survey and Integrated Household Survey to provide up-to-date estimates. According to the GP Patient Survey for 2012, 12 % of Black African men were regular or occasional smokers compared with 3 % of Black African women. Moreover, never smokers were 72 % and 94 %, respectively. Analysis of the Integrated Household Survey for England and Wales for 2009/2010–2011/2012 showed that Black African men born outside the UK had lower smoking rates than the UK-born (14.3 % vs 18.5 %), a prevalence ratio (UK-born: non-UK-born, 95 % CI) of 1.29 (1.06–1.57). The differential was even larger for Black African females: 4.4 % of the non-UK-born were current cigarette smokers compared with 11.1 % of the UK-born, a prevalence ratio of 2.54 (1.97–3.28). There is only slight evidence of a social class (NS-SEC) gradient in smoking prevalence for Black African men and none for Black African women.

Alcohol

The 2004 Health Survey for England asked about usual drinking frequency amongst respondents aged 16 and over. Seventeen per cent of Black African men drank on 3 or more days a week, a substantially lower proportion than Black Caribbean men (28 %) and men in the general population (41 %). A third (32 %) of Black African men were non-drinkers, compared with 15 % of Black Caribbean men and 8 % of men in the general population. Only 6 % of Black African women drank on 3 or more days a week, lower than Black Caribbean women (11 %) and women in the general population (26 %). Forty-five per cent of Black African women were non-drinkers, compared with 21 % of Black Caribbeans, and just 14 % of women in the general population.

Male past week drinkers in all minority ethnic groups except the Irish were less likely than those in the general population to exceed 4 (i.e. government recommendations on daily drinking amounts) and 8 units (i.e. those who had been binge drinking) on their heaviest drinking day in the past week. The pattern for women was similar. Among past week drinkers,

Irish women were the most likely to drink more than 3 (53 %), the government recommended limit, or 6 (23 %) units, that is, binge drinking, on their heaviest drinking day, and were the only group more likely than the general population to exceed these levels. Black African women were somewhat less likely to exceed 3 (25 %), or 6 (4 %) daily units compared with Black Caribbean, Chinese, and Indian women.

Overweight and Obesity

The mean body mass index (BMI)[3] of men and women in the general population was 27.1 kg/m^2 and 26.8 kg/m^2, respectively. For some minority ethnic groups (Chinese and Bangladeshi men and Chinese women), the mean BMI was significantly lower than that of the general population. Black African men had a mean BMI somewhat lower (26.4) than men in the general population. However, mean BMI was markedly higher among Black Caribbean (28.0 kg/m^2) and Black African (28.8 kg/m^2) women. Indeed, Black African women had the highest mean BMI amongst all minority ethnic groups.

In the general population, 22.7 % of men and 23.2 % of women were obese (a BMI over 30 kg/m^2). Men from minority ethnic groups had markedly lower obesity prevalence rates than those in the general population, with the exception of Black Caribbean and Irish men. Black African men had a rate substantially lower (17.1 %) than the Black Caribbean group (25.2 %) and the general population, though higher than the South Asian and Chinese group. Amongst women, obesity prevalence was highest in the Black African (38.5 %) group but also high in the Black Caribbean (32.1 %) and Pakistani (28.1 %) groups. The largest difference in prevalence of obesity between men and women was found in Black Africans, where women's prevalence was higher than that in men by over 20 percentage points (38.5 % vs 17.1 %).

The prevalence of overweight including obesity (BMI over 25 kg/m^2) was 66.5 % among men and 57.1 % among women in the general population. Black African men (61.8 %) had a substantially lower overweight (including obesity) rate than Black Caribbean (67.4 %) men, indeed the lowest rate apart from South Asian and Chinese men. Among women, the prevalence of overweight, including obesity, was higher than the general

---

[3] BMI is a widely accepted measure that takes into account weight and height: it is calculated as weight (kg) divided by squared height (m^2).

population in the Black Caribbean (64.5 %), Black African (69.8 %), and Pakistani (62.3 %) groups. The other minority ethnic groups had lower rates than the general population. Indeed, the Black African rate was the highest amongst all the groups.

Waist–hip ratio (WHR) is defined as waist circumference divided by hip circumference, that is, waist girth (m)/hip girth (m). Among the general population, the mean WHR was 0.92 in men and 0.82 in women. Amongst men, mean WHR was lowest in Black African men (0.87) and Chinese men (0.87) and highest in Irish men (0.93). There was less variation among women, mean values ranged from 0.81 (Black African and Chinese) to 0.85 (Bangladeshi women).

Mean waist circumference was 96.5 cm for men and 86.4 cm for women in the general population. Mean waist circumference ranged from 86.8 cm in Chinese men to 97.3 cm in Irish men, Black African men (90.6) occupying an intermediate position. Amongst women, mean waist circumference ranged from 77.6 cm in Chinese women to 90.2 cm in Black African women.

In the general population, 33 % of men and 30 % of women had *raised* WHR (defined as 0.95 or more for men and 0.85 or more in women). The lowest rate in men was found among Black Africans (16 %) and the highest among Pakistanis (37 %). Amongst women, 32 % of Black Africans had a raised WHR, higher than in the general population but intermediate in the range from Chinese (22%) to Bangladeshi women (50%).

The prevalence of *raised* waist circumference (102 cm or more in men, and 88 cm or more in women) was 31 % in men and 41 % in women in the general population. Nineteen per cent of Black African men had raised waist circumference, the lowest rates being recorded among Chinese (8 %) and the highest among Irish men (33 %). Prevalence ranged from 16 % among Chinese women to 53 % among Black African women.

Blood Pressure

In the 2004 Health Survey for England, mean systolic blood pressure (SBP) was higher among men (131.4 mmHg) than women (125.9) in the general population and in each minority ethnic group. Amongst men, mean SBP was highest among Black Caribbean (133.3) and Irish (131.5) respondents and men in the general population and lowest in Bangladeshi men (121.0). SBP in Black African men (128.0) was lower than for Black Caribbeans. Women in the general population had the highest mean

SBP (125.9 mmHg), Black Caribbean (123.0) and Irish women (124.6) having the highest SBP amongst minority ethnic groups. Black African women (118.1) had lower SBP, along with South Asian (116.4–119.2) and Chinese women (115.1).

Mean diastolic blood pressure (DBP) was higher in Black Caribbean informants (74.7 mmHg in men and 73.7 mmHg in women) than the other minority ethnic groups and the general population (74.3 and 73.2 in men and women, respectively). Black African men had a mean DBP (73.5) below that of the general population and the lowest amongst minority ethnic groups. Among women, Black Africans had a mean DBP of 72.8, only the Chinese having a lower mean DBP (70.0).

With respect to detection and treatment of high blood pressure (hypertension), hypertension is defined as having raised blood pressure (SBP≥140 mmHg or DBP≥90 mmHg) or on medication to treat hypertension. Participants were considered hypertensive if their SBP was 140 mmHg or over, their DBP was 90 mmHg or over, or they were taking medicine prescribed for high blood pressure. Four levels were used in the HSE 2004 Report: normotensive-untreated (SBP<140 mmHg and DBP<90 mmHg and not taking medicine prescribed for high blood pressure) and three hypertension levels (hypertensive-controlled: SBP<140 mmHg and DBP<90 mmHg and taking medicine prescribed for high blood pressure; hypertensive-uncontrolled: SBP≥140 mmHg or DBP≥90 mmHg and taking medicine prescribed for high blood pressure; and hypertensive-untreated: SBP≥140 mmHg or DBP≥90 mmHg and not taking medicine prescribed for high blood pressure).

Black Caribbean informants had the highest prevalence of hypertension (38 % men, 32 % women), followed by the Irish (36 % men, 29 % women) and similar to the general population (32 % men, 29 % women). Black Africans were somewhat lower than these groups (25 % men, 19 % women) but above the South Asian and Chinese groups. The HSE also reported the proportion of informants who had BP≥160/100 mmHg, but were not on drug treatment for hypertension. Five per cent of men within the general population had untreated BP≥160/100 mmHg. The proportion of men in minority ethnic groups with untreated BP≥160/100 mmHg ranged from 1 % of Bangladeshis to 5 % of Irish men, the proportion amongst Black Africans being 4 %, none of these differences being statistically significant.

The proportion of women in the general population with untreated BP≥160/100 mmHg was also 5 %. Amongst minority ethnic women, the prevalence of hypertensive-untreated ($\geq 160/100$ mmHg) participants was highest for Black Africans (4 %) and lowest amongst Black Caribbean and Chinese women, though none of the differences found between the minority ethnic groups and the general population was statistically significant.

Participation in Physical Activity

In the general population, 37 % of men and 25 % of women had high activity levels, that is, a level defined as achieving the recommendations of participating in activity of moderate to vigorous intensity for at least 30 minutes on 5 or more days a week on average. Among minority ethnic groups, Irish (39 %) and Black Caribbean (37 %) men had the highest rates of adherence to the recommendations, Black Africans having only a slightly lower rate (35 %). Black Caribbean, Black African, and Irish women had the highest rates (31 %, 29 %, and 29 %, respectively). South Asian men and women had lower rates.

Two-thirds of general population men reported regular participation in any physical activity (at least once a week on average). Regular participation was reported by about two-thirds of those in the Irish, Black Caribbean, and Black African minority ethnic groups. Six in ten women in the general population participated regularly in physical activity, the proportion amongst Black African women being 57 %.

Eating Habits

The recommended guidelines of consuming five or more portions of fruit and vegetables a day were met by 23 % of men in the general population, the proportion of men meeting the guidelines being significantly higher among all minority ethnic groups (with the exception of Irish men). Thirty-one per cent of Black African men met the five-a-day recommendation, similar to Black Caribbean men (32 %), with somewhat higher rates in the Indian and Chinese groups. Similar patterns were found in the mean number of portions consumed. In the general population, a significantly higher proportion of women (27 %) met the five-a-day recommendation. Amongst Black African women 32 % met the recommendation, slightly higher than Black Caribbean women (31 %), though exceeded by Chinese and Indian women (42 % and 36 %, respectively).

The mean fat intake score amongst men in the general population was 24 but lower in men in minority ethnic groups, Black African men had a score of 20 (only Indian and Chinese men having a lower score). Mean fat score was also lower among women in minority ethnic groups than those in the general population (21), ranging from 17 among Indian respondents to 20 among Black African, Irish, and Pakistani women.

Fifty-six per cent of men in the general population reported use of salt in cooking. This proportion was higher—with the exception of Irish men—among men in minority ethnic groups (from 74 % among Black African men to 95 % among Bangladeshi men). A similar pattern of salt use in cooking was observed for women. The prevalence of salt use in cooking was also higher for women in minority ethnic groups (with the exception of Irish women), within a range from 69 % among Black Caribbean women to 92 % among Indian women, than those in the general population (53 %). Black African women (83 %) occupied an intermediate position.

Complementary and Alternative Medicines

Among the general population, women were more likely than men to have used any of a list of 24 complementary or alternative medicines (CAMs) in the last 12 months (33 % of women compared with 21 % of men). A lower proportion of Black African women (19 %) and Black African men (16 %) had used CAMs.

CHILDREN'S HEALTH

Key findings were reported by the 2004 Health Survey for England. Within the general population, 24 % of boys and 20 % of girls aged 15 or under had a longstanding illness. It was lower among children in all of the ethnic minority groups and lowest amongst Black African boys (11 %) and girls (7 %). Among the general population 36 % of boys aged 15 or under had ever wheezed, compared with 29 % of girls of this age. The proportions were amongst the lowest in the Black African group (20 % and 12 %, respectively). In the general population, 23 % of boys and 18 % of girls had had asthma diagnosed by a doctor. Prevalence was lower amongst Black African boys and girls (17 % and 9 %, respectively). In the general population, 18 % of boys and 19 % of girls aged between 8 and 15 had ever smoked. Again, the proportions in the Black African group were lower

(12 % and 9 %, respectively). In the general population, 45 % of boys and 40 % of girls aged between 8 and 15 said that they had ever had a whole proper alcohol drink, the proportions being substantially lower in the Black African group (17 % and 15 %, respectively). Within the general population, 30 % of boys and 31 % of girls were classified as overweight or obese. The proportion of overweight or obese boys was highest in the Black African population (42 %), and Black African girls were also one of the ethnic groups most likely to be overweight or obese (40 %) (exceeded only by Black Caribbeans). There were few differences across the ethnic groups in the proportions who participated in any physical activity. Finally, among the general population, 11 % of boys and 12 % of girls aged between 5 and 15 ate five or more portions of fruit and vegetables a day. These proportions were exceeded by Black Africans (18 % and 20 %, respectively).

INFECTIOUS DISEASES

HIV/AIDS

The African continent has been the epicentre of the global HIV epidemic and numbers of affected people are set to increase due partly to improved HIV medicines which lead to better health outcomes for people living with the virus. The heterosexual nature of the Black African epidemic in sub-Saharan Africa is reflected in the heavy burden of heterosexually contracted HIV amongst Black Africans in the UK. HIV/AIDS has dominated the discourse on Black African health over the last two or three decades. However, the epidemiology and burden of the disease have changed substantially during this period, as new therapeutic regimes have changed the disease from an acute to a chronic or long-term condition.

The HIV and AIDS Reporting Section (HARS) data collection provides comprehensive data on HIV-diagnosed individuals receiving HIV care; first HIV and AIDS diagnoses; deaths among HIV-positive individuals; and CD4 surveillance, available by regions and strategic health authority, specific prevention groups, and other demographic factors.

Table 8.2 gives numbers of HIV-diagnosed persons seen for HIV care in the UK by ethnicity and route of exposure in 2013. The table shows that the highest number of HIV-diagnosed people seen for care in 2013 was the White group (42,966 persons) but Black Africans were second with 26,617 persons. Clearly, Black Africans were substantially overrepre-

Table 8.2 The numbers of HIV-diagnosed persons seen for HIV care in the UK by ethnicity and route of exposure in 2013

	Sex between men	Sex between men and women	Injecting drug use	Blood/blood products	Mother-to-child transmission	Other/not reported	Total
White	30,915	9,032	1,434	409	117	1,059	42,966
Black Caribbean	741	1,608	19	6	27	48	2,449
Black African	555	24,172	36	139	1,238	477	26,617
Other Black/Black unspecified	394	1,279	31	7	51	48	1,810
Indian/Pakistani/Bangladeshi	484	729	12	34	18	64	1,341
Other Asian/Oriental	684	727	20	16	8	68	1,523
Other/Mixed	2,122	1,429	128	42	145	138	4,004
Not known	336	193	6	3	22	242	802
Total	36,231	39,169	1,686	656	1,626	2,144	81,512

Source: The HIV and AIDS Reporting Section (HARS) data collection

sented, given that they comprise only 1.8 % of the UK population. Black-Caribbeans, Other Black/Black unspecified, South Asians, and Other Asians (mainly East and SE Asians) had much lower numbers. In addition, route of exposure was very different in the White group compared with Black Africans. In the White group, sex between men accounted for 72.0 % of all persons seen for care, with sex between men and women comprising just 21.0 %. Amongst Black Africans, sex between men and women accounted for 90.8 % of all persons seen for care and sex between men just 2.1 %.

There are important geographical differences across England in the extent to which Black Africans contribute to HIV cases. Amongst upper tier local authorities in London in 2013 with a prevalence of diagnosed HIV infection of 2 or more per 1,000 population (aged 15–59 years), the proportion of Black Africans among people living with diagnosed HIV infection was highest in Bexley (64 %), Enfield (61 %), Newham (58 %), Greenwich (54 %), and Croydon (54 %). Outside London, the proportions were highest in Thurrock (68 %), Luton (67 %), Coventry (67 %), Southend-on-Sea (67 %), and Leicester (65 %).

In 2013, an estimated 38,700 Black Africans were HIV positive and this group constitutes two-thirds (65 %, 38,700) of all heterosexual people living with HIV (Public Health England 2014). The HIV prevalence rate among Black African heterosexuals is 56 per 1,000 population aged 15–59 years (41 per 1,000 men and 71 per 1,000 women). This is a rate 30 times higher for Black African men and women compared to the general population in England. Almost two in five (38 %) Black African men and one in three (31 %) Black African women living with HIV remained unaware of their infection. The lower rate of undiagnosed infection among heterosexual women is largely due to the effectiveness of the UK antenatal screening programme. Rates of undiagnosed infection among heterosexual Black Africans were higher outside London, estimated at 49 % (4,400), the comparative proportions inside London being estimated to be 13 % (500). Similar patterns were observed among women outside London, where 41 % (6,700) of HIV positive Black African women were unaware of their infection, and in London where 10 % (800) were unaware.

Other characteristics of the disease that disproportionately affect Black Africans include late diagnoses. The proportion of adults diagnosed with a CD4 count <350 cells/mm^3 was particularly high among Black African men (66 %) and women (57 %), compared with 61 % and 42 %, respectively, in the White group. Further, while the annual incidence rates of

HIV and tuberculosis co-infection have been declining in recent years, elevated rates persist amongst people of Black African ethnicity (7.7 per 1,000).

In Black African communities, high levels of HIV testing have been reported. In 2010, 46 % and 44 % of Black African men and women, respectively, reported having had an HIV test done in the last 5 years. A community survey of Black African populations has observed self-reported protective behaviours of HIV testing in the last year (39 %) and regular condom use which may, however, be too low to reduce HIV transmission in this population (Bourne et al. 2014). HIV screening in STI (sexually transmitted infections) services is effective. For example, of those who did not have an HIV test at their first STI clinic attendance in 2011, but who had a test at a subsequent attendance at that same clinic, Black African heterosexual men and women showed the diagnosis rate at reattendance was around 5 per 1,000 (7/1,290), indicating the importance for Black African heterosexual men and women of obtaining very high HIV test uptake rates at STI clinics. However, less than one in five of the Black African population attended an STI clinic in the previous 5 years, underlying the importance of improving access to HIV testing in other settings, including the use of national HIV self-sampling services.

However, despite improvements in the diagnosis and care of Black Africans with HIV, there remain a number of issues that continue to contribute to inequalities, including the high prevalence of comorbidities, mental health issues, and experiences with stigma and discrimination. Amongst structural factors, challenges experienced by Black Africans at the social level, notably stigma, are amongst the most important. They continue to impact on disclosure patterns and on everyday life experiences (Anderson and Doyal 2004).

In the UK, children living with HIV have always constituted a small but significant group of people affected by HIV. The UK-based National Study of HIV in Pregnancy and Childhood (NSHPC) has, since 1989, collected data on children presenting with HIV infection and infants born to HIV-infected women in the UK. The number of reported pregnancies in women with diagnosed HIV in the UK increased from 80 in 1990 to over 1,400 in 2010; the majority were among women born in sub-Saharan Africa. Most children reported to the NSHPC are also reported to the 17 UK centres that participate in the Paediatric European Network for Treatment of AIDS (PENTA) trial. By October 2002, 627 children were alive and in follow-up at PENTA trials and most of the children were resident in London and were of Black African parent heritage. A high uptake of HIV testing in pregnancy has reduced the numbers of babies being born with HIV, with the estimate being that only 2 % of children born to HIV-positive mothers in the UK between 2005 and 2011 were HIV positive. However, as Table 8.2 shows, the largest number of mother-to-child transmission cases was in the Black African group and these accounted for over three-quarters (76 %) of all such cases.

Tuberculosis

Tuberculosis (TB) case reports and rates by place of birth and ethnic group for the UK are published by Public Health England.[4] The 2013 data show that for the UK-born population in the UK Black Africans (with 98 cases) had a rate of 31 per 100,000, higher than Black Caribbeans (92 cases) with a rate of 23 cases per 100,000 but substantially lower than the Other Black group (26 cases) with a rate of 61 per 100,000. Only Pakistanis had a higher rate, of 38 cases per 100,000. However, if the burden of disease is measured by number of case reports, the greatest burden was found in the White group (1,345 cases), followed by Pakistanis (223 cases) and Indians (162 cases).

However, cases and rates have traditionally been higher in the non-UK-born population. Non-UK-born Black Africans have a rate of 170 per 100,000 (based on 1,020 cases), substantially higher than Black Caribbeans (29 per 100,000, 63 cases) and Other Black (127 per 100,000, 34 cases). The highest rates were found in non-UK-born South Asians, with rates of 286 per 100,000 for Pakistanis and 220 per 100,000 for Indians. These two countries also had the highest burdens (as defined by case reports), with 1,765 in the case of Indians and 1,117 for Pakistanis.

Country of birth data show important variations across African countries in number of cases and percentage of cases and the median time since entry to the UK and interquartile range (Public Health England 2014, p. 14). In 2013, Somalia (292 cases) had 5.4 % of non-UK-born cases in the UK and a median time since entry of 9 years (4–13). Nigeria had 164 cases, 3.0 % of all cases, and a median time since entry of 7 years (3–11). Zimbabwe had 105 cases, 1.9 % of all cases, and a median time since entry of 11 years (7–12). Kenya (a country of birth group that includes both

---

[4] https://www.gov.uk/government/uploads/system/uploads/attachment_data/file/358250/TB_place_of_birth_and_ethnic_group_UK_2013.pdf. Data as on May 2014.

Black Africans and East African Asians) accounted for 84 cases, 1.6 % of all cases, and a median time since entry of 22 years (8–37). Finally, Eritrea had 62 cases, 1.1 % of all cases, and a median time since entry of 4 years (2–7). The numbers of reported cases for people born in Zimbabwe and Somalia have declined due to change in migration patterns and policies.

The number of TB cases in the non-UK-born population has been influenced by detection methods. From 2012, the UK rolled out a pre-entry screening programme for migrants from high-incidence countries, and this programme has seen an increase in the number of cases identified in the pre-entry screening for all countries compared to the programme that targeted migrants from high TB incidence countries. Multidrug-resistant TB is a public health threat, the social factors that can contribute to this including interrupted adherence to treatment and contracting multiresistant TB. Migrants from Somalia, Nigeria, Sudan, and Sierra Leone were amongst the countries of birth for people who had developed drug-resistant TB. TB affects children and most cases of TB reported in the 0–14 age group were in UK-born children (69 %), with the highest proportion amongst the Black African (23 %) and Indian groups.

Sexually Transmitted Infections

One of the major drawbacks in establishing the incidence of STIs in the Black African population is that data are reported by Public Health England for an aggregate 'Black' group, while it is known that rates vary across the different Black groups. The highest rates of STI diagnoses (genital warts, gonorrhoea, genital herpes, and syphilis) are found among persons of Black ethnicity, and the majority of these cases were among persons living in areas of high deprivation, especially in urban areas (Public Health England 2014). This high rate of STI diagnoses among Black ethnic communities is likely to be the consequence of a complex interplay of cultural, economic, and behavioural factors.

Risk behaviours and STI epidemiology vary markedly between Black African and Black Caribbean ethnic groups (Fenton et al. 2005; Low et al. 2001). However, the setting up of new surveillance systems provided data available by ethnic group for genital Chlamydia infection, gonorrhoea, genital warts, genital herpes simplex virus, and syphilis. Early releases did provide tabulations for the separate Black groups (Aspinall and Jacobson 2004). The extent to which different groups are affected varies substantially, with especially high rates of STIs in the Black Caribbean and Other Black ethnic groups.

The 2002 Gonococcal Resistance to Antimicrobials Surveillance Programme (GRASP) collection showed that Black and minority ethnic groups continue to bear a disproportionate burden of *gonorrhoea* infections, with Black Caribbeans accounting for 32.55 and 41.2 % of the total infections in females and heterosexual males, respectively, and ethnic minorities accounting for 47 % of the total diagnoses. Data from the ProgrESS surveillance initiative show a similar distribution by ethnic group for *genital Chlamydia infection*. The highest diagnosed rates in London were seen in the Black Caribbean and Other Black groups. Amongst both male and female Black Caribbeans rates were over 900/100,000 population; the male rate in the Other Black group exceeded 1,200/100,000 and reached 1,500 amongst females in this group.

For *genital warts*, data from ProgrESS for London again show uneven rates of diagnoses across the different ethnic groups. The highest rates for both males and females were seen in the Other Black group—exceeding 300/100,000 population—and rates were also high in the Black Caribbean group (around 150 and 200/100,000 in males and females, respectively). Once again, with respect to *Genital herpes simplex virus (HSV) infection*, ProgrESS data for rates of diagnoses (first attack) in London show highest rates amongst Black ethnic groups: over 300/100,000 population amongst Other Black females and 150/100,000 amongst Black Caribbean females; around 175/100,000 and 100/100,00, respectively, amongst males. Enhanced surveillance data for *syphillis* show that between April 2001 and September 2003 almost half of heterosexual diagnoses of syphilis were attributed to Black or Black British ethnic groups.

SOCIAL AND COMMUNITY CARE

The term 'children in care' includes all children being looked after by a local authority, including those subject to care orders under section 31 of the Children Act 1989, and those looked after on a voluntary basis through an agreement with their parents. Routinely collected statistics show the number of children looked after in England gradually increased from 60,900 in 2009 to 68,110 in 2013 (Table 8.3). White British children comprised around three-quarters of these children, Black or Black British 7 %, and Black African 3 % of the total. Black African children, oscillating in numbers around 2,100 a year, comprised the largest of

Table 8.3   Children looked after as on 31 March by ethnic origin, England 2009–2013

Ethnic origin	2009	2010	2011	2012	2013
All children looked after	60,900	64,450	65,500	67,080	68,110
Rate/10,000 children <18 years[a]	54	57	58	59	60
White	46,180	49,000	50,410	52,150	53,030
White British	44,470	47,170	48,530	50,020	50,620
Mixed	5,300	5,670	5,760	6,040	6,090
White and Black African	510	550	630	660	690
Asian or Asian British	3,220	3,420	3,110	2,820	2,620
Black or Black British	4,400	4,580	4,550	4,500	4,470
Caribbean	1,560	1,660	1,630	1,550	1,530
African	2,100	2,120	2,070	2,110	2,080
Any other Black background	740	800	840	840	860
Other ethnic groups	1,660	1,660	1,490	1,300	1,390
Other[b]	140	130	190	270	500

Source: Department for Education and Children Looked After in England, year ending March 2013

Notes: Numbers have been rounded to the nearest 10. Percentages have been rounded to the nearest whole number. Figures exclude children looked after under an agreed series of short-term placements
[a]The rates per 10,000 children under 18 years have been derived using the mid-year population estimates for 2012 provided by ONS
[b]'Other' comprises Refused and Information not yet available

the Black groups, exceeding Black Caribbean and Other Black children throughout the 5 years.

For all children the rate was 58 per 100,000 children under 18 in 2011. Using 2011 Census data as denominators, the Black African rate was over 633 per 100,000, almost 11 times the White British rate. Moreover, the White and Black African rate was 739 per 100,000, over 12 times the White British rate.

Owen and Statham (2009) have provided one of the most comprehensive analyses of the disproportionality in child welfare with respect to ethnic group, including a synthesis of the relevant research literature and new analyses conducted on three national data sets (the Children in Need Census, children on the child protection register, and children looked after). Looked after children's care histories were examined to see if over- or underrepresentation could be explained by factors such as differing rates of entering or leaving care. The disproportionate presence of Black African children in children in need, children looked after, and other statistics has been the subject of inquiry by a number of investigators.

A large-scale study of placement stability, involving analysis of data on over 7,000 children from 13 English local authorities, found that children who were not White (a quarter of the sample) were 'more likely to enter the care system at least in part for reasons of poverty or other social disadvantage' (Sinclair et al. 2007, p. 50). In a review of poverty and ethnicity research, Platt (2007) found that the risk of poverty was highest for Bangladeshis, Pakistanis, and Black Africans. This review also found variations in levels of social contact by ethnic group, Black Caribbeans and Black Africans appearing to be lacking in informal social contact, particularly women.

Amongst the key literature findings reported by Owen and Statham (2009), African children were much more likely to enter placements as teenagers (Sinclair et al. 2007). A study by Gibbons and Wilding (1995) identified that inadequate supervision or 'home alone' cases disproportionally involved more African families, possibly influenced by parents' income and inability to access affordable childcare. With respect to cultural attitudes and practices within families, Bernard and Gupta (2008) argue that strongly gendered norms placing women in a subordinate position within African families may operate to constrain mothers in their ability to protect their children in the context of domestic violence. However, Owen and Statham (2009) found little research evidence to support or contradict this, domestic violence being recorded as a cause for concern in the court files of half the children of Black African mothers (Masson et al. 2008), very similar to the rate for all mothers in the sample. Though the sample size for this analysis was small, concerns about drug abuse were much more likely to be recorded in the case files of Black Caribbean mothers and much less likely to be recorded as a concern in the case of Black African or South Asian mothers.

With respect to children looked after, Owen and Statham (2009) pooled data for 2004, 2005, and 2006 and provide a much more detailed picture than that available through the published statistics. They reported that Black African children looked after, starting to be looked after, and ceasing to be looked after comprised 3.0 %, 4.1 %, and 3.8 % of the national totals, while comprising 1.4 % in the national census. The proportions for White/Black Africans were 0.8 %, 0.9 %, and 0.8 %, respectively, compared with a presence in the population of 0.3 %. The Mixed groups and the Black groups are starting to be looked after at rates higher than their presence in the total population. With respect to the total length of time a child is looked after, Black African children had amongst the shortest total length of time looked after (449 days), only the 'Other' group having a shorter time (418 days). This compares with 993 days for White Irish children (the longest), 832 days for Black Caribbeans, 812 for Other Black children, and 801 days for White/Black African children.

While the average age of first entering care for the children in this data set was almost 7, Black African (8.7) children were the oldest and the 'Mixed' group the youngest (White and Black Africans 5.7). For all ethnic groups the main reason for starting to be looked after is abuse or neglect (60.2 %), though less than 50 % for the Black African group (along with 'Other' ethnic group, Chinese, and 'Other' Asian). However, the Black African group (along with these other ethnic groups) have very much higher rates for absent parenting (20.6 % in case of the Black African group), only exceeded by the 'Other' category (24.0 %), substantially higher than the Black Caribbean group (7.6 %) and the White British group (3.3 %). Though unaccompanied asylum seekers were excluded from these analyses, Owen and Statham (2009) speculate that some of these children were unaccompanied asylum seekers but not coded as such. Black African children also had a high percentage with parental illness or disability (12.1 %), above the national average (7.0 %).

Whilst being looked after, the two main categories of care placements are fostering and residential care, with fostering being the more common. Overall 85.3 % of children looked after experienced foster care, with quite small variation by ethnic group. Overall 86.1 % of Black Africans were ever fostered, similar to Black Caribbeans (86.4 %) and White British (85.2 %). The pattern for residential placements is quite different. While the overall percentage of children who experienced residential care was 23.1 %, there were large ethnic differences. Overall 22.4 % of Black Africans were ever in residential care, compared with 30.2 % of Black Caribbeans (the highest proportion), 21.7 % of White and Black Africans, and 23.0 % of White British. Owen and Statham (2009) also explore which children are most likely to be adopted according to their ethnic group, adoption being an outcome strongly favoured by social workers. Black children and those of Pakistani and Bangladeshi origin are the least likely to be adopted. Just 2.5 % of Black Africans were ever adopted, the lowest of any ethnic group. This proportion compares with 5.3 % of Black Caribbeans, 7.1 % of Other Black, 11.8 % of White/Black Africans, and 13.3 % of White British.

Finally, on average 17.9 % of looked after children cease being looked after by returning to their parents, returning to parents varying much more by ethnic group than being adopted. Black African children (along with Chinese, 'Other', and Black Caribbean children) were much less likely to be returned to their parents than the other ethnic groups. Black Africans (9.4 %) had next to the lowest proportion ever returned to parents (Chinese had the lowest proportion, at 9.0 %). These proportions compare with Black Caribbeans (11.9 %), Other Black (15.2 %), and White British (18.8 %). Owen and Statham (2009) speculate that reasons for such large differences in the rates at which children looked after were returned to their parents may lie in the fact that the parents were absent, or that they were not deemed suitable to take back their children.

The importance of Owen and Statham's (2009) analysis is that they disaggregate the broad categories of ethnicity reported in the annual published data, allowing the Black African group to be identified and both disproportionality and disparity by detailed ethnicity to be established for looked after children. Moreover, a local-level analysis showed that over-representation of certain minority ethnic groups is not simply a function of living in areas with overall low or high levels of children involved with the child welfare system. The investigators conclude that 'it is not clear from this analysis why the Black group should be so over-represented amongst the looked after population' (in contrast to the extreme under-representation of Asian children in the care population). Moreover, they consider it likely that many different factors interact to contribute to the differences, making it impossible to draw straightforward conclusions. There clearly remains a need to explore what might be producing these differences between ethnic groups, through a partnership with members of these communities.

The other important conclusion is that the investigators' analyses highlight the need to disaggregate minority ethnic groups: 'the ethnic groups put together in the four summary categories do not all have the same experiences and trajectories, so that the summary classification may be masking important differences' (Owen and Statham 2009, p. 47). Currently, the main collections report data only for aggregated or pan-ethnic groupings. Data on Children in Need (CiN) are collected in the Children in Need Census. The censuses take place in a 'typical' week and record details of all children who received services from Social Services during that week. The numbers of children are reported by ethnic group but only in five categories (White, Mixed, Asian, Black, and Other), less detailed than the categorisation used to collect the data because many local authorities have few Black and minority ethnic children. With respect to the Child Protection Register (CPR), each local authority in England sends details annually of children on its CPR to government on form CPR3. However, the table for England by ethnic group uses the same five categories as the CiN census. Information on Children Looked After (CLA) is collected on the SSDA903 statistical return annually, a longitudinal record of each looked after child. The Department for Children, Schools and Families (DCSF) website includes figures by ethnic group for each local authority using the same five-group classification as the CiN census and the CPR figures.

Unaccompanied asylum-seeking children (UASC) (defined by the UN High Commissioner for Refugees in 1994 as children under 18 years of age who have been separated from both parents and are not being cared for by an adult) were excluded from Owen and Statham's (2009) analyses. However, some statistics are available from the Department for Education (2014). There were 1,970 UASC looked after by local authorities as on 31 March 2014. This number has decreased by 43 % since 2010, numbers falling from 3,480 in 2010 to 2,740 in 2011, 2,220 in 2012, and 1,930 in 2013. In 2014, 89 % were male and three-quarters (76 %) were aged 16 and over. The largest proportion were from other ethnic groups. However, data for Q1, in 2011, show that there were 345 applications received from UASC, of whom 100 (29.0 %) were African nationals (15 Algerians, 25 Eritreans, 5 Ethiopians, 5 Nigerians, 20 Somalians, 5 Sudanese, and 20 Other Africa).

CHAPTER 9

Social, Cultural, and Civic Life

The effects of social networks within the Black African community have been underresearched with respect to their outcomes on community members. We have already seen in Chap. 5 the positive 'ethnic density' effects that stem from improved social support, improved social networks, and improved access to culturally specific facilities and services. The term 'social capital' has gained popularity and describes social networks that exist amongst populations, groups, and organisations. Kwon and Adler state (2014, p. 412) its effects 'lie in information, influence, and solidarity benefits that accrue to members of a collectivity ("bonding" social capital) and to actors, whether individual or collective, in their relations to other actors ("bridging" social capital)'. Its sources lie in the social relations among those actors which can be differentiated (notionally) from relations of market exchange and of hierarchical authority.

These investigators identify different dimensions of social capital which exist in different forms of networks. These include 'cognitive networks' which are based on shared memories of what life was or is in Africa, or the imaginings of what it means to be an African. These shared memories speak to shared identities, which splinter to reflect various colonial, migrational, and other lived experiences in the UK and transnational links with the African continent. Such networks may also be potential or mobilised networks, the latter occurring, for example, when Black Africans diagnosed with a stigmatised health condition unilaterally socially exclude themselves from the wider African community at a time when they most

© The Editor(s) (if applicable) and The Author(s) 2016   201
P.J. Aspinall, M.J. Chinouya, *The African Diaspora Population in Britain*, DOI 10.1057/978-1-137-45654-0_9

need support. Also, it is important to recognise the role of physical space in interactions within social networks. This issue is now often mediated by technology, the use of Skype and smart phones having made it possible for Black Africans to belong to multiple global, local, and virtual networks, thereby transforming the imagined 'African community'.

The notion of civic engagement is also complicated. Enquete-Kommission (2002) identify key activities that characterise civic engagement. These are activities which are carried out voluntarily without the aim of personal material gain, are oriented towards shared responsibility for the welfare of others, take place in public space, are transparent, can be joined by other people, are community based, and have a cooperative character. This may be an idealised form of civic engagement as it is often problematic to measure the altruistic nature of civic engagement. Civic engagement may, in turn, lead to Black African involvement in governance and a role in policymaking.

Organisations thus set up face many challenges, especially funding which is key to sustainability. In developing a survey sampling frame for those involved in healthcare and welfare issues (Aspinall et al. 2015), a high proportion of identified organisations (including those registered as charities) were found to be either no longer operating or subsumed by other organisations. Others had a poor financial or compliance history and were operating with minimal income, few having their own dedicated websites. A study commissioned by the Joseph Rowntree Foundation (Seok-Woo and Adler 2014) reported that Black and ethnic minority groups experience difficulties in accessing core funding, funders not fully comprehending the work of these agencies. For African-led organisations, this lack of funding, overscrutiny, and the perception of skill deficits in running organisations have resulted in some of them having very short lives, continuing to operate informally, and relying heavily on volunteers. This is clearly an important policy issue as African-led organisations provide an important link between decision makers, statutory providers, and the wider African public in Britain and are important 'tools' that promote civic engagement within this public.

SOCIAL RELATIONSHIPS

Friendships and Conviviality

It was Paul Gilroy who introduced to us the concept of 'conviviality' to refer to 'the processes of cohabitation and interaction that have made multiculture an ordinary feature of social life in Britain's urban areas and in postcolonial cities elsewhere' (Gilroy 2004). He sees the idea as successor to multiculturalism. It provides a different space to that occupied by issues of tolerance and racism and 'a measure of distance from the pivotal term "identity"'. It focuses on 'radical openness' rather than 'a nonsense of closed, fixed, and reified identity' and 'is orientated by routine, everyday exposure to difference'. In the words of Williams (2013, p. 6), 'it is produced when people are so used to mingling with myriad languages, religions and skin colours that difference becomes commonplace and automatically accepted'. This suggests that it is manifested in specific locales in large British cities that have diverse populations. It is no surprise, then, that Gilroy considers London the home and prime example for the study of conviviality but concerning that he has little to say about its manifestations in other British cities.

This grass roots spontaneous tolerance and openness that characterises convivial culture is difficult to capture in surveys and research undertakings and, as Gilroy concedes, the London experience is not generalizable elsewhere. However, there have been systematic attempts to capture experiences and patterns of friendships across different ethnic groups and in a variety of settings, particularly by the Citizenship Survey and the Ethnic Minority British Election Survey (EMBES). The 2010–2011 Citizenship Survey reported percentages of respondents mixing regularly (at least once a month) with people from different ethnic or religious backgrounds. Mixing is defined as mixing socially with people from different ethnic or religious backgrounds at work, school, or college; a child's crèche, nursery, or school; the pub, club, café, or restaurant; a group, club, or organisation; the shops; a place of worship; through formal or informal volunteering, but not at home. Proportions amongst Black Africans (95 % of 1,132 respondents) in 2010–2011 were similar to other minority ethnic groups (94–97 %) but higher than the White group (80 %). These proportions have remained stable across recent surveys (2007–2008, 2008–2009, 2009–2010, and 2010–2011).

With respect to sphere of mixing with people from different ethnic/religious backgrounds, the 2010–2011 Citizenship Survey reveals that Black Africans differed little from other ethnic groups with one or two exceptions (Table 9.1). Such mixing at home or in their home (65 %) was similar to the proportion (63 %) for ethnic minority groups, but much lower than for the Mixed Race group (81 %). Such mixing at work, school, or college was highest for Black Africans (78 %), compared with 73 % for all ethnic minority groups. This type of mixing at child's crèche, nursery, or school was higher

Table 9.1 Mixing with people from different ethnic or religious backgrounds by sphere of mixing: ethnicity, England, 2010–2011

	Home or their home	Work, school, or college	Child's crèche, nursery, or school	Pub, club, café, or restaurant	Group, club, or organisation	Shops	Place of worship	Formal volunteering	Informal volunteering	Any mixing (excluding at home)	Respondents
White	32	51	15	44	31	61	11	19	13	80	8,809
All Asian	60	72	34	57	41	83	44	21	23	94	3,985
Indian	63	75	30	64	48	82	44	25	23	94	1,424
Pakistani	55	67	40	47	32	85	42	20	25	95	1,475
Bangladeshi	54	65	44	50	33	87	44	13	21	96	561
All Black	66	73	36	57	49	87	61	28	30	95	2,099
Caribbean	68	65	32	60	49	87	45	28	33	96	907
African	65	78	38	57	48	87	72	28	29	95	1,132
Mixed Race	81	76	29	76	59	85	29	29	32	97	491
Chinese/Other	64	74	28	61	39	86	38	13	20	95	884
Ethnic minority groups	63	73	33	59	44	85	46	23	25	95	7,459
White	32	51	15	44	31	61	11	19	13	80	8,809

Source: Citizenship Survey, 2010–2011

for Black African (38 %), Pakistani (40 %), and Bangladeshi (44 %) groups, reflecting the higher fertility rates in these groups. Mixing with people from different ethnic/religious backgrounds in pub, club, café, or restaurant was 57 % for Black Africans, similar to ethnic minority groups (59 %) but almost 20 percentage points lower than the Mixed Race group (76 %). Such mixing at groups, clubs, or organisations was again disproportionately high for the Mixed Race group (59 %) but proportions for Black Africans (48 %) were similar to ethnic minority groups (44 %). However, one of the most notable differences across the range of settings was the high proportions of Black Africans engaging in such mixing in churches (72 %), substantially higher than ethnic minority groups (46 %) and the Mixed Race group (29 %). Finally, Black Africans engaged with different groups at similar levels for formal (28 %) and informal (29 %) volunteering, higher than for ethnic minority groups (23 % and 25 %, respectively).

The Ethnic Minority British Election Survey asked respondents how many of their friends have the same ethnic background as the respondent (with response categories of all, most, about half, a few, and none). Amongst Black African middle-class respondents, 48 % of respondents had all or most friends from the same ethnic background, lower than Pakistanis (51 %) and Bangladeshis (58 %) but higher than Indians and Caribbeans (each 43 %). Asian working-class respondents reported higher proportions (Indian, 57 %, Pakistani, 66 %, and Bangladeshi, 71 %) than middle-class respondents, though the differences were small for the Black groups (Caribbean, 44 %, and African, 51 %). For ethnic minority respondents as a whole, the proportion with all or most friends from the same *ethnic/religious* background decline across generations (from 72 % in the first generation to 40 % in third+ generations).

Interethnic Unions

Interethnic unions (cohabitation and marriage) represent the most intimate form of interethnic friendship. The percentage of couples in interethnic unions in England and Wales (married, in a civil partnership, or cohabiting) has been increasing in recent decades, from, for example, 7 % in 2001 to 9 % or 2.3 million in 2011. However, the proportion of people in an interethnic relationship varies markedly across ethnic groups. In 2011, 59,000 Black Africans (over the age of 16) were in an interethnic relationship, 22 % of all Black Africans living as a couple. This was substantially lower than Black Caribbeans (73,000, 43 %) and Other Black people

(30,000, 62 %). The proportion of Black Africans was little different from that in 2001 (29,000, 23 %), while the proportion of Black Caribbeans in interethnic unions had increased markedly from 58,000 (34 %) in 2001. The proportion of Other Black people in such unions was higher in 2001 (12,000, 71 %). The only exception to this low rate amongst Black Africans was the 'Mixed: White and Black African' group, where 23,000 (79 %) were living as a couple in interethnic relationships in 2011. Such high proportions were common to all four 'mixed' groups (88 % in the 'White and Black Caribbean', 87 % in the 'White and Asian' group, and 87 % in the 'Other Mixed' group), though lowest in the 'White and Black African' group. This was also the case in 2001, when 77 % of White and Black Africans were living as a couple in interethnic relationships.

The most common interethnic relationships amongst Black Africans were with White British (24,000 or 9 % of all people living as a couple in the Black African group), Other White (10,000 or 4 %), and Other Black (7,000 or 2 %). There were also 6,000 Black Africans in interethnic unions with Black Caribbeans. The top three interethnic relationships in the case of the Mixed: White and Black African group were somewhat different. Of all people living as a couple in that ethnic group, 13,000 'White and Black Africans' (44 %) were in interethnic relationships with White British, 3,100 with Black Africans (11 %), and 3,000 (10 %) with people in the Other White group. Thus, of the two constituent heritages in the 'White and Black African' group, White partners outnumbered Black Africans by a ratio of over 5:1.

The pattern of interethnic relations also differs by gender across some ethnic groups. In the Chinese group, for example, in 2011 women were twice as likely (39 %) to be in an interethnic relationship as men (20 %), and this was also the case with Other Asian women (38 % vs 23 %). In the Arab group, men (43 %) were more likely than women (26 %) to be in an interethnic relationship. Amongst the Black/African/Caribbean/Black British groups, somewhat higher proportions of men than women were in interethnic relationships, 25 % versus 19 % in the case of Black Africans, compared with 48 % versus 37 % in the case of Black Caribbeans, and 64 % versus 59 % in the case of Other Black people. There are also some important differences by age across ethnic groups, though across most groups people in the older age range (50 and over) were less likely to be in an interethnic relationship than those aged 16–24 and 25–29. The major exception was the 'Other White' group, where older age groups were more likely to be in an interethnic relationship than the 16–24-year-olds.

The 16–24-year-olds had higher rates of interethnic union formation than other age groups across all the Black/African/Caribbean/Black British groups and the Mixed White and Black African group. For example, amongst Black Africans living as a couple, 29 % of 16–24-year-olds were in an interethnic relationship, compared with 22 % of 25–49-year-olds, 18 % of 50–64-year-olds, and 21 % of the 65+ group.

Caring for Family Members, Friends, and Neighbours

The role of Black Africans as carers for family members, friends, and neighbours provides another point of access to friendships and informal social relationships. The 2011 England and Wales Census asked respondents: 'Do you look after, or give any help or support to family members, friends, neighbours or others because of either long-term physical or mental ill-health/disability or problems related to old age?' (but not counting anything they do as part of their paid employment). If they did so, they were asked if it was 1–19 hours a week, 20–49 hours a week, or 50 or more hours a week. The proportion was quite low in the Black African group (5.6 %, comprising: 3.1 % 1–19 hours; 1.3 % 20–49 hours; and 1.2 % 50 or more hours) and the Mixed: White and Black African ethnic group provided the least (4.9 %) (ONS 2013b). This may be explained by the relatively young age structure of the Black African group and the fact that, in 2011, it had the highest proportion of people with 'very good' (64.2 %) or 'good' health (27.4 %) and the lowest proportion of 'Not Good' general health (8.4 %), of all ethnic groups. These proportions compare with 11.1 % in the White British group and 11.0 % in the White Irish group. The Black African ethnic group had the lowest proportion of people providing 50 hours of unpaid care who reported 'Not Good' general health, at 20.3 %.

Moral Conviviality: The Case of Home Associations

There are now diverse African organisations in Britain, including groups organised around a place of origin ('home associations' frequently regarded as having an orientation to an ethnic homeland), place of settlement, religious communities (Swahili groups, as noted in Chap. 4), professions, and various voluntary groups focused on particular 'home' countries/countries of origin. These organisations may vary from large national umbrella organisations to small informal groups of friends and extended kin. Such diversity is also reflected in matters such as the involvement of these organisations in broader political issues and in the involvement of the welfare of their members, while most share an attachment to a shared 'home' place.

African diaspora groups may play a key role in developments in Africa by channelling and delivering developmental benefits, including the sending of collective remittances. They may also influence integration in Britain by, for example, fostering 'bonding capital' amongst members. However, Mercer and Page (2010) shift the focus from ethnicity to place and 'morality of convivial relations' in the African diaspora, by focusing on home associations' debate about 'what is an intrinsically good way to live in the diaspora', drawing on research with Cameroonian and Tanzanian home associations in Britain and a thriving associational life in these communities.[1] These investigators found that Cameroonian home associations are more commonly organised around a smaller geographical home in Africa (such as a village) while Tanzanian home associations claim a common affinity to the nation or region, bringing together Tanzanians living in a particular city in the UK. They are 'engaged in constructing a sense of coherence and community for themselves in the context of being in Britain'. Both the Cameroonian and Tanzanian diasporas are small and struggling for recognition, respect, and a foothold compared to the larger African diasporas.

The Tanzanian diaspora associations aimed to give the community a focus, to encourage diaspora investment at home, and to help community members (welcoming newcomers, offering support in times of need, such as illness and death, gathering contributions for the bereaved to attend burials at home, organising wedding planning committees to raise funds, and providing a space in which ideas about how best to proceed within the diaspora community can be debated). Cameroonian associations similarly provided a forum for discussing the responsibilities of those in the diaspora towards each other and the organising of annual cultural galas as a way of expressing solidarity amongst Cameroonians.

African community organisations also practise 'moral conviviality as extraversion through various strategies of "reaching out" to British societies' (Mercer and Page 2010, p. 122) and for many integration into British society was a central aim. Such activities might include the acquisition of practical skills, inviting professionals to talk to the association, the legal

---

[1] Other well-established diaspora communities in Britain include the Nigerian, Ghanaian, Somalian, and Sierra Leonean diasporas.

constitution of associations to receive funding from local government and charities, the negotiation of the British legal system, and the general enablement of finding a way to live in Britain within the context of a shared identity, including the use of language in the diaspora, and helping members maintain confidence in their background. Thus, Mercer and Page (2010) transform the view of ethnic associations as encouraging an inward-looking attachment to an African homeland to one of creating a sense of community *and* belonging to Britain, in which integration is one of their key aims.

BROADER AFRICAN ORGANISATIONS

Health and Welfare Organisations and Networks

One of the most important areas where African organisations have taken a lead role in the provision of services is in health and healthcare, though frequently under threat of closure due to lack of funds. The African Health Policy Network (AHPN) is an umbrella agency that has a membership network of over 200 mostly African community-based organisations who work at local, regional, and national levels in the UK, such partnership and collaboration being key to the AHPN's values including the engagement of Black Africans in policymaking. The AHPN has led the involvement of Black Africans through these organisations in developing health and other policies that reflect the lives of Black Africans. The membership organisations were historically consulted by statutory providers in the development of HIV policy documents and prevention frameworks. While initially focusing on HIV/AIDS and sexual health, the AHPN widened its remit to include mental health, tuberculosis, stroke, diabetes, and cancer.

The communities in Britain most affected by the AIDS/HIV pandemic were nationals of Uganda, Zambia, Zimbabwe, Kenya, and Congo. In the early days of the epidemic in Britain, Africans were arguing that HIV services at the time were not culturally appropriate as they had initially been set up for gay White men. Ugandans in particular began to set up organisations to support people in their migrant community who were presenting with AIDS in British clinics as well as those who were dying or bereaved. They included, for example, the Uganda AIDS Action Fund (UAFF), registered in 2001. Some of these organisations worked with the wider African population affected by HIV/AIDS issues, while other groups led by other nationals began to emerge, catering for the diverse

African population in the UK. These groups included organisations such as Pamodzi (a Zambian group led by women and dedicated to helping and protecting the health and well-being of the Southern African communities) and Simba (a Zimbabwean group). These organisations and cognitive networks amongst Africans in the UK had the language skills and other competences that made them culturally relevant for this population. However, funding issues have forced many such organisations to close or to work together in the provision of HIV support to Black Africans in the UK.

Experiences of living with cancer amongst Black African communities or knowing someone affected by cancer has also led to the development of formal support organisations or registered charities. Language barriers as well as limited knowledge about illness and its management in African communities have made these African-led organisations more culturally relevant in working with African clients. As an example, Ponayi (the Shona word for rebirth, recovery, or healing) was set up by a breast cancer survivor. Personal experiences of suffering brought on by cancer and of ways of preventing such suffering brought together people from Zimbabwe around the values of the founder and the Shona name of the organisation.

Different networks have in some cases evolved to support women and men, reflecting their different migration experiences. Gender-based networks were often started informally with a group of individuals who came together to address a particular need in their communities (e.g. such as a specific health issue). Subsequently, some of these networks registered themselves as a charity, grew in the numbers they supported, and expanded the geographical areas they covered. As an example, seven migrant African women living in Ireland, operating without funding or support, started the Akina Dada wa Africa (Swahili for sisterhood) in 1999–2001 to address feelings of exclusion, isolation, racial abuse, discrimination, and issues related to gender-based violence (De Tona and Lentin 2011). A similar group—Akina Mama wa Africa—was set up as a small community-based organisation for African women in London in 1985, which now describes itself as an 'international Pan African, non-governmental organisation for African women'. Personal experiences of health issues and parents' concerns about their children (e.g. their poorer sexual health) have also been catalysts for the formation of formal and informal networks of support.

Social networks were also formed to support asylum seekers and other migrants who came to Britain for education, work reasons, and family reunification, including knowledge about their respective communities in Britain and opportunities for the exchange of ideas on welfare rights. When significant numbers of Zimbabweans started coming to the UK seeking asylum from the economic and political strife in their country, organisations catering for their welfare were established, such as the Zimbabwe Welfare Association. Others from Somalia facing difficulties related to migration set up the Somali Refugee Action Group. Similarly, the Zambian Nationals Welfare Association (UK) was formed in 1996 with the aim to address issues of poverty and advance education amongst Zambians living in the UK. The Nigerian Women's Welfare Association in London, the United Nigerian Welfare Association in Birmingham, and the Ghanaian Welfare Association in London are further examples. The latter was set up to help Ghanaians improve their language and interview skills for employment, help them adjust to life in the UK, and to promote an inclusive community that is 'proud of its origins'. All these groups recruit management committee members who gain skills in project management, community engagement, and in the wider issues that affect the lives of Black Africans in Britain. These roles can be seen as expressions of belonging to transnational identities, where events in their home country and life in the UK create particular identities that require collective action for negotiation and exercise of their rights.

African Churches: Missionary Zeal and Migrant Needs

Spiritual spaces and activities provide opportunities for the development of networks and social capital. The migration of Africans to the UK has been accompanied by the movement of spiritual beliefs that were originally planted by early Christian missionaries during the colonisation of Africa. However, it is now within the Pentecostal movement that some seek solutions to the effects of witchcraft, generational curses, and bad spirits that bring poverty and poor health. Though church attendance in missionary churches such as the Anglican, Methodist, and Catholic Churches is low in Britain, migration from the African continent has however brought some revitalisation to these traditional missionary churches through a process of 'Africanisation'. In some cities such as Newcastle, Leeds, and London, there are special worship days led by an African priest or clergy. Catholics, Anglicans, and Methodists from Zimbabwe have developed their own spaces in these churches (such as the Zambian Anglican Fellowship UK), with services led by Zimbabwean clergy and conducted in Shona and Ndebele (Zimbabwean languages). The culture of uniforms in these churches, introduced by the colonial missionary churches, has been brought back to Britain. For example, the Zimbabwe *mabachi*, especially worn by worshippers such as church-married women and members of the mothers' union (Chinouya 2007), have been introduced into British places of Anglican, Methodist, and Catholic worship. Women and men attend special African services wearing these garments at which public announcements of their identities as members of *vabvui* (fishers of men) or members of the mothers' union might be made.

In addition to the revitalisation of these African missionary churches in Britain, there has been a marked growth in the Pentecostal movement. Pentecostalism has transformed the religious landscape in Africa with most African-born Pentecostal movements becoming 'vigorously transnational', as David Maxwell (2006, p. 3) has noted, 'planting assembles in neighbouring countries and European cities through its diaspora and missionaries'. Despite its appearance as a 'new phenomenon' African Pentecostalism has its roots in the colonial past, offering a mixture of political and economic themes and the American commodification of religion. It is also linked to the American gospel of prosperity which preaches that financial and material blessings are the will of God and that through faith, tithes, and donations, one's wealth multiplies. African Pentecostalism has now grown to be part of popular culture through the use of social media, tele-evangelism, music, miracle cures, the casting out of demons, and prophesy.

African Pentecostal churches have been set up in two waves. Some are linked to the first wave of migration from the 1950s. The Church of the Lord in London was started by the Apostle Adejobi in 1964 and whose headquarters is in Nigeria. The Cherubim and Seraphim Church, with headquarters also in Nigeria, was started in 1965. The rapid growth of Pentecostal churches is also associated with the second (recent) wave of migration. African-migrant-initiated transnational (though some are independent) Pentecostal churches imported from Nigeria and other West African countries and planted by denominations or individuals in British cities have catered for the needs of migrant populations, but have also been accompanied by a conscious missionary zeal, a kind of 'reverse mission' (Burgess 2015). Four of Britain's ten largest mega-churches are led by Nigerians. The largest single congregation in Western Europe is the London-based Kingsway International Christian Centre (KICC), founded by a Nigerian Pentecostal, and one of the fastest growing Pentecostal denominations in Britain is the Nigerian-initiated Redeemed Christian Church of God, with over 390 congregations.

Indeed, in the period 2005–2012 there has been a 50 % increase in the numbers of people attending Pentecostal churches in London (due largely to African migrants) (Brierley Consultancy 2013). A total of 230,000 people attended Pentecostal services in 2012, Pentecostal churchgoers making up 32 % of Sunday worshippers in London. Indeed, Pentecostal churches now make up 30 % of the total number of churches in London, more than 1,450 of them, the only other denomination with more than 1,000 churches in the capital being the Church of England.

Other newer diasporas have also established their own churches such as the Forward in Faith Ministries, Agape, and the Masowe from Zimbabwe. These forms of spirituality intersect religion, entrepreneurship, and other forms of social capital. The African Pentecostal churches are significant sources of information regarding business start-ups, nurturing and networking for business, and sharing business ideas. Pentecostal networks based on trust and ritualised church occasions offer opportunities for enacting a sense of belonging and the development of entrepreneurship and, indeed, some of these churches offer a ready market for goods and services.

CIVIC AND POLITICAL PARTICIPATION

There has been considerable research showing ethnic inequalities in political and civic participation. In many areas, these inequalities have narrowed over recent years, though a deficit remains in voting, political participation, and representation at both the national[2] and regional levels. Similarly in the civic sphere, activism is less common in minority groups. Ethnic inequalities are driven by socio-economic factors, patterns of party mobilisation, interpersonal mobilisation, and social networks, and are affected by political opportunity structures and changes in national and local population structures, including migration in particular.

A key source on political and civic participation is the 2010 Ethnic Minority British Election Survey (EMBES), led by Anthony Heath (Heath et al. 2013).

[2] There is small but significant number of Africans who are involved in politics including Sam Gyimah (British Ghanaian and MP for East Surrey), Paul Boateng (British Ghanaian and Member of the House of Lords), Kwasi Kwarteng (British Ghanaian and MP for Spelthorne), Kate Osamor (British Nigerian and MP for Edmonton), Victor Adebowale (British Nigerian and Member of the House of Lords), and Lola Young (British Nigerian and member of the House of Lords). Those serving in the House of Commons and House of Lords are from more settled communities of Nigerians and Ghanaians.

While regular British Election Surveys (BES) have been conducted following every general election since 1964, the probability samples of around
2,000–3,000 respondents are not sufficiently large to yield reliable estimates (around 200 in 2010) of ethnic minority political attitudes and
behaviour. A 'booster' sample of ethnic minorities was undertaken in the
1997 BES to allow a more detailed investigation but none since then. The
EMBES was established to obtain a nationally representative post-election
probability sample of the main established ethnic minorities (including
Black Africans), with oversampling in areas of high ethnic minority density. The main focus was on registration, turnout, vote choice, other forms
of political participation, trust in parliament, satisfaction with democracy,
and sense of British identity. A total of 2,787 responses were achieved
in all, a response rate of 58–62 %, including 525 responses from Black
Africans (compared with only 38 in BES). BES was used to supply the
comparator White British (3,126) and Other White (57) samples.

A further important source on civic participation is the Citizenship
Survey. Between 2001 and its cancellation after March 2011, this survey was the main source of information for people living in Britain on
their attitudes towards and experiences of migration, integration, race,
faith, volunteering, and civic life. Based on a survey of a large random
sample of the British population, interviewees are a nationally representative sample of about 10,000 adults in England and Wales, plus an additional booster sample of about 5,000 people from ethnic minority groups
to enable this population to be analysed in detail. The survey is a key
source on community life and, while it does not include information on
respondents' legal citizenship or immigration status, it does include self-
identified nationality, country of birth, country of parent's birth, and self-
identified ethnic group.

Civic Participation

Civic participation may encompass volunteering and other civic engagement activities like civic activism. The last (final) report of the Citizenship
Survey, for 2010–2011, provides evidence of civic engagement and volunteering across eight ethnic categories (Fig. 9.1). Black African respondents
to the survey in 2010–2011 numbered 1,132. In 2011, Black Africans
(51 %) ranked fifth in all civic engagement activities (civic participation,
civic consultation, civic activism, and formal volunteering) after the White

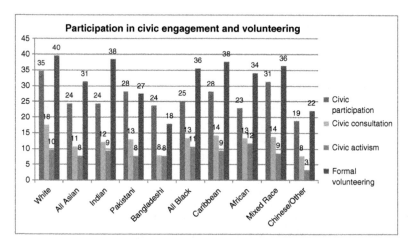

Fig. 9.1 Participation in civic engagement and volunteering.
Source: 2010–2011 Citizenship Survey

group (58 %), Black Caribbeans and Mixed Race (54 %), and Indians (53 %), but substantially higher than Bangladeshis and the Chinese/Other group. This participation level in all activities has declined over the last few years, from 57 % in 2007–2008 to 56 % (2008–2009), 54 % (2009–2010), and 51 % (2010–2011). This trend is in common with the Black group as a whole, ethnic minorities, and the White group.

With respect to civic participation, Black Africans (23 %) had the lowest rate across all ethnic groups, except for the Chinese/Other group (19 %). Nevertheless, they were akin to the All Black and Asian group rates but substantially lower than the White (35 %) and Mixed Race (31 %) rates. With respect to civic consultation, 13 % of Black Africans participated in the last year, which was similar to other ethnic groups except White (18 %), Bangladeshis (8 %), and Chinese/Other (8 %). On the measure of civic activism, 12 % of Black Africans participated in the last year, higher than any other ethnic group, including White (10 %). 34 % of Black Africans engaged in volunteering in the year prior to the interview, the lowest proportion in the Black group, but higher than Pakistanis, Bangladeshis, and Chinese/Other. By comparison, the White group had the highest level (40 %) of volunteering amongst respondents in England in 2010–2011.

Political Participation

In the 2010 EMBES survey (Heath et al. 2013), the Black African sample had the lowest level of validated registration at their current address (59 %). This compared with 72 % amongst Black Caribbeans and 78 % for Indians and Pakistanis, though the proportion amongst the White British sample was much higher (90 %). Such a low Black African proportion may be partially accounted for by eligibility, around 11 % of Black Africans falling outside the categories of British/dual citizenship or Commonwealth but not British citizenship. Other factors may include lack of knowledge about eligibility and lack of fluency in the English language amongst recent African migrants. Registration was higher amongst second-generation Black Africans (85 %) than the first generation (79 %). Saggar's research into the 1997 general election also found that Black Africans had one of the lowest registration levels at 87.1 % compared to Black Caribbean (96 %), White (96.9 %), Indian (96.9 %), Pakistani (90.2 %), and Bangladeshi (91.3 %) groups (Saggar 1998). In Anwar's (1998) face-to-face sample survey across five local authority areas, non-registration was, again, lowest amongst the Black groups (Black Caribbean, 26 %; Black African, 25 %; and Other Black, 45 %).

Turnout amongst those registered to vote was the lowest for Black Africans (self-reported, 73 %, validated, 72 %), similar to Black Caribbeans but lower than the South Asian groups and the White British group (self-reported, 82 %, validated 78 %). There was no difference by generational status amongst Black Africans. The key barrier to political engagement was therefore registration and not turnout. Amongst other reasons for not voting was the perception that no party really represented their views, around 50 % of second-generation Black Africans holding this view. Low turnout for the Black African and Black Caribbean group has been a key finding of other surveys (though the 2001 Electoral Commission Survey included Black Africans in an aggregated 'Black' group). Saggar's research into the 1997 general election (based on the British Election Survey which contained a booster sample of minority ethnic groups) reported turnout levels for Black Africans of 64.4 %, lower than for Black Caribbeans (68.7 %), Asians (73.9–82.4 %), and White group (78.7 %).

In the 2010 EMBES sample, Black Africans overwhelmingly (85 %) voted Labour, higher than Black Caribbeans (78 %), Asians (59–71 %), and the White British group (29 %). Just 6 % of Black Africans voted Conservative, 7 % Liberal Democrat, and 2 % Other. There were differences across generation, 87 % of the first generation voting Labour but 76 % of the second generation. Thus, vote choice is very different for the Black African group compared with the Asian and White groups. This represents a continuity with respect to previously reported patterns.

Galandini's (2013) focus is on Black African organisations but particularly on the relationship between these organisations, co-ethnic residential concentration, and political participation. Using a mixed methods study, he explores these relationships in the well-established and generally well-integrated Ghanaian community and the more recent Somali group facing greater barriers to integration. Living in high concentration areas was found to be a relevant factor facilitating individual participation in, and the creation of, ethnic organisations amongst Somalis but not Ghanaians. Somali organisations were found to cluster in areas where the community is clustered, while Ghanaian organisations (outside London) appeared to be spread more widely across the country.

The structure and function of the voluntary groups also differed between communities. Somali organisations provided community members with regular support to tackle specific issues and needs, while Ghanaian organisations primarily played a social role and operated less visibly, with support to members being provided through informal connections and mechanisms similar to mutual aid societies. Moreover, Somali organisations positively impacted on both non-electoral and electoral engagement by facilitating political information, increasing group consciousness, and promoting the emergence of ethnic candidates. On the contrary, Ghanaian associations were generally described as apolitical bodies. Thus, Somali organisations played an advocacy function, community leaders expressing the need to be engaged as a community in the political arena in order to voice and tackle their needs. Such a mobilising effect was not present in Ghanaian organisations, Ghanaians seeing political, and specifically electoral, participation as an individual, and not a collective, process. Galandini (2013, p. 15) concludes that 'Future research should take into account the internal diversity characterising the Black African community and, more generally, the impact exerted by immigration-related factors on the direct connection between residential concentration and political participation as well as the "missing links" underpinning this relationship.'[3]

---

[3] Galandini (2013, p. 17) suggests as missing links factors such as group consciousness and political mobilisation.

LINKS WITH AFRICAN HOMELANDS

Black Africans in the diaspora frequently maintain links with Africa by travelling back to countries of origin to see family and friends (as well as communications through telephone, Skype, and other technologies) and through the payment of remittances to family members. Over the years, as Africans become settled in Britain, they frequently keep contact with relatives in their home countries and travel there for short visits away from the UK. The participatory Mayisha study conducted amongst 756 migrants from Kenya, Uganda, Zimbabwe, Congo, and Zambia living in Inner London found that 43 % of the men and 46 % of the women had travelled to their home countries or countries of birth in the last 5 years (Fenton et al. 2001).

The study found that the likelihood of travelling to one's country of origin was significantly associated with nationality ($P < 0.0005$) and length of residence in the UK ($P = 0.0001$), varying from 30 % (25/83) in those who have lived in the UK for 0–2 years to 60 % (96/159) among those who have lived in the UK for 10 years or more. Clearly, home visits are more likely with increasing settlement in Britain, in addition to other favouring factors such as the attainment of secure immigration status and secure financial resources. Employment status and higher educational qualifications were significantly associated ($P < 0.0005$) with the likelihood of travelling back to homelands as was the case with those with further education or professional training (vs those with school-level education). Of those in full-time employment, 54 % (160/297) had visited their countries of origin versus 25 % (12/47) of those not in full-time employment.

More than half of Bloch 2008's sample of 500 Zimbabweans living in the UK (55 %) had returned to Zimbabwe for a visit. Of this proportion, a quarter returned more than once a year and more than half (55 %) every 1–2 years, those with transnational business activities being much more likely to visit. However, visits to Zimbabwe reflected immigration status rather than being an indicator of other transnational activities, such as economic remittances.

After social contact with close family members, economic remittances form the most regular exchanges (Bloch 2008). Remittances paid to family members or organisations by individuals and home associations also help to maintain relationships with people in countries of origin. In Bloch's (2008) sample, 80 % of respondents remitted money to Zimbabwe, most often to support family members. With respect to other economic activities that were not sent as remittance, 19 % made donations to charities and 10 % donated to community organisations in Zimbabwe.

The propensity to send economic remittances was not significantly associated with the personal and demographic characteristics of age, gender, and length of time outside Zimbabwe. However, the main activity at the time of the survey, especially whether respondents were unemployed or not working, was strongly associated with the sending of remittances, increasing this activity 1.7-fold. Security of immigration status was more significant and had a stronger level of association than legal access to the labour market, those without secure status (including those on working and student visas) being the most likely to send remittances. Close ties to Zimbabwe indicated by the presence of close family members, owning property or land, interest in returning to Zimbabwe to live, and interest in contributing to development were all highly associated with remittance activities. In a logistic regression analysis, the highest odds ratio was between sending remittances and legal access to the labour market.

With respect to regularity of remittances, 41 % in Bloch's sample sent remittances more than once a month, 38 % between every 1–2 months, and 22 % less than every 2 months. The average monthly remittances varied by income, the largest proportion (37 %) sent being between £100 and £199 every month. There was a significant relationship between the amount of remittances sent and both levels of income and the regularity of contact with close family members (especially where there were children involved). Remittances also include goods and social exchanges in the form of ideas and social capital, 74 % of respondents in Bloch's study sending non-monetary gifts (notably clothes and books) to Zimbabwe. Other help and support included providing accommodation, advice and financial help about moving, and assistance with visas with respect to leaving Zimbabwe. UK Zimbabweans also participated in transnational social, cultural, and political exchanges, both with Zimbabweans in the UK and in Zimbabwe. Informal social activity in the UK was the main activity, followed by church and religious participation (with women being more likely than men to participate), and Internet discussion groups with others in Zimbabwe.

African communities in Britain which have developed networks and set up community groups frequently raise funds to help families and individuals in Africa. There are many such organisations, including Health Concern Zimbabwe, Ghana Outlook, Nigeria Mercy Education Trust, and Widows and Orphans International, the latter a London-based agency that works with street children, orphans, and vulnerable children and aims to reduce poverty and suffering in the UK and abroad. Furthermore, a collective sense of struggle has led to activism, often manifested in volunteering in different liberation causes, sometimes in collaboration with non-African groups (including concerts at Hyde Park and elsewhere, marches, and demonstrations). The release of Nelson Mandela from prison and the official end of apartheid resulted in the rebuilding of networks and forging of alliances amongst South Africans and the African diaspora in the UK in an effort to create spaces for celebrating independent Africa and addressing poverty and the impact HIV/AIDS on the African continent. To raise awareness of the latter, Nelson Mandela's prison number 46664 was used in campaigns in Africa. Such activities are redolent of the 1985 Live Aid concerts in London and Philadelphia to address famine in Ethiopia. Most recently, when Sierra Leone and other West African countries were devastated by the Ebola epidemic, Western musicians responded by raising money for this public health issue.

CHAPTER 10

Implications for Policy and Practice

In 2011, the Black African population in England and Wales stood at almost 1 million (989,628), larger than the Black Caribbean (594,825) and Other Black (280,437) groups combined. Moreover, there were an additional 165,974 persons who were of Mixed 'White and Black African' ethnicity. Further, non-UK-born Black Africans (666,000) exceeded UK-born Black Africans (323,000) by a factor of more than two. The story of the large increase in the Black African population is largely one of recent migrations. Ninety-five per cent of the current non-UK-born Black African population arrived after 1981 and around 60 % in the decade 2001–2011. Indeed, around a fifth (17 %) of the foreign-born population of England and Wales was born in Africa. Around a half (47 %) of the non-UK-born population from the African region was Black African. There have also been changes in where these international migrants have settled: Over the decade 2001–2011, the Black African population has become much less concentrated in London, 58.0 % now living in the capital compared with around 80 % in 2001. Thus, the policy implications of the analysis presented in this book largely (but not solely) arise from the position of the Black African population as a recent migrant population, including significant numbers of asylum seekers and refugees.

So, within this broad statistical picture, what does it mean to be a Black African living in Britain? This book has shown the complex layers of identification that are masked by the official census and racial category. It has revealed how this group, that settled in Britain in large numbers from the

   221
P.J. Aspinall, M.J. Chinouya, *The African Diaspora Population in Britain*, DOI 10.1057/978-1-137-45654-0_10

1960s onwards, is an embodiment of colonial and post-colonial histories and politics that continue to shape aspects of their lives through a variety of structural processes. Being a Black African also means living the legacy and penalty of being racially assigned as Black, in a society where racial discrimination is embedded in structures and cultures of organisations. The chapters have shown that for most Black Africans, key features of their lives are embedded in social exclusion, poverty, limited opportunities for work, which are not commensurate with their qualifications, poor housing, and increased risk of some infectious diseases. Indeed, with respect to how Black Africans are connected to the fabric of life in modern Britain, an enduring characteristic has been the impact of persistent social exclusion driven by racism, that is, the belief that qualities of superiority and inferiority apply to population groups with all their distorting, dehumanising, and disadvantaging consequences.

What Kind of Ethnicity Data Is Needed?

Accurate statistics on the Black African population are needed to inform policy analyses and to develop policy. One of the major barriers to undertaking research and policy analysis on the Black African community in Britain is the limitations with respect to category in data collections and, in the past, the omission of the Black African group in surveys (they were excluded, for example, from the Health Education Authority's first [1992–1993] and second [1994] Black and Minority Ethnic Groups in England Health and Lifestyles Surveys, the 1994 Fourth National Survey of Ethnic Minorities, the 1999 Health Survey for England, and the 2000 Ethnic Minority Psychiatric Illness Rates in the Community [EMPIRIC] survey). While all three decennial censuses which have asked an ethnic question (1991, 2001, and 2011) have included 'Black African' as a discrete category and under a Black overarching label since 2001, the output from the census (standard tables) has sometimes resorted to the use of a collective 'Black' group which aggregates the Black African, Black Caribbean, and Other Black categories. As all three groups have very distinctive population profiles, this pan-ethnic grouping has little utility with respect to an analysis of the Black African population. This is a particular drawback in equality and diversity reports, which would be expected to privilege separate Black groups, given the focus on *diversity*. Instead, they almost invariably report on an aggregate 'Black' group in their workforce statistics. This has resulted in an increasing number of freedom of information requests to obtain this disaggregated information, in some cases for very substantial fees, in circumstances where it should be readily available. This problem of concealed heterogeneity is also the case with the Health and Social Care Information Centre's (HSCIC) workforce statistics on the National Health Service (NHS) medical and non-medical workforce, where in the published data categories like Black African nursing, midwifery, and health visiting staff and doctors remain invisible through aggregation into a 'Black or Black British' grouping. This is also the case with staff employed directly and indirectly by adult social services departments in England. Many other data suffer this problem, including the national analysis of the National Child Measurement Programme, where the seven groupings include 'Black or Black British'.

A further major drawback is that, when the 'Black African' category *is* used, it conceals substantial heterogeneity with respect to country of origin, migration experience, time of arrival in the UK, generational status, religion, main language, and national/transnational identity. This criticism has been made not only by users of census data but also by Black Africans themselves, who argue that the label fails to encapsulate their complex identities. While representations were made to the ONS ahead of the last two England and Wales censuses to obtain a more finely granulated classification that might, for example, separately capture Nigerians, Ghanaians, Somalis, and Zimbabweans as the largest communities of descent, these were unsuccessful. In 2011, Scotland, with its much smaller Black African population, offered two options under the overarching label of 'African': 'African, African Scottish, or African British' and 'Other, please write in'. Thus, in England and Wales, a single 'Black African' ethnic category will serve policy needs until around 2023 when the first results are released from the 2021 Census. Against this critique, the 'Black African' label clearly encapsulates in a single term the identities of people who have directly migrated from the African continent, have a connective ancestral history with it, and are racially categorised as 'Black', providing an identity around which to coalesce in their fight against racism and disadvantage.

While the 2011 Census contained a free-text option in the Black/African/Caribbean background (and for all the other pan-ethnic groups), few identifiable Black African respondents used it, besides Somalis and Nigerians, but may conceal others with a community of descent in Africa. At present, the fraction of the Black African population which does not report in the Census 'African' category is very small. However, the popularity of the free-text option increased markedly between 2001 (98,068) and 2011 (280,437), and this trend is likely to continue in the future. As the Black African population becomes more diverse, more respondents may choose to eschew the predesignated category to write in their ethnic group. Only a few data sets make additional provision for more detailed reporting by offering 'extended' or more detailed codes. These include the Department for Education (DfE) classification codes for the Annual School Census (Angolan, Congolese, Ghanaian, Nigerian, Sierra Leonean, Somalian, Sudanese, and Other Black African), those used within the Rio and System One child health information systems, and Read Codes used on the Vision and EMIS general practice IT computer systems for primary care, such as Nigerian, Somali, and Mixed Black, though requiring aggregation to the standard census ethnic codes for national reporting. Health and other statutory bodies have also made use of distinctive names to yield a more granular classification of population groups than that yielded by the Census. In particular, Pablo Mateos (2014) has derived 66 Onomap Subgroups, including a dozen identifying African communities (Nigerian, Ghanaian, Somalian, African, Sierra Leonean, Afrikaans, Black South Africa, Muslim North Africa, Eritrean, Ethiopian, Ugandan, and Congolese).

It is unclear what can be done to address these drawbacks in future censuses. While the number of categories used in the decennial census could be increased, these have risen from 9 categories in 1991 to 16 in 2001 and 18 in the 2011 England and Wales Census: More categories may confuse form-fillers, increase respondent burden, and add to the administrative burden of producing ethnic statistics from the census. One option may be to add an open response ethnic origin/ancestry question to the census, of the kind which has been used in Canada and the USA, which would permit multiple reporting. However, the cultural question set in the census is already extensive—national identity, main language, and proficiency in spoken English having been added in 2011—and scope to add to it in the future seems limited.

When 'Black African' data are used from the decennial census, certain quality issues need to be taken into account. For example, in the 1991 Census, the published estimate of Black Africans in England and Wales was 209,665. To adjust for estimated undercount, this was increased to 220,603 through a raising factor of 1.052. Indeed, based on various estimates/adjustments, there is a 1.1-fold difference in the size of the 1991 'Black African' population and a 1.2-fold difference in percentage estimates of intercensal change (Office for National Statistics 2006a). In the

2001 Census, the Black African population in particular had high rates of underenumeration and in consequence 29.1 % of the Black African population was imputed, the highest proportion of any ethnic group. For that reason (and the fact that 34 % were young adults in 2007), ONS located the Black African group in the 'high' category of 'enumeration difficulty' in 2010 (ONS 2010). Census response rates in the England and Wales 2011 Census were estimated at 88.2 % for Black Africans, lower than for Black Caribbeans (91.9 %) and White British (95.1 %). Imputed responses comprised 6.7 % of all Black African responses. An analysis of change and stability in ethnic group between the 2001 and 2011 Census in the ONS LS found that 8.2 % of Black African records were imputed in either year. Moreover, analysis by Simpson has shown that the proportion of people changing their ethnic group between censuses doubled between 1991–2001 and 2001–2011, even though changes in the classification were limited between 2001 and 2011, and this is likely to increase in the future as the diversity of the country increases and the population increasingly chooses to express their ethnicity in their own way.

While a 'Black African' category has been widely adopted in data collections, including those in health and healthcare, concern has been expressed about data quality in some settings (Saunders et al. 2013). When ethnicity in hospital (hospital episode statistics [HES]) records was compared with the gold standard of 'self-reported' ethnicity in the English Cancer Patient Experience Survey for a total of 58,721 patients, substantial discordance was identified. HES-recorded 'Indian', 'Pakistani', 'Bangladeshi', 'Chinese', 'Black Caribbean', and 'Black African' ethnicity had only intermediate levels of sensitivity (65–80 %) and positive predictive value (PPV) (80–89 %), respectively. That is, routine hospital data will miscode between 20 and 35 % of all patients who self-report that they belong to these ethnic groups.

These quality issues concerning the reproducibility of the data, concealed heterogeneity under the hegemonic banner 'Black African', and concealment of the category in an aggregate 'Black' group all pose challenges in research and policy analysis. Simpson and Jivraj (2015b) have stated that 'Reliance on the ethnic group question to ensure equality of opportunity and allocation of resources is being stretched to a limit' (p. 223). These limitations are a particular drawback for population profiling at local and national levels, in assessing and planning the provision of services to address needs, and in allocating resources, especially with respect to community groups and other organisations that work with specific communities. To cite just one example of these drawbacks, the decennial census asks a question: One year ago, what was your usual address? This question has the potential to provide data on residential stability and movement. It is known from previous censuses that Black Africans have a particularly low level of residential stability. However, in the England and Wales 2011 Census, data were only reported for a Black African/Black Caribbean/Other Black group, thereby concealing this important measure for the Black African group.

As the chapters have shown most official data collections, including HES, most contract minimum data sets administered by the NHS Information Centre, the former Mental Health Count-Me-In Census, and Annual School Census (though with provision for extended categories) continue to use the 'Black African' census category. Against such usage is the growing internal diversity of the group. There is clearly a research need to explore some of the factors that contribute to ethnic identity, singly, in combination, and intersectionally, following the recommendation of Burton et al. (2010), to obtain a better understanding of processes like integration and acculturation and of how Black Africans live their lives in Britain.

Use of country of birth as a proxy for ethnicity lacks utility though this measure has some utility in its own right, especially through census data, in a population group where two-thirds of the population are foreign-born. To address concealed heterogeneity further, country of birth combined with additional proxy measures such as national identity, main language, and religion merits further exploration. Language in its own right, when cross-tabulated by ethnic group, offers substantial scope to unpack diversity amongst Black Africans, as has been shown in *Language Capital*'s analyses of pupils in London using the Annual School Census. Whilst most Africans in Britain speak English, there are certain languages that can be traced to particular regions in Africa, which could add increased granularity to the diversity profile of the Black African group. Census data have the potential to contribute to such analyses though they only capture 'main language' (rather than all speakers) and the number of African languages reported is limited. Moreover, the many languages spoken within Africa and their frequent lack of coterminosity with territorial boundaries complicate the use of this variable in health and other surveys (Nazroo 2005), though grouping strategies may yield proxy measures of diversity.

RACISM AND DISADVANTAGE

Racism has a long history in Britain which has been addressed since the 1960s by the development of legislation and practice frameworks to promote equality and non-discriminatory practice. The first Race Relations Act of 1965 made discrimination on the grounds of race, ethnic, or national background illegal and this act has been followed by many others, culminating in the radical Race Relations Amendment Act of 2000. Since then, additional groups have received protection under the 2010 Equality Act. However, it is clear that these legal frameworks have not adequately addressed the racism that has become embedded in British life and continues to be one of the major contributors to health and other social inequalities. A systematic approach that involves tackling racial discrimination at every level of the NHS has been recommended but it is less clear how this has worked and what its impact has been.

The Labour Market

Chapter six that addressed *the labour market* clearly showed that disadvantage persists for the Black African group compared with the experience of the White British group. Black African men and women experience lower levels of labour market participation and higher rates of unemployment while available for work. In 2011, Black African men's unemployment among 25–49-year-olds was one in six, 10 percentage points higher than the 6 % amongst White British men of the same age. These inequalities persist despite Black Africans' high educational attainment.

Studies of the experiences of Black African nurses in the NHS found that racism, bullying, discrimination, and lack of equal opportunities are common, in spite of the Equality Act (2010). Likupe (2015) has argued that 'robust measures to combat racism and discrimination are urgently needed'. She also argues that managers need training on how to interpret and put the Act into practice and the effect of the Act on the experiences of overseas nurses needs to be evaluated so that managers at all levels can plan a way forward. Part of the problem may, as noted, lie in the limited utility of annual equality and diversity reports that frequently render the 'Black African' workforce invisible in an aggregate 'Black' group. Few of these reports for NHS providers offer such basic information as the number of Black African nurses and hardly any break-down of these statistics by recruitment, promotion, learning activity/training, and leavers.

In the light of Likupe's findings, it is a matter of concern that Black African nurses are being referred disproportionately to the nursing regulator (Nursing and Midwifery Council [NMC]) over their fitness to practise: Black nurses are 50 % more likely to be referred to the NMC than their White counterparts. Black African nurses are also overrepresented in disciplinary procedures. The Nursing and Midwifery Admissions Service (NMAS) statistics suggest that Black African applicants continue to find it harder than their White counterparts to be accepted on to diploma courses. While 17.6 % of applicants to adult nursing described themselves as Black Africans, they made up only 7.2 % of successful applicants. By contrast, White people made up 64 % of applicants but 79 % of those were accepted (Anonymous 2007). Black African nurses continue to be under-represented in the higher echelons of nursing.

There have, indeed, been numerous reports of racism within the NHS, with some evidence that it is embedded in its organisational culture despite the anti-discriminatory policies that openly drive the work of the NHS. Racism within the NHS not only is confined to nurses but also occurs at every level from recruitment of medical personnel, to their training and promotion. Almost 20 years ago, the *BMJ* reported cited examples of racial discrimination across the NHS for over a decade (Esmail and Carnall 1997). There have also been experimental studies with regard to applications to medical schools and posts that show that minority ethnic groups with the same qualifications as White British applicants are discriminated against.

Further, differences in language difficulty in finding or keeping a job across different Black African subgroups indicate the need for more extensive provision of courses on English as a second language (Mitton and Aspinall 2011). While only 2 % of Ghanaians and <1 % of Zimbabweans aged 16+ in the UK reported these difficulties in Labour Force Survey (LFS) data for 2003/2006/2009, the percentage was 17 % amongst Somalis.

The Housing Market

Black Africans have been shown to be particularly disadvantaged in *the housing market*, notably with respect to the rise in private renting. This tenure offers only limited security and is frequently associated with poor maintenance and repair. Black African households (along with Chinese households) have more than twice the proportion renting privately than the White British group (17 %) and substantially higher than the South Asian groups (22 % or more). Moreover, Black Africans have the highest levels of overcrowding (along with the Pakistani and Bangladeshi groups). Finney and Harries (2015, p. 159) have written that it is 'imperative that action is taken to address the insecurity of private renting, for example, in terms of rent control, length of tenancy agreements and quality of housing, if deepening of the "housing crisis" is to be avoided'.

Health and Health Care

With respect to *health*, the Black African group (along with the Chinese) has consistently reported better generic health status (as measured by limiting long-term illness and general health) compared with other ethnic groups and by a substantial margin. Research indicates that these differences are real and not artefactual based on different cultural interpretations of the measure. However, it is not wholly a success story.

HIV continues to dominate the health agenda for the Black African community. The most recent (2014) Public Health England report on HIV in the UK highlights continuing high prevalence rates for Black African heterosexual women (25,100 people; prevalence of 7.1 %) and Black African heterosexual men (13,600 people; prevalence of 4.1 %). An estimated 38,700 Black Africans were HIV positive and this group constitutes two-thirds (65 %) of all heterosexual people living with HIV. There are a number of key implications for public health policy.

Firstly, there are high rates of undiagnosed infection in Black African communities. In 2013, 31 % of Black African heterosexual women and 38 % of Black African heterosexual men who had HIV were unaware of their infection, and so remain at risk of passing on their infection. Rates of undiagnosed infection were somewhat lower among heterosexual people of other ethnicities: 27 % in men and 23 % in women. Twenty-four per cent of all people living with HIV in the country were undiagnosed and so were unaware of their HIV status. The report also shows that rates of undiagnosed infection were much worse outside London, where 41 and 49 % of African men and women, respectively, were undiagnosed, compared with 10 and 13 % undiagnosed in London, though the estimates are approximate. These differences could reflect stronger community networks and more accessible health services, including targeted prevention, in London.

Secondly, public health policies need to address high rates of undiagnosed and late diagnosis through the further promotion of HIV testing and increased coverage in the Black African community. Rates of late diagnosis—people diagnosed with a CD4 cell count below 350 cells/mm^3—were highest among heterosexual men (62 %) and heterosexual women (51 %), with Black Africans especially likely to be diagnosed late. Black-African communities collectively contain the largest number of people with undiagnosed HIV infection (13,000) in the UK. Non-Londoners were more likely to be diagnosed late.

At present, the UK meets two of the three targets announced by UNAIDS (United Nations Programme on HIV and AIDS) in November 2014: for 90 % of all people living with HIV to know their status, 90 % of those to be on treatment, and 90 % of those to have an undetectable viral load. However, it has a significant problem due to the high rates of undiagnosed infection.

While the age/sex structure of the Black African population conforms to the traditional population pyramid of a primarily youthful population (but with a bulge in the 30–34 to 45–49 age groups), there is, nevertheless, a small ageing population with some 3 % in the 65+ age group. Additional surveillance is merited for certain subgroups. Stagg et al.'s (2012) study of the uptake of primary health care amongst recent migrants, through a record linkage study of port health screening records and the Personal Demographic Services database, found low levels of registration amongst Africans. Compared with those from Europe, individuals of nationalities from Africa (0.74 [0.69–0.79]) were less likely to be registered with a GP practice, as were students, and asylum seekers and their dependants. Given the high proportion of African migrants who are asylum seekers, their frequently poorer health, including post-traumatic stress disorder (PTSD) and depression, and the barriers they face in registering, it is important that steps are taken to increase registration to avoid costly emergency health care and increased public health risks.

Disadvantage amongst users of NHS services has also been reported, though not markedly different from the White British group in the case of Black Africans. The NHS surveys of patient experience provide some evidence though the Black sample is small (2 % in the 2012 and 2013 surveys of adult inpatients) and Black Africans are only infrequently distinguished as a separate group in the published reports. In the 2012 Survey the overall patient experience scores for each ethnic group show that Black Africans scored 75.2 (similar to Black Caribbeans, 75.3, but below White

British [76.7] and Mixed White and Black Africans, 80.2, though not significantly so in the case of the latter). These disadvantages with respect to health care have implications for Public Health Practice. The Public Health Outcome Framework, with the main objectives of reducing inequalities in life expectancy and improving the quality of lives throughout the life course, places responsibility for improving and protecting health within communities, the government and individuals. The domains or indicators of the framework are based on how well the wider determinants of health are addressed, health improvement for the population, health protection, and reducing the numbers of premature deaths between communities.

This book has shown that poor access to the labour and housing markets are key determinants of health, as are structural issues like racism, poverty, social exclusion, and deprivation. The impact of AIDS/HIV (now affecting 7 % of Black African women) has clear public health implications with between 31 % (women) and 38 % (men) with infections unknown to the person and thus exposing others to the risk of infection. Similarly, past and current perceived restrictions on asylum seekers gaining access to treatment for HIV/AIDS is likely to place the wider population at greater risk and reluctance to undergo testing or present for treatment may be exacerbated by those claimants who feel such behaviour may be prejudicial to their cases.

Social Care

Prominence has been given in Chap. 8 to the case of Victoria Climbié, a young girl born in the Ivory Coast, who died after being abused by her great-aunt and her great-aunt's partner who believed that the child was possessed by a demon. Following her death, Lord Laming was commissioned to conduct an inquiry. The subsequent Laming Report (Laming 2003) demonstrated that health and social care professionals had failed to protect Victoria and social workers could have prevented the abuse and death. There was a systematic failure to prevent the death of a child who was in need of protection. The report led to the child protection reforms and the creation of child protection databases that detailed children who were at risk of abuse, which had not hitherto existed. The Victoria Climbié case demonstrated how families and children in need, such as those from the Black African community, could easily escape from being protected by health and social care professionals and the police, particularly when there are language barriers. The Victoria Climbié case highlighted the need for interprofessional collaboration and working between health and social care professionals. It also emerged that health professionals who play a critical role in child protection, were often not trained in these matters. The Victoria Climbié case led to the formulation of various legislations and policies such as 'Every Child Matters' and the Children Act, 2004. The policy initiative 'Every Child Matters' seeks to improve the lives of children and sets out five outcomes that matter most to the lives of children: being healthy; enjoying good physical and mental health and living a healthy lifestyle; staying safe, being protected from harm and neglect; enjoying and achieving; getting the most out of life and developing the skills for adulthood; making a positive contribution, being involved with the community and society and not engaging in antisocial or offending behaviour; and economic well-being, not being prevented by economic disadvantage from achieving their full potential in life (Every Child Matters 2003, pp. 6–7).

Health and social care practitioners and the police in Britain are now guided by complex ethical and practice-specific guidelines that are embedded in these legal and policy frameworks. The case of Victoria Climbié exposed how at times care workers often blame 'cultures' for not intervening in child protection cases. For example, social workers saw Victoria Climbié's timidity in the presence of adults as culturally appropriate. Similarly, medical practitioners who noticed marks on Victoria Climbié's body considered the possibility that children who have grown up in Africa may be expected to have more such marks than those who have been raised in Europe (Laming 2003, p. 345). 'African cultures' should be underscored by professional common sense about what abuse is. There is no room for blaming a hegemonic and imagined African culture in cases of abuse. Practitioners must be able to identify abuse of children and place the needs of vulnerable children first before an imagined African culture. However, there are also good cultural practices in every ethnic group that promote the positive development of children.

Considerable debate about the issues of private fostering followed the death of Victoria Climbié. It was estimated that there were then more than 10,000 West African children in Britain in private fostering arrangements 'who are unknown to social services, and therefore potentially highly vulnerable' (Health Committee 2003). The Committee endorsed the recommendation made by the Social Care Institute for Excellence (2003) in their position paper on private fostering, that those who provide private fostering services should be subject to a registration process that, as a minimum safeguard, ensures they meet certain basic standards of care.

Living in Deprived Neighbourhoods

The above areas of disadvantage, especially those relating to the labour and housing markets, are reflected in Jivraj and Khan's (2015) analysis of the extent to which people from minority ethnic groups live in deprived neighbourhoods. Their analysis showed that Black Africans were amongst the most concentrated in the 0–3 % of most deprived neighbourhoods and, indeed, in the 50 % most deprived neighbourhoods. Moreover, unlike the Bangladeshi, Pakistani, and Black Caribbean groups, the Black African group showed no improvement in the proportion living in the 10 % most deprived neighbourhoods between 2001 and 2011. These findings suggest that Black Africans are forced to find a home in deprived neighbourhoods when they arrive as migrants and that few are able to afford to move away from these areas to better quality housing.

If one accepts the research findings that suggest that there are negative effects of neighbourhood disadvantage on labour market and housing prospects, so-called 'neighbourhood effects', then, as Jivraj and Khan suggest, there is clearly a case for targeted interventions at those who, like Black Africans, get stuck in the most deprived neighbourhoods. Further, there are differences in the concentration of minority ethnic groups in deprived neighbourhoods across the English regions, such regional variations particularly affecting Black Africans. Again, such findings also have implications for policymakers to alleviate disadvantage in those regions where disadvantage is most concentrated. However, as Jivraj and Khan (2015) show, the disadvantage that Black Africans experience relative to the White British group are less when living in deprived neighbourhoods compared with all others, in respect to unemployment and economic activity, requiring the need for policies to target Black Africans *wherever* they live.

Asylum Seekers

While the number of asylum seekers has fallen in recent years, there has been a marked upturn in applicants from Eritrea and the Sudan. The number of asylum seekers from Eritrea in 2014 was the largest number from any country. This trend is likely to continue throughout 2015 and the foreseeable future: the International Organization for Migration has stated that more than 350,000 migrants have made the journey across the Mediterranean in the first 8 months of 2015, fleeing turmoil and poverty in the Middle East and Africa in search of a better life in Europe. This total includes large numbers of Eritreans, many making their way through Europe to Calais with the intention of entering the UK. Eritreans now constitute the second largest national group (after Syrians) taking this sea route. The UN human rights report on Eritrea (UN 2015) offers a clear challenge to European asylum policy. It concluded that 'the Government of Eritrea is responsible for systematic, widespread and gross human rights violations on a scope and scale seldom witnessed elsewhere, and some of the violations may even constitute crimes against humanity'. On the issue of national service, the report states: 'the indefinite duration of national service, its terrible conditions—including arbitrary detention, torture, sexual torture, forced labour, absence of leave and the ludicrous pay—and the implications it has for the possibility of any individual to found a family, conduct a family life and have favourable conditions of work make national service an institution where slavery-like practices are routine'.

It is of concern that the Home Office has recently issued guidance (Home Office 2015a, b) that countermands the UN human rights report. According to the new guidelines, National Service: no longer constitutes persecution or degrading or inhuman treatment and hence, people who flee to seek protection will not be granted refugee status in the UK; does not constitute forced labour; and is not indefinite but between 18 months and 4 years. Conscripts or draft evaders who exit illegally either to avoid conscription or to desert from the National Service will not be granted refugee status. Such guidance (and other restrictive immigration policies) is foregrounded by the coalition administration's 2010 election pledge to reduce net migration to less than 100,000 a year. In August 2015, the ONS announced that net migration to the UK was 330,000 in the year ending March 2015, up from 236,000 in the year ending March 2014. In the year ending March 2015, 636,000 people immigrated to the UK, a statistically significant increase compared with 552,000 in the previous year. The prime minister reaffirmed his commitment to this 'ambition' to reduce the numbers in the Conservative manifesto and in a May 2015 address at the Home Office.

This political agenda to substantially reduce migration to the UK (around 45 % of this migration comprised non-EU and non-British citizens in the year to March 2015) selects for policies which are in some cases ill-considered, rapidly introduced, and ultimately unfair to asylum seekers and other migrants. One consequence of the government's policy approach to asylum seekers has been the declaration that the detained fast-track immigration appeals procedure has been declared unlawful and 'structurally unfair' by the high court, notably the process under which rejected asylum seekers arriving in Britain are detained and given 7 days to appeal. The judge found that the rules put asylum seekers 'at a serious procedural disadvantage' and that the procedure 'looks uncomfortably akin to … sacrificing fairness on the altar of speed and convenience'. This process was first introduced in 2000 but has rapidly expanded in recent years, the latest published figures, for 2013, showing that 4,286 asylum seekers who were assessed to have 'manifestly unfounded' claims were detained in Yarl's Wood, Colnbrook or Harmondsworth detention centres under the scheme, a 72 % increase over the number put through the detained fast track in 2012.

The UK government's response to the European Commission's call on EU member states to take in 40,000 asylum seekers from Syria and Eritrea who land in Italy and Greece over the next 2 years—a policy of 'fair distribution'—has met with a response from the UK to take just 20,000 refugees from Syria by 2020. Such positioning is likely to antagonise the Black African population in Britain. In the Ethnic Minority British Election Survey (EMBES), Black Africans tended to be most supportive on asylum issues.

Restrictive Immigration Policies

What is happening with asylum seekers is part of the wider issue of immigration, that is, 'a concept measured by a date of entering the UK, for those not born in the UK or not returning to it' (Simpson and Jivraj 2015b). Attempts to meet the net immigration target have resulted in restrictive and punitive policies. Changes to the immigration rules in 2012 will have a detrimental effect on the retention of nurses already working in the UK and on the future recruitment of nurses from outside the European Economic Area (EEA). As of 6 April 2012, the immigration rules were amended by the Statement of Changes HC188 on 15 April 2012.[1] These changes state that any nurse who entered the UK after 6 April 2011,

[1] Home Office and The Rt Hon Damian Green. Reforms are vital next step towards sustainable migration. 15 March 2012.

on a tier 2 visa[2] will need to earn £35,000 to apply for indefinite leave to remain. Under the new rules, a nurse may only remain in the UK for as maximum of 6 years if the high-income threshold is not satisfied. After this time, the nurse will need to leave the UK, as further leave cannot be obtained based on employment (RCN 2015).

The Royal College of Nursing has attempted to estimate the impact of these changes on overseas nurses in the NHS. From April 2011 to March 2015, 3,365 nurses registered to work in the UK from outside the EEA. The RCN argues that the majority of these nurses will not reach the £35,000 threshold to be eligible to apply for indefinite leave to remain and may have to leave as a direct result of the 2012 immigration changes. Even if 10 % of these nurses were to progress to a mid-upper band 7 nurse salary, 3,029 nurses would still potentially need to leave the UK. Based on an average of £6,000 per nurse to recruit, the 3,365 nurses already working in the UK who may be impacted by the changes would cost the NHS around £20.2 million. This may result in yet a further cycle of overseas recruitment which has characterised the nursing profession over recent decades. Indeed, the prediction that these changes would precipitate an immediate crisis in nursing staffing resulted in these restrictions on recruiting nurses from overseas being temporarily lifted in October 2015. Nurses from outside the European Economic Area (EEA) will have their work visa applications prioritised.

With a similar intent, the Home Office introduced new rules regarding UK spouse immigration in July 2012, ostensibly to ease the financial burden of migration on the state. Under the new family migration policy only British citizens, or those with refugee status, who earn at least £18,600 a year can sponsor their non-European spouse's visa.[3] This rises to £22,400 for families with a child, and a further £2,400 for each extra child. In 2013, the High Court ruled that the UK family immigration rules are not unlawful but are 'onerous... and unjustified'. However, the Home Secretary decided to appeal the decision, providing some measure of the government's commitment to reduce net migration.

[2] A tier 2 visa is initially granted for a period of 3 years. So long as the nurse is needed in their position, an extension can be applied for, which may be granted for a maximum of 3 years.

[3] This policy was subject to a judicial review decision which questioned the proportionality of the new rules. For the evidence, see: on the minimum income requirement contained in para e-ECP.3.1 of Appendix FM of the Immigrant Rules. The Queen vs Secretary of State for the Home Department. Claim No: CO/7031/2012. High Court of Justice. Expert Report of Peter J Aspinall. 3 December 2012.

THE PREFERENCES AND ASPIRATIONS OF THE BLACK AFRICAN COMMUNITY

Finally, as Simpson and Jivraj (2015b) have pointed out, a further important area of policy addresses the diversity of preferences and needs associated with ethnicity that may be different from mainstream expectations and the need for respect for these differences. They provide the following as examples: housing size and style; cultural specific requirements of paid and unpaid carers, supported housing, care homes, and hospital care; preferred residential location; and traditional beliefs about contact between Muslim women and the commercial world and engagement in economic activity. Such diversity of preferences and aspirations are expressed through both organisations and individuals, recognition and respect for which may yield more nuanced responses in the provision of services.

One such example is where Black Africans in the UK have appropriated their evolving traditions and cultures in the diaspora to facilitate support for those with HIV. The context of stigma may affect health-seeking behaviour, the associated fear preventing participants from attending for HIV testing and care and seeking emotional and social support after diagnosis. Participatory programmes involving Black African communities (e.g. Ffena), irrespective of migration status and seropositivity, help develop a critical consciousness that exposes inequalities. Ffena (the Luganda word for 'we/togetherness') is a UK-based network of Africans living with and affected by HIV that enables members to participate in personal development, influence policy, and engage in national debates and influence change.[4] Such programmes, informed by sensitivity, do much to transform processes of imposition to ones of mutuality and negotiation. Others have harnessed traditional concepts that were in part shaped by memories from home, to address HIV related stigma, for example, amongst Zimbabweans culturally competent health-promotion interventions have been developed that moved away from individualistic approaches to those that promoted community relations with members of this community, a group highly affected by HIV (Bloch 2008). The engagement with cultural resources that sustained community life before migration appeared to help the participants to move on with life, with memories of home providing hope.

[4] AHPN: African Health Policy Network. Ffena. See http://www.ahpn.org.uk/ffena.php

References

Agbetu, T. (2004). *Letter, The Ligali Organisation, to Richard Alldritt, Statistics Commission, January 12, 2004.* African British Identity. Retrieved from www. ligali.org/pdf/richard%20alldritt%20-%20african%20british%20identity.pdf

Ager, A., & Strang, A. (2004). *Indicators of integration: Final report* (Development and Practice Report 28). London: Home Office.

Agyemang, C., Bhopal, R., & Bruijnzeels, M. (2005). Negro, Black, Black African, African Caribbean, African American or what? Labelling African origin populations in the health arena in the 21st century. *Journal of Epidemiology and Community Health, 59,* 1014–1018.

AHPN (African HIV Policy Network). (2007). *UK website.* Retrieved from www. ahpn.org

Alexis, O., & Vydelingum, V. (2009). Experiences in the UK National Health Service: The overseas nurses' workforce. *Health Policy, 90*(2–3), 320–328.

Anderson, J., & Doyal, L. (2004). Women from Africa living with HIV in London: A descriptive study. *AIDS Care, 16*(1), 95–105.

Anonymous. (1999, October 4). One in five Britons has black ancestor. *Bionews 028.*

Anonymous. (2007, May 16). Fewer males and Black Africans get on to courses. *Nursing Standard, 21*(36), 6-6.

Anonymous. (2012, November 14). BME nurses more likely than White staff to face NMC. *Nursing Standard, 27*(11), 7-7.

Anwar, M. (1998). *Ethnic Minorities and the British Electoral System.* Warwick: CRER and OBV, University of Warwick.

Aspinall, P. J. (2000). The new 2001 Census question set on cultural characteristics: Is it useful for the monitoring of the health status of people from ethnic groups in Britain. *Ethnicity & Health, 5*(1), 33–40.

Aspinall, P. J. (2007a). Language ability: A neglected dimension in the profiling of populations and health service users. *Health Education Journal, 66*(1), 90–106.

Aspinall, P. J. (2007b). Is it time to abandon colour categories for ethnic groups. *Journal of Epidemiology & Community Health, 61*, 91.

Aspinall, P. J. (2008). The categorization of African descent populations in Europe and the USA: Should lexicons of recommended terminology be evidence-based? *Public Health, 122*(1), 61–69.

Aspinall, P. J. (2009). *Estimating the size and composition of the lesbian, gay, and bisexual population in Britain* (Research report 37). Manchester, England: Equality & Human Rights Commission.

Aspinall, P. J. (2013). When is the use of race/ethnicity appropriate in risk assessment tools for preconceptual or antenatal genetic screening and how should it be used? *Sociology, 47*(5), 891–909.

Aspinall, P. J., & Chinouya, M. (2008). Is the standardised term 'Black African' useful in demographic and health research in the United Kingdom?'. *Ethnicity and Health, 13*(3), 182–202.

Aspinall, P. J., Dyson, S. M., & Anionwu, E. (2003). The feasibility of using ethnicity as a primary tool for antenatal selective screening for sickle cell disorders. Pointers from the research evidence. *Social Science and Medicine, 56*, 285–297.

Aspinall, P. J., & Jacobson, B. (2004, July). *Ethnic disparities in health and health care: A focused review of the evidence and selected examples of good practice.* Canterbury, England: Centre for Health Services Studies.

Aspinall, P. J., & Mitton, L. (2010). *The migration history, demography, and socio-economic position of the Somali community in Britain* (Countries, regional studies, trading blocks, unions, world organizations series). New York: Nova Science Publishers.

Aspinall, P. J., & Mitton, L. (2014). Smoking prevalence and the changing risk profiles in the UK ethnic and migrant minority populations: Implications for stop smoking services. *Public Health, 128*(3), 297–306.

Aspinall, P. J., Mitton, L., & Chinouya, M. (2015). *Constructions of 'Black African' health in Britain by health professionals, African community members, and African organisations.* Unpublished paper. Canterbury, England: Centre for Health Services Studies.

Aspinall, P. J., & Song, M. (2013). *Mixed race identities* (Identity studies in the social sciences series). Basingstoke, England: Palgrave Macmillan.

Aspinall, P. J., & Watters, C. (2010). *Refugees and asylum seekers: A review from an equality and human rights perspective* (Research Report 52). Manchester, England: Equality and Human Rights Commission.

Bagley, C. (1972). Patterns of Inter-Ethnic Marriage in Great Britain. *Phylon, 33*, 373–379.

Bains, B., & Klodawski, E. (2006). *GLA 2005 round: Interim ethnic group population projections* (DMAG Briefing 2006/22). London: Greater London Authority.

Baker, P., & Eversley, J. (Eds.). (2000). *Multilingual capital*. London: Battlebridge Publications.

Bansal, N., Bhopal, R., Netto, G., Lyons, D., Steiner, M. F., & Sashidharan, S. P. (2014). Disparate patterns of hospitalisation reflect unmet needs and persistent ethnic inequalities in mental health care: The Scottish health and ethnicity linkage study. *Ethnicity and Health, 19*(2), 217–239.

Barth, F. (1969). *Ethnic groups and boundaries*. London: George Allen and Unwin.

Bashford, J., Buffin, J., & Patel, K. (2003) *The Department of Health's drug misuse needs assessment project. Community engagement. Report 2: The findings*. Preston, England: Centre for Ethnicity and Health, University of Central Lancashire.

Bécares, L. (2013, October). *Which ethnic groups have the poorest health? Ethnic health inequalities 1991 to 2011. Dynamics of diversity: Evidence from the 2011 Census*. Manchester, England: ESRC Centre on Dynamics of Ethnicity.

Bécares, L. (2015). Which ethnic groups have the poorest health? In J. Jivraj & L. Simpson (Eds.), *Ethnic identity and inequalities in Britain. The dynamics of diversity* (pp. 123–139). Bristol, England: Policy Press.

Bécares, L., Nazroo, J. Y., & Stafford, M. (2011). The ethnic density effect on alcohol use among ethnic minority people in the UK. *Journal of Epidemiology & Community Health, 65*(1), 20–25.

Ben-Shlomo, Y., Evans, S., Ibrahim, F., Patel, B., Anson, K., Chinegwundoh, F., et al. (2008). The risk of prostate cancer amongst black men in the United Kingdom: The PROCESS Cohort Study. *European Urology, 53*, 99–105.

Bernard, C., & Gupta, A. (2008). Black African children and the child protection system. *British Journal of Social Work, 38*(3), 476–492.

Bhopal, R. (2004). Glossary of terms relating to ethnicity and race: For reflection and debate. *Journal of Epidemiology & Community Health, 58*, 441–445.

Bhui, K., Craig, T., Mohamud, S., Warfa, N., Stansfeld, S. A., Thornicroft, G., et al. (2006). Mental disorders among Somali refugees: Developing culturally appropriate measures and assessing socio-cultural risk factors. *Social Psychiatry & Psychiatric Epidemiology, 41*(5), 400–408.

Birley, A. (1979). *The people of Roman Britain*. London: Batsford.

Blacknet, UK. (n.d.). Retrieved from http://www.blacknet.co.uk/

Bloch, A. (2008). Zimbabweans in Britain: Transnational activities and capabilities. *Journal of Ethnic & Migration Studies, 34*(2), 287–305.

Boatswain, S. J., & Lalonde, R. N. (2000). Social identity and preferred ethnic/racial labels for Blacks in Canada. *Journal of Black Psychology, 26*(2), 216–234.

Bobo, L. (1993). Report of Rapporteurs. In Statistics Canada & US Bureau of the Census (Eds.), *Challenges of measuring an ethnic world: Science, politics, and reality. Proceedings of the Joint Canada-United States Conference on the Measurement of Ethnicity, April 1–3, 1992*. Washington, DC: US Government Printing Office.

Boliver, V. (2015a, May 12). Exploring ethnic inequalities in admission to Russell Group universities. *Sociology*. doi: 10.1177/0038038515575859.

Boliver, V. (2015b). Why are British ethnic minorities less likely to be offered places at highly selective universities? In C. Alexander & J. Arday (Eds.), *Aiming higher: Race, inequality and diversity in the academy* (pp. 15–18). London: Runnymede Trust.

Bouchardy, C., Wanner, P., & Parkin, D. M. (1995). Cancer mortality among sub-Saharan African migrants in France. *Cancer Causes & Control, 6*, 539–544.

Bourne, A., Reid, D., & Weatherburn, P. (2014). *African Health & Sex Survey 2013–2014: Headline findings*. London: Sigma Research and London School of Hygiene and Tropical Medicine. Retrieved from http://www.sigmaresearch. org.uk/files/report2014c.pdf.

Boydell, J., van Os, J., McKenzie, K., Allardyce, J., Goel, R., McCreadie, R. G., et al. (2001). Incidence of schizophrenia in ethnic minorities in London: Ecological study into interactions with environment. *British Medical Journal, 323*, 1336–1338.

Brierley Consultancy. (2013). *What the London Church Census reveals*. London: Brierley Consultancy/London Church Census/London City Mission.

Brimicombe, A. (2007). Ethnicity, religion and residual segregation in London: evidence from a computational typology of minority communities. *Environ Plann B, 34*(5), 884–904.

Brown, D. (2008, June). *More destitution in Leeds: Repeat survey of destitute asylum seekers and refugees approaching local agencies for support*. York, England: Joseph Rowntree Charitable Trust.

Bulmer, M. (1996). The ethnic group question in the 1991 Census of population. In D. Coleman & J. Salt (Eds.), *Ethnicity in the 1991 Census of population*. London: HMSO.

Burgess, R. (2015). *Transnational Nigerian Pentecostal churches, networks and believers in three northern countries: Migrant churches as a potent social force*. Birmingham, England: University of Birmingham. Retrieved from http:// www.birmingham.ac.uk/schools/ptr/departments/theologyandreligion/ research/projects/transnational-nigerian-pentecostal.aspx.

Burgess, S., Greaves, E., & Wilson, D. (2009). *An investigation of educational outcomes by ethnicity and religion. Report for the National Equality Panel*. Bristol, England: University of Bristol, CMPO.

Burton, J., Nandi, A., & Platt, L. (2010). Measuring ethnicity: Challenges and opportunities for survey research. *Ethnic and Racial Studies, 33*(8), 1332–1349.

Butz, W. P., Goldmann, G. J., & Lapham, S. (1993). Introduction. In Statistics Canada & US Bureau of the Census (Eds.), *Challenges of measuring an ethnic world: Science, politics, and reality. Proceedings of the Joint Canada-United States Conference on the Measurement of Ethnicity, April 1–3, 1992*. Washington, DC: US Government Printing Office.

Callister, P. (2015). 'The New Zealand *"melting pot"'. January 2015*. Retrieved from http://callister.co.nz/the-new-zealand-melting-pot.pdf.

Cantor-Graae, E. (2007). Is there an increased risk of psychotic illness in ethnic minority groups in the UK. *Evidence-Based Mental Health, 10*, 95.

Cantor-Graae, E., & Selten, J. P. (2005). Schizophrenia and migration: A meta-analysis and review. *The American Journal of Psychiatry, 162*, 12–24.

Castles, S., Korac, M., Vasta, E., & Vertovec, S. (2002). *Integration: Mapping the field*. London: Home Office.

Catney, G. (2015). Has neighbourhood ethnic residential segregation decreased? In S. Jivraj & L. Simpson (Eds.), *Ethnic identity and inequalities in Britain. The dynamics of diversity* (pp. 109–122). Bristol, England: Policy Press.

Catney, G., & Simpson, L. (2010). Settlement area migration in England and Wales: assessing evidence for a social gradient. *Transactions of the Institute of British Geographers, 35*(4), 571–584.

Cattell, M. G. (1997). The discourse of neglect: Family support for the elderly in Samia. In T. S. Weisner, C. Bradley, & P. L. Kilbride (Eds.), *African families and the crisis of social change*. Westport, CT: Greenwood.

Cebulla, A., Daniel, M., & Zurawan, A. (2010, July). *Spotlight on refugee integration: Findings from the survey of new refugees in the United Kingdom* (Research Report 37). London: Home Office.

Cebulla, A., Rice, B., Tomaszewski, W., & Hough, J. (2009, July). In T. Savage (Ed.), *Profiling London's rough sleepers: A longitudinal analysis of CHAIN data*. London: Broadway Homelessness and Support.

CEMACH. (2004). *Why mothers die 2000-2002. Report on confidential enquiries into maternal deaths in the United Kingdom*. London: CEMACH.

Centre for Maternal and Child Enquiries (CMACE). (2011, March). 'Saving mothers' lives. Reviewing maternal deaths to make motherhood safer: 2006-2008 The Eighth Report of the Confidential Enquiries into Maternal Deaths in the United Kingdom. *British Journal of Obstetrics and Gynaecology, 118*(Suppl 1), 1–203.

Chief Secretary to the Treasury. (2003, September). Every Child Matters. Cm 5860. London: The Stationery Office.

Child Exploitation and Online Protection Centre (CEOP). (2011, October). *Child trafficking update*. Retrieved from http://ceop.police.uk/Documents/ceopdocs/child_trafficking_update_2011.pdf

Chinouya, M. (2007). Ubuntu and the helping hands for AIDS. In O. Wambu (Ed.), *Under the tree of talking: Leadership for change in Africa*. London: Counterpoint.

Chinouya, M. (2010). Maintaining transnational families: HIV positive Zimbabwean women's narratives of obligation and support. In J. McGregor & R. Primorac (Eds.), *Zimbabwe's new diaspora: Displacement and the cultural politics of survival*. New York: Berghahn.

Chinouya, M., Ssanyu-Sseruma, W., & Kwok, A. (2003). *The SHIBAH report: A study of the sexual health issues affecting Black Africans living with HIV in Lambeth, Southwark and Lewisham.* London: Health First.

Chouhan, K., & Lusane, C. (2004). *Black voluntary and community sector funding: Its impact on civic engagement and capacity building.* London: Joseph Rowntree Foundation.

Cohen, R. (2008). *Global diasporas: An introduction.* Abingdon, England: Routledge.

Cole, I., & Robinson, D. (2003). *Somali housing experiences in England.* Sheffield, England: Sheffield Hallam University.

Coleman, D. (2006). Immigration and ethnic change in low-fertility countries: A third demographic transition. *Population and Development Review, 32*(3), 401–446.

Coleman, D. (2010). Projections of the ethnic minority populations of the United Kingdom 2006–2056. *Population and Development Review, 36*(3), 441–486.

Coleman, D., & Dubuc, S. (2010). The fertility of ethnic minority populations in the United Kingdom, 1960s–2006. *Population Studies, 64*(1), 19–41.

Coleman, D. A., & Smith, M. D. (2005). *The projection of ethnic populations: Problems and data needs* (Working paper 13, Background paper 2). Oxford, England: Oxford Centre for Population Research.

Communities and Local Government. (2009). *2007-08 Citizenship Survey. Identity and Values Topic Report.* London: Communities and Local Government.

Council of Europe. (1997). *Measurement and indicators of integration.* Strasbourg, France: Council of Europe Publishing.

Cresswell, J. A., Yu, G., Hatherall, B., Morris, J., Jamal, F., Harden, A., et al. (2013). Predictors of the timing of initiation of antenatal care in an ethnically diverse urban cohort in the UK. *BMC Pregnancy and Childbirth, 13*, 103.

Cruise O'Brien, D. B. (2003). *Symbolic Confrontations: Muslims Imagining the State in Africa.* London: C Hurst and Company (Publishers) Ltd.

Daley, P. (1996). Black-African: Students who stayed. In C. Peach (Ed.), *Ethnicity in the 1991 Census. The ethnic minority populations of Great Britain* (pp. 44–65). London: HMSO.

Daley, P. (1998). Black Africans in Great Britain: Spatial concentration and segregation. *Urban Studies, 35*(10), 1703–1724.

De Tona, C., & Lentin, R. (2011, April). Networking sisterhood, from the informal to the global: AkiDwA, the African and migrant women's network, Ireland. *Global Networks, 2*, 242–261.

Demie, F. (2006). *The achievement of African heritage pupils: Good practice in Lambeth schools.* London: London Borough of Lambeth.

Demie, F., Lewis, K., & McLean, C. (2007, July). *Raising the achievement of Somali pupils: Challenges and school responses.* London: Lambeth Research and Statistics Unit.

Department for Education. (2014, December). *Children looked after in England (including adoption and care leavers) year ending 31 March 2014: Additional tables* (SFR 36/2014). London: Department for Education. Retrieved from

https://www.gov.uk/government/uploads/system/uploads/attachment_
data/file/384300/SFR362014_AdditionalText.pdf

Department for Education and Skills (DfES). (2005). *Children in need guidance 2005: Annex B. Ethnicity and religion categories.* London: DfES. Retrieved from http://www.dfes.gov.uk/datastats1/guidelines/children/ANNEX%20B_2005.pdf

Department for Education and Skills (DfES). (2006a). *Final key list of extended ethnic groups.* Retrieved from http://www.standards.dfes.gov.uk/ethnicminorities/resources/Extended_Eth_Codes_V1_Oct06.xls

Department for Education and Skills (DfES). (2006b). *Ethnicity and education. The evidence on minority ethnic pupils aged 5-16.* London: Department for Education and Skills.

Department of Health. (2005). *HIV and AIDS in African communities: A framework for better prevention and care.* London: Department of Health, National Aids Trust, & African HIV Policy Network.

Dobbs, J., Green, H., & Zealey, L. (2006). *Focus on ethnicity and religion.* Basingstoke, England: Palgrave Macmillan.

Dodds, C., Hickson, F., Weatherburn, P., Reid, D., Hammond, G., Jessup, K., et al. (2008). *BASS Line 2007 survey: Assessing the sexual HIV prevention needs of African people in England.* London: Sigma Research.

Dougan, S., & Harris, J. P. (2003). Overcounting of Black Africans in the UK: The problem of undetected record duplication. *Communicable Disease and Public Health, 6*(2), 147–151.

Dubuc, S. (2009). Application of the own-children method for estimating fertility by ethnic and religious groups in the UK. *Journal of Population Research, 26*(3), 207–225.

Dubuc, S. (2012). Immigration from high fertility countries: Intergenerational adaptation and fertility convergence in the UK. *Population and Development Review, 38*(2), 353–368.

Dubuc S. (2016, forthcoming). Fertility and migration. In F. Bean, S. Brown, & P. MacDonald (Eds.), *Encyclopedia of migration.* Dordrecht, The Netherlands: Springer.

Dubuc, S., & Haskey, J. (2010). Fertility and ethnicity in the UK: Recent trends. In J. Stilwell & M. van Ham (Eds.), *Understanding population trends and processes: Vol. 3. Ethnicity and integration* (Chapter 4). Dordrecht, The Netherlands: Springer.

Duncan, O. D., & Duncan, B. (1955). A methodological analysis of segregation indices. *Am Sociological Review, 20*(2), 210–217.

Ekwe-Ekwe, H. (2012). What exactly does 'sub-Saharan Africa' mean? *Pambazuka News, 566.* Retrieved from http://www.pambazuka.net/en/category.php/features/79215

Ekwulugo, F. (2006). Entrepreneurship and SMEs in London (UK): Evaluating the role of Black Africans in this emergent sector. *Journal of Management Development, 25*(1), 65–79.

Elam, G., Chinouya, M., & The Joint Health Surveys Unit. (2000). *Feasibility study for health surveys among Black African populations living in the UK: Stage 2—Diversity among Black African communities.* London: Department of Health.

Elam, G., McMunn, A., Nazroo, J., Apwonyoke, M., Brookes, M., Chinouya, M., et al. (2001). *Feasibility study for health surveys among Black African people living in England. Final report.* London: Department of Health.

Enquete-Kommission "Zukunft des bürgerschaftlichen Engagements." (2002). Bürgerschaftliches Engagement: auf dem Weg in eine zukunftsfähige Bürgergesellschaft [Civic engagement: On the way to a sustainable civil society]. Retrieved from http://www.bmi.bund.de/SharedDocs/Downloads/DE/Themen/Politik_Gesellschaft/GeselZusammenhalt/enquete_be.pdf?__blob=publicationFile

Esmail, A., & Carnall, D. (1997). Tackling racism in the NHS. We need action not words. *British Medical Journal, 314,* 618.

Evans-Pritchard, A. (2004, December 21). Frustrated Somalis flee Holland for the freedom of Britain. *Daily Telegraph.*

Eversley, J., Mehmedbegovic, D., Sanderson, A., Tinsley, T., von Ahn, M., & Wiggins, R. D. (2010). *Language capital: Mapping the languages of London's schoolchildren.* London: The National Centre for Languages (CILT).

Fearon, P., Kirkbride, J. B., Morgan, C., Lloyd, T., Hutchinson, G., Tarrant, J., et al. (2006). Incidence of schizophrenia and other psychoses in ethnic minority groups: Results from the MRC AESOP study. *Psychological Medicine, 36,* 1541–1550.

Fenton, K. A., Chinouya, M., Davidson, O., Copas, A., & Mayisha Research Team. (2001). HIV transmission risk among sub-Saharan Africans in London travelling to their countries of origin. *AIDS, 15*(11), 1442–1445.

Fenton, K. A., Mercer, C. H., McManus, S., Erens, B., Byron, C. J., & Copas, A. J. (2005). Sexual behaviour in Britain: Ethnic variations in high-risk behaviour and STI acquisition risk. *Lancet, 365*(9466), 1246–1255.

Finch, J., & Mason, J. (1993). *Negotiating family responsibilities.* London: Routledge.

Finney, N., & Harries, B. (2015). Which ethnic groups are hardest hit by the housing crisis? In S. Jivraj & L. Simpson (Eds.), *Ethnic identity and inequalities in Britain: The dynamics of diversity* (pp. 141–160). Bristol, England: Policy Press.

Finney, N., & Simpson, L. (2009). *'Sleepwalking to segregation'? Challenging myths about race and migration.* Bristol, England: Policy Press.

Frissa, S., Hatch, S. L., Gazard, B., Fear, N. T., Hotopf, M., & SELCoH Study Team. (2013). Trauma and current symptoms of PTSD in a South East London community. *Social Psychiatry and Psychiatric Epidemiology, 48*(8), 1199–1209.

Fryer, P. (1984). *Staying power: The history of Black people in Britain.* Concord, MA: Pluto Press.

Fumanti, M., & Werbner, P. (2010). The moral economy of the African diaspora: Citizenship, networking and permeable ethnicity. *African Diaspora, 3,* 3–12.

Gaffney-Rhys, R. (2011). Polygamy and the rights of women. *Women in Society, 1,* 1–15.

Galandini, S. (2013). *Residential concentration, ethnic organisations and political participation: A mixed-method study of Black Africans in Britain.* Paper prepared for presentation at the Political Studies Association conference, Cardiff, Wales, March 25–27, 2013.

General Register Office for Scotland. (2006). *2006 Census test forms.* Edinburgh, Scotland: GRO(S). Retrieved from http://www.gro-scotland.gov.uk/files/2006-census-test-form.pdf

Gibbons, J., & Wilding, J. (1995). *Needs, risks and family support plans: Social Services Departments' responses to neglected children. Interim report to the Department of Health.* Norwich, England: University of East Anglia.

Gilroy, P. (1993). *The Black Atlantic: Modernity and double consciousness.* Cambridge, MA: Harvard University Press.

Gilroy, P. (2004). *After empire. Melancholia or convivial culture?* Abingdon, England: Routledge.

Hahn, R. A., & Stroup, D. F. (1994). Race and Ethnicity in Public Health Surveillance: Criteria for the Scientific Use of Social Categories. *Public Health Reports, 109*(1), 7–15.

Harker, R., & Heath, S. (2014, August). *Children in care in England: Statistics* (Standard Note SN/SG4470). London: House of Commons Library.

Harrison, F. V. (1994). Racial and gender inequalities in health and health care. *Medical Anthropology Quarterly, 8*(1), 90–95.

Hayase, Y., & Liaw, K. (1997). Factors on polygamy in sub-Saharan Africa. *The Developing Economies, 35*(3), 293–327.

Health and Social Care Information Centre. (2014, November). *Mental health bulletin. Annual report from MHMDS returns 2013-14.* Leeds, England: HSCIC.

Health and Social Care Information Centre. (2015, February 11). *Personal social services: Staff of social services departments at 30 September—England, 2014.* Leeds, England: Health and Social Care Information Centre. Retrieved 15:53 July 15–09:30 February 11, 2015 from http://www.hscic.gov.uk/article/2021/Website-Search?productid=17291&q=social+services+staff&sort=Relevance&size=10&page=1&area=both#top

Health Protection Agency. (2006). *South East London Health Protection Unit annual review 2005.* London: HPA.

Heath, A. F., Fisher, S. D., Rosenblatt, G., Sanders, D., & Sobolewska, M. (2013). *The Political Integration of Ethnic Minorities in Britain.* Oxford: Oxford University Press.

Hickman, M., Crowley, H., & Mai, N. (2008). *Immigration and social cohesion in the rhythms and realities of everyday life.* York, England: Joseph Rowntree Foundation.

Higher Education Funding Council for England (HEFCE). (2004). *Equality and diversity monitoring in higher education institutions: A guide to good practice. Good practice April 2004/14.* London: HEFCE.

Higher Education Statistics Agency (HESA). (2007a). *Students and qualifiers data tables: Ethnicity.* Cheltenham, England: HESA. Retrieved from http://www.hesa.ac.uk/holisdocs/pubinfo/student/ethnic0506.htm.

Higher Education Statistics Agency (HESA). (2007b). *Students in higher education institutions 2004/5 & 2005/6.* Cheltenham, England: HESA.

Holloway, L. (2007). *Black is my colour. London: The 1990 trust.* Black Information Link. Retrieved from http://www.blink.org.uk/print.asp?key=14034

Holman, C., & Holman, M. (2003, April). *First steps in a new country: Baseline indicators for the Somali community in London Borough of Hackney.* London: Sahil Housing Association.

Home Office. (2004). *Integration matters: A national strategy for refugee integration* (Draft consultation). London: Home Office.

Home Office. (2006). *Home Office statistical bulletin: Asylum statistics United Kingdom 2005. 14/06* (see also earlier bulletins). London: Home Office.

Home Office. (2009). *Control of Immigration: Quarterly statistical summary, UK. July-September.* London: Home Office.

Home Office. (2010, July). *Spotlight on refugee integration: Findings from the survey of new refugees in the United Kingdom.* London: Home Office.

Home Office. (2015a, February 18). *Migrant journey: Fifth report.* London: Home Office. Retrieved from https://www.gov.uk/government/publications/migrant-journey-fifth-report/migrant-journey-fifth-report

Home Office. (2015b, March). *Country information and guidance. Eritrea: Illegal exit.* London: Home Office.

Home Office. (2015c, March). *Country information and guidance. Eritrea: National (including military) service.* London: Home Office.

Homes, A., & Murray, L. (2008). *Cognitive question testing Scotland's Census ethnicity classification. Research findings no. 2/2008.* Edinburgh, Scotland: Scottish Government Social Research.

Hopper, N. A., & D'Souza, E. (2012). *Written translation support in the 2011 Census: Evidence used to rank languages in England and Wales according to estimated relative volume of need and use.* London: Office for National Statistics.

Hoskins, R. (2012). *The boy in the river.* Basingstoke, England: Pan Books.

House of Commons. (2002). *Hansard.* Commons Debates, 30 January 2002 (Col. 365).

House of Commons. (2006). *Hansard.* Written answer of 14 July 2006 (Col. 2116W).

House of Commons Health Committee. (2003, June 5). *The Victoria Climbie inquiry report. Sixth report of session 2002-03. Report, & formal minutes together with oral evidence* (HC 570). London: The Stationery Office.

Hubbard, M., & Haines, L. (2004). *A national programme of neonatal audit: Report of a feasibility study*. London: Department of Health, Healthcare Commission, and Royal College of Paediatrics and Child Health.

Human Rights Council. (2015, June 5). *Report of the detailed findings of the commission of inquiry on human rights in Eritrea* (Human Rights Council, 29th session, Agenda item 4). Human Rights Council (also: United Nations General Assembly. Report of the commission of inquiry on human rights in Eritrea. Human Rights Council, 4 June 2015).

ICAR. (2007, July). *ICAR briefing—The Somali refugee community in the UK*. London: ICAR

Ifekwunigwe, J. (1999). *Scattered belongings*. London: Routledge.

Improvement and Development Agency. (2003). *Taking forward community cohesion in Leicester*. London: The Improvement and Development Agency.

Institute for Public Policy Research (IPPR). (2007, September). *Britain's immigrants: An economic profile*. London: IPPR.

Ipsos Mori Social Research Institute. (2010, September). *A survey of refugees living in London. Report for the Greater London authority*. London: Ipsos Mori.

Jenkins, R. (1996). *Social identity*. London: Routledge.

Jivraj, S. (2013, January). *How can we count immigration*. Manchester, England: Centre on Dynamics of Ethnicity.

Jivraj, S., & Byrne, B. (2015). Who feels British? In: Jivraj, S., & Simpson L. *Ethnic Identity and Inequalities in Britain: The Dynamics of Diversity* (pp. 65–78). Bristol: Policy Press.

Jivraj, S., & Khan, O. (2015). How likely are people from minority ethnic groups to live in deprived neighbourhoods. In S. Jivraj & L. Simpson (Eds.), *Ethnic identity and inequalities in Britain. The dynamics of diversity*. Bristol, England: Policy Press.

Johnson, R., Voas, D., & Poulsen, M. (2003). Measuring spatial concentration: the use of threshold profiles. *Environ Plann B, 30*(1), 3–14.

Jones, J. (2006). *Somewhere to go? Something to do? London Borough of Newham young peoples survey*. Northampton, England: Mattersoffact.

Karlsen, S., & Nazroo, J. (2008). *Being a Muslim in Europe: Attitudes and experiences: Full research report* (ESRC End of Award Report, RES-163-25-0009). Swindon, England: Economic and Social Research Council.

Killingray, D. (Ed.). (1994). *Africans in Britain*. Ilford, England: Frank Cass.

Killingray, D. (2012). Significant Black South Africans in Britain before 1912: Pan-African organisations and the emergence of South Africa's first Black lawyers. *South African Historical Journal, 64*(3), 393–417.

Killingray, D., & Plaut, M. (2010). *Fighting for Britain: African soldiers in the Second World War*. Woodbridge, England: James Currey.

King, T. E., Parkin, E. J., Swinfield, G., Cruciani, F., Scozzari, R., Rosa, A., et al. (2007). Africans in Yorkshire? The deepest-rooting clade of the Y phylogeny within an English genealogy. *European Journal of Human Genetics, 15*, 288–293.

Krieger, N., Williams, D., & Zierler, S. (1999). "Whiting out" white privilege will not advance the study of how racism harms health. *American Journal of Public Health, 89*(5), 782–785.

Kyambi, S. (2005). *Beyond Black and White: Mapping new immigrant communities*. London: IPPR.

Laming Lord. (2003, January). *The Victoria Climbié inquiry: Report* (Command Paper CM5730). Norwich, England: HMSO.

Leach, S., Eckardt, H., Chenery, C., Müldner, G., & Lewis, M. (2010). A Lady of York: Migration, ethnicity and identity in Roman Britain. *Antiquity, 84*(323), 131–145.

Leicester City Council and Leicester Partnership. (2007, June 28). *The diversity of Leicester: A demographic profile. Final draft* (1st ed.). Leicester, England: Leicester City Council and Leicester Partnership.

Levitt, P. (2013). A new social contract: Social welfare in an era of transnational migration. *Tikkun, 3*, 44.

Lewis, H. (2007). *Destitution in Leeds: The experiences of people seeking asylum and supporting agencies*. York, England: Joseph Rowntree Charitable Trust.

Li, Y. (n.d.). *The socio-economic integration of second-generation immigrants in Britain and the USA*. Manchester, England: Institute for Social Change, University of Manchester. Retrieved from https://cream.conference-services. net/resources/952/2371/pdf/MECSC2011_0391_paper.pdf

Likupe, G. (2006). Experiences of African nurses in the UK National Health Service: A literature review. *Journal of Clinical Nursing, 15*(10), 1213–1220.

Likupe, G. (2011, May). *Motivations, migration and experiences of Black African nurses in the United Kingdom*. Thesis submitted for the degree of Doctor of Philosophy, University of Hull.

Likupe, G. (2015). Experiences of African nurses and perceptions of their managers in the NHS. *Journal of Nursing Management, 23*(2), 231–241.

Likupe, G., Baxter, C., Jogi, M., & Archibong, U. (2014). Managers' perspectives on promotion and professional development for Black African nurses in the UK. *Diversity and Equality in Health and Care, 11*(2), 113–124.

Lindley, A., & van Hear, N. (2007). *New Europeans on the move: A preliminary review of the onward migration of refugees within the European Union* (Working Paper No. 57). Oxford, England: Centre on Migration, Policy and Society, University of Oxford.

Ligali Media Network. (2005). *African British identity tops polls*. Retrieved April 30, 2005, from http://www.ligali.org/article.php?id=279

London Development Agency. (2004). *The educational experiences and achievements of Black boys in London schools 2000-2003. A report of the Education Commission*. London: LDA.

London Health Commission. (2004). *Health in London. Review of the London Health Strategy high level indicators: 2004 update*. London: London Health Commission.

London School of Hygiene and Tropical Medicine. (2007). *Directory of clinical databases (DoCDat)*. Retrieved from http://www.lshtm.ac.uk/docdat/page.php?t=index

Lorde, A. (1984). Age, race, class, and sex: Women redefining difference. In A. Lorde (Ed.), *Sister outsider*. New York: Crossing Points.

Low, N., Sterne, J. A. C., & Barlow, D. (2001). Inequalities in rates of gonorrhoea and chlamydia between black ethnic groups in south east London: Cross sectional study. *Sexually Transmitted Infections, 77*, 15–20.

Lukes, S., & Perry, J. (2014). *What shapes migrant destitution and what can be done about it*. Oxford, England: COMPAS, University of Oxford.

Lymperopoulou, K., & Parameshwaran, M. (2014, March). *How are ethnic inequalities in education changing? (The dynamics of diversity: Evidence from the 2011 Census)*. Manchester, England: ESRC Centre on Dynamics of Ethnicity.

Mamdani, M. (2001). Beyond settler and native as political identities: Overcoming the political legacy of colonialism. In O. Enwezor (Ed.), *The short century: Independence and liberation movements in Africa* (pp. 1945–1994). Munich, Germany: Prestel.

Massey, D. S., & Denton, N. A. (1988). The dimensions of residential segregation. *Social Forces, 67*, 281–315.

Masson, J., Pearce, J., & Bader, K. (2008). *Care profiling study. Ministry of Justice Research Series 4/08*. London: Ministry of Justice.

Mateos, P. (2014). *Names, ethnicity and populations. Tracing identity in space*. Berlin, Germany: Springer.

Maxwell, D. (2006). *African gifts of the spirit: Pentecostalism and the rise of the Zimbabwean transnational religious movement*. Oxford, England: James Curry.

Mayor of London. (2012, February). *The Mayor's education inquiry. First report. London context and call for evidence*. London: Greater London Authority.

Mayor of London. (2015). *Chain annual report. Greater London. April 2014- March 2015*. London: Greater London Authority.

McKenzie, K. (2008, 12 January). Being black is bad for your health. *The Guardian*.

Mercer, C., & Page, B. (2010). African home associations in Britain: Between political belonging and moral conviviality. *African Diaspora, 3*(1), 110–130.

Mhende, T. C. (2013, October). *The cows are coming home. African wedding customs still have value for the diaspora*. Retrieved from http://blogs.lse.ac.uk/africaatlse/2013/10/23/the-cows-are-coming-home-african-wedding-customs-still-have-value-for-the-diaspora/

Mitton, L. (2011). The languages of Black Africans in England. *Journal of Intercultural Studies, 32*(2), 151–172.

Mitton, L., & Aspinall, P. J. (2010). Black Africans in England: A diversity of integration experiences. In J. Stillwell & M. van Ham (Eds.), *Ethnicity and integration: Understanding population trends and processes* (Vol. 3, pp. 179–202). Dordrecht, The Netherlands: Springer.

Mitton, L., & Aspinall, P. J. (2011, January). *Black Africans in the UK: Integration or segregation? Research findings.* Understanding Population trends and Processes [UPTAP]/ESRC.

Momatrade. (2004, October 1). *European conference on integration and migration: The Somali Community in focus.* Amsterdam: Momatrade Consultancy.

Moret, J., & Van Eck, C. (2005). *Somali refugees in the Netherlands. Strategies of exile and policy responses* (SFM Studies No. 46, Country Report 4). Geneva: Swiss Forum for Migration and Population Studies.

Muttarak, R. (2004). Marital assimilation: *Interethnic marriage in Britain.* Paper presented at 12th Biennial Conference, Australian Population Association, Canberra, September 15–17, 2004.

Nair, M., Kurinczuk, J. J., & Knight, M. (2014, April). Ethnic variations in severe maternal morbidity in the UK—A Case Control Study. *PLoS One, 9*(4), e95086.

Nangoli, M. (1986). *No more lies about Africa.* East Orange, NJ: African Heritage Publishers.

National Statistics and Health and Social Care Information Centre. (2005). *Health survey for England 2004: The health of minority ethnic groups—Headline tables.* Leeds, England: National Statistics and NHS Health and Social Care Information Centre.

Nazroo, J. (1997). *The health of Britain's ethnic minorities: Findings from a national survey.* London: Policy Studies Institute.

Nazroo, J. (2005). *A longitudinal survey of ethnic minorities: Focus and design. Final report to the ESRC and ONS.* London: UCL (Department of Epidemiology & Public Health).

Ndofor-Tah, C. (2000). *Capital assets: A community research intervention by the African Forum in Redbridge and Waltham Forest (London).* London: Sigma Research.

Newman, J., & Demie, F. (2006, June). *The Africans in Lambeth. Historical and empirical evidence.* London: Lambeth Research and Statistics Unit.

NHS Information Authority. (2001). *DSC notice: 02/2001. CDS, HES & workforce: Ethnic data. Finalised coding frame.* Birmingham, England: NHS Information Authority.

NHS Perinatal Institute. (2004). *Maternity core data index. Data item, basis, explanation and values.* Birmingham, England: NHS Perinatal Institute.

Nwajiaku-Dahou, K. (2012, July 6). *Same difference? Nigerian Brits, French Senegalese: What they said? What the research said?* (Workshop paper, St Anthony's College, Oxford). Oxford, England: University of Oxford Podcast. Retrieved from https://podcasts.ox.ac.uk/people/kathryn-nwajiaku-dahou

Nwajiaku-Dahou, K. N. (2013). *Being and becoming ethnic in Europe and Africa: State and politics of recognition in Nigeria, France and the UK* (ESRC End of Award Report, RES-063-27-0136). Swindon, England: ESRC.

Nwankwo, S. (2005). Characterisation of Black African entrepreneurship in the UK: A pilot study. *Journal of Small Business & Enterprise Development, 12*(1), 120–136.

Nzira, V. (2011). *Social care with African families in the UK.* Abingdon, England: Routledge.

Obbo, C. (1980). *African women: Their struggle for economic independence.* London: Zed Press.

Office for National Statistics. (2003). *Ethnic group statistics. A guide for the collection and classification of ethnicity data.* London: Office for National Statistics.

Office for National Statistics. (2004). *Commissioned table M221b. Ethnic group (detailed categories based on ethnic group write-in). 2001 Census.* Crown Copyright.

Office for National Statistics. (2006a). *A guide to comparing 1991 and 2001 Census ethnic group data.* London: ONS.

Office for National Statistics. (2006b). *Focus on ethnicity and religion.* London: Office for National Statistics and Basingstoke/Palgrave Macmillan.

Office for National Statistics. (2006c). *Commissioned table C0644. Religion by detailed country of birth.* Crown Copyright reserved.

Office for National Statistics. (2006d). *2011 Census. Assessment of initial user requirements on content for England and Wales. Individual responses to consultation.* London: ONS. Retrieved from http://www.statistics.gov.uk/about/consultations/2011Census_response.asp

Office for National Statistics. (2006e). *Census 2011: Questions to be included in the 2007 Census test.* London: ONS. Retrieved from http://www.statistics.gov.uk/census2001/pdfs/2007_test_H1_form.pdf

Office for National Statistics (ONS). (2008). *Equality impact assessment. Ethnicity, national identity, language and religion question development. 2011 Census in England and Wales.* London: ONS.

Office for National Statistics. (2009, March). *Information paper. Deciding which tick boxes to add to the ethnic group question in the 2011 England and Wales Census.* London: ONS.

Office for National Statistics. (2010, December). *Framework for getting the count right for key population groups. Stakeholder management and communication.* London: ONS.

Office for National Statistics. (2013a, January). *2011 Census variable and classification information: Part 6.* London: ONS.

Office for National Statistics. (2013b, July 17). *Ethnic variations in general health and unpaid care provision, 2011.* London: ONS.

Office for National Statistics. (2014a, June 24). *2011 Census analysis: How do living arrangements, family type and family size vary in England and Wales?* London: ONS.

Office for National Statistics. (2014b). *Beyond 2011: Statistical research update (M13).* London: Office for National Statistics.

Office for National Statistics. (2014c, November 4). *2011 Census analysis: Social and economic characteristics by length of residence of migrant populations in England and Wales*. London: Office for National Statistics.

Office for National Statistics. (2015, August). *Births in England and Wales by parents' country of birth*. London: ONS.

Office for National Statistics and Welsh Assembly Government. (2007). *Census advisory group for Wales. Ethnicity testing in Wales by the Welsh Assembly Government. CAGW(07) 02*. Cardiff, Wales: Welsh Assembly Government.

Office for Standards in Education. (2003, October). *The education of asylum-seeker pupils* (HMI 453). London: OFSTED.

Oheneba-Sakyi, Y., & Takyi, B. K. (2006). *African families at the turn of the 21st century*. Westport, CT: Praeger Publishers.

Ojo, S. (2012). Ethnic enclaves to diaspora entrepreneurs: A critical appraisal of Black British Africans' transnational entrepreneurship in London. *Journal of African Business, 13*(2), 145–156.

Olusoga, D. (2015, July 15). *Britain's forgotten slave owners*. Film transcript, transmitted BBC2.

Ong, A. (1999). *Flexible citizenship: The cultural logic of transnationality*. Durham, NC: Duke University Press.

Onyeani, C. (2009). *Contemptousness of Sub-Saharan Africa*. Retrieved July 16, 2009, from http://worldpress.org/Africa/3382.cfm

OPCS. (1980). *Tests of an ethnic group question. OPCS monitor CEN 80/2*. London: Office of Population Censuses and Surveys.

Owen, C., & Statham, J. (2009, June). *Disproportionality in child welfare. The prevalence of Black and minority ethnic children within the 'looked after' and 'children in need' populations and on child protection registers in England* (Research Report DCSF-RR124). London: Thomas Coram Research Unit, Institute of Education, University of London.

Parekh, B. (2000). *The future of multi-ethnic Britain. The Parekh report*. London: Profile Books.

Petersen, W. (1987). Politics and the measurement of ethnicity. In W. Alonso & P. Starr (Eds.), *The politics of numbers*. New York: Russell Sage Foundation.

Phillimore, J., & Goodson, L. (2008). Making a place in the global city: The relevance of indicators of integration. *Journal of Refugee Studies, 21*(3), 305–325.

Phillips-Mundy, H. M. (2011). *An exploration of the mothering experiences among first generation Somali Muslim immigrant mothers in Bristol, England*. PhD Thesis, University of Bristol, England.

Pickett, K. E., Shaw, R. J., Atkin, K., Kiernan, K. E., & Wilkinson, R. G. (2009). Ethnic density effects on maternal and infant health in the Millennium Cohort Study. *Social Science and Medicine, 69*(10), 1476–1483.

Piggott, G. (2006). *2001 Census: Health by ethnic group, religion and country of birth. DMAG briefing 2006-3*. London: Greater London Authority (Data Management & Analysis Group).

Pissarra, M. (2004). The luggage is still labelled. *Third Text, 18*(2), 183–191.

Platt, L. (2007). *Poverty and ethnicity in the UK*. Bristol, England: Policy Press.

Platt, L. (2009). *Ethnicity and family. Relationships within and between ethnic groups: An analysis using the Labour Force Survey*. Colchester, England: Institute for Social and Economic Research, University of Essex.

Platt, L., Simpson, L., & Akinwale, N. (2005). Stability and change in ethnic groups in England and Wales. *Population Trends, 121*, 35–46.

Prewitt, K. (2013). *What is your race? The Census and our flawed efforts to classify Americans*. Princeton, NJ: Princeton University Press.

Public Health England. (2014, November). *HIV in the United Kingdom: 2014 report*. London: Public Health England.

Raftery, J., Roderick, P., & Stevens, A. (2005). Potential use of routine databases in health technology assessment. *Health Technology Assessment, 9*(20), 1–92.

Refugee Council. (2004). *The Refugee Council's response to the Government's consultation document published in July 2004: "Integration matters: A national strategy for refugee integration"*. London: Refugee Council.

Royal College of Nursing. (2015, June). *International recruitment 2015*. London: Royal College of Nursing. Retrieved from http://www.rcn.org.uk/__data/assets/pdf_file/0007/629530/International-Recruitment-2015.pdf

Rudat, K. (1994). *Black and minority ethnic groups in England. Health and lifestyles*. London: Health Education Authority.

Rutter, J. (2004). *Refugee Communities in the UK: Somali Children's Educational Progress and Life Experiences*. London: London Metropolitan University.

Rutter, J., Cooley, L., Jones, N., & Pillai, R. (2008a). *Moving up together: Promoting equality and integration among the UK's diverse communities*. London: IPPR.

Rutter, J., Cooley, L., Reynolds, S., & Sheldon, R. (2008b). *From refugee to citizen: 'Standing on my own two feet'*. London: IPPR.

Sabater, A., & Simpson, L. (2009). Enhancing the population census: a time series for sub-national areas with age, sex, and ethnic group dimensions in England and Wales, 1991-2001. *Journal of Ethnic and Migration Studies, 35*(9), 1461–1477.

Sadler, K., Fenton, K. F., Elam, G., McGarrigle, C., Mercey, D., & Davidson, O. (2005). *Mayisha II main study report: Assessing the feasibility and acceptability of community based prevalence surveys of HIV among Black Africans in England*. London: Health Protection Agency.

Saggar, S. (1998). *The General Election 1997: Ethnic Minorities and Electoral Politics*. London: Commission for Racial Equality.

Saunders, C. L., Abel, G. A., El Turabi, A., et al. (2013). Accuracy of routinely recorded ethnic group information compared with self-reported ethnicity: Evidence from the English Cancer Patient Experience survey. *BMJ Open, 3*, e002882. doi:10.1136/bmjopen-2013-002882.

Save the Children. (2006). *One million more: Mobilising the African diaspora health care professionals for capacity building in Africa*. London: Save the Children.

School of Health and Human Sciences. (2000). *Ethnicity profiling in primary care. The Princes Park Health Centre model.* Liverpool, England: Public Health Sector, School of Health and Human Sciences, John Moores University.

Scott, J., & Marshall, G. (Eds.). (2005). *Oxford dictionary of sociology.* Oxford, England: Oxford University Press.

Seok-Woo, K., & Adler, P. S. (2014). Social capital: Maturation of a field of research. *Academy of Management Review, 39*(4), 412–422.

Serious Organised Crime Agency (SOCA). (2013, August). *UKHTC: A strategic assessment on the nature and scale of human trafficking in 2012.* London: SOCA. Retrieved from http://www.ecpat.org.uk/sites/default/files/ext-6538_ukhtc_strategic_assesssment_on_human_trafficking_2012_v1.01.pdf

Shahadah, A. (2012, May) *Linguistics for a new African reality: Language and African Agency.* Retrieved from http://www.africanholocaust.net/news_ah/language%20new%20reality.htm

Shevky, E., & Williams, M. (1949). *The social areas of Los Angeles, analysis and typology.* Berkeley, CA: University of California Press.

Shirley, M. H., Barnes, I., Sayeed, S., & Ali, R. (2014). Incidence of breast and gynaecological cancers by ethnic group in England, 2001-2007: A descriptive study. *BMC Cancer, 14,* 979.

Sigelman, L., Tuch, S. A., & Martin, J. K. (2005). What's in a name? Preference for 'Black' versus 'African-American' among Americans of African descent. *Public Opinion Quarterly, 69*(3), 429–438.

Sillitoe, K., & White, P. (1992). Ethnic group and the British Census: The search for a question. *Journal of the Royal Statistical Society: Series A (Statistics in Society), 155*(1), 141–163.

Simpson, L. (2012, December). *More segregation or more mixing? Dynamics of diversity: Evidence from the 2011 Census (code) series.* Manchester, England: ESRC Centre on Dynamics of Ethnicity.

Simpson, L. (2013, June). *What makes ethnic group populations grow? Age structures and immigration. Dynamics of diversity series.* Manchester, England: ESRC Centre on Dynamics of Ethnicity.

Simpson, L. (2014, March). *How have people's ethnic identities changed in England and Wales?.* Manchester, England: Centre on Dynamics of Ethnicity.

Simpson, L., & Finney, N. (2009). Spatial patterns of internal migration: evidence for ethnic groups in Britain. *Population, Space and Place, 15*(1), 37–56.

Simpson, L., & Jivraj, S. (2015a). Why has ethnic diversity grown. In L. Simpson & S. Jivraj (Eds.), *Ethnic identity and inequalities in Britain. The dynamics of diversity* (pp. 33–47). Bristol, England: Policy Press.

Simpson, L., & Jivraj, S. (2015b). Policy implications. In S. Jivraj & L. Simpson (Eds.), *Ethnic identity and inequalities in Britain. The dynamics of diversity* (pp. 217–225). Bristol, England: Policy Press.

Sinclair, I., Baker, C., Lee, J., & Gibbs, I. (2007). *The pursuit of permanence: A study of the English child care system.* London: Jessica Kingsley.

Smart, K. (2009, January). *The second destitution tally: An indication of the extent of destitution among asylum seekers, refused asylum seekers and refugees* (Asylum Support Partnership).

Social Care Institute for Excellence. (2003, January). *Effectiveness of childminding registration and implications for private fostering.* London: Social Care Institute for Excellence.

Sporton, D., Valentine, G., & Nielsen, K. B. (2006, July). *Post-conflict identities: Practices and affiliations of Somali refugee children. Briefing note 2c. Identities on the move: Mobility of young Somalis in Sheffield.* Sheffield, England: University of Sheffield.

Stafford, M., Bécares, L., & Nazroo, J. (2010, July). *Racial discrimination and health: Exploring the possible protective effects of ethnic density. UPTAP research findings.*

Stagg, H. R., Jones, J., Bickler, G., & Abubakar, I. (2012). Poor uptake of primary healthcare registration among recent entrants to the UK: A retrospective cohort study. *BMJ Open, 2,* e001453. doi:10.1136/bmjopen-2012-001453.

Statistics Commission. (2005). *Approaches to the Commission (SC/2005/13): Action for meeting* (Item 3). African British Identity.

Stephen Jivraj & Ludi Simpson (Eds.). (2015). *Ethnic Identity and Inequalities in Britain.* Bristol: Policy Press.

Strand, S., Malmberg, L., & Hall, J. (2015, January). *English as an additional language (EAL) and educational achievement in England: An analysis of the National Pupil Database.* Oxford, England: Department of Education, University of Oxford.

Sykes, B. (2006). *Blood of the Isles. Exploring the genetic roots of our tribal history.* London: Bantam Press.

Thompson, L. A. (1972). Africans in northern Britain. Museum africum. *West African Journal of Classical and Related Studies, 1,* 28–38.

Tindal, S., Findlay, A., & Wright, R. (2014, May). *The changing significance of EU and international students' participation in Scottish higher education* (Working Paper 49). Southampton, England: ESRC Centre for Population Change.

Tingay, K., & Stein, S. M. (2005). *National CAMHS dataset. Data dictionary. Version 1.1.* Dunstable, England: Durocobrivis Publications.

Tucker, C., McKay, R., Kojetin, B., Harrison, R., de la Puente, M., Stinson, L., et al. (1996). *Testing methods of collecting racial and ethnic information: Results of the current population survey supplement on race and ethnicity.* Washington, DC: Bureau of Labor Statistics.

UK Collaborative Group for HIV and STI Surveillance. (2004). *Focus on prevention. HIV and other sexually transmitted infections in the United Kingdom in 2003.* London: Health Protection Agency Centre for Infections.

UK Parliament. (2006). House of commons. *Hansard.* Written answer of 14 July 2006. Column 2116W.

UN (Department of Economic & Social Affairs). (2007). *Composition of macro geographical (continental) regions, geographical sub-regions, and selected economic and other groupings*. Retrieved from http://unstats.un.org/unsd/methods/m49/m49regin.htm

Valentine, G., Sporton, D., & Nielsen, K. (2009). Identities and belonging: A study of Somali refugee and asylum seekers living in the UK and Denmark. *Environment and Planning D: Society and Space, 27*, 234–250.

Van den Reek, E., & Hussein, A. I. (2004). *Somaliërs op doorreis—Verhuisgedrag van Nederlandse Somaliërs naar Engeland*. Tilburg, The Netherlands: Wetenschapswinkel, University of Tilburg.

Van Liempt, I. (2007). *Navigating borders: Inside perspective on the process of human smuggling into the Netherlands*. Amsterdam: Amsterdam University Press.

Von Ahn, M., Lupton, R., Greenwood, C., & Wiggins, D. (2010a, June). *Languages, ethnicity, and education in London* (DoQSS Working Paper No. 10-12). London: Department of Quantitative Social Science, Institute of Education.

Von Ahn, M., Lupton, R., Greenwood, C., & Wiggins, D. (2010b, July). *Languages, ethnicity and education in London. Research findings*. UPTAP/ESRC.

Walvin, J. (2000). *Making the Black Atlantic: Britain and the African diaspora*. London: Cassell.

Ward-Perkins, B. (2005). *The Fall of Rome and the End of Civilization*. Oxford: Oxford University Press.

Werbner, R. (2002). Cosmopolitan ethnicity, entrepreneurship and the nation: Minority elites in Botswana. *Journal of Southern African Studies, 28*(4), 731–753.

White, P. M., Badets, J., & Renaud, V. (1993). Measuring ethnicity in Canadian Censuses. In Statistics Canada & US Bureau of the Census (Eds.), *Challenges of measuring an ethnic world: Science, politics and reality* (pp. 223–269). Washington, DC: US Government Printing Office.

Wild, S. H., Fischbacher, C. M., Brock, A., Griffiths, C., & Bhopal, R. (2006). Mortality from all cancers and lung, colorectal, breast and prostate cancer by country of birth in England and Wales, 2001-2003. *British Journal of Cancer, 94*, 1079–1085.

Wild, S. H., Fischbacher, C., Brock, A., Griffiths, C., & Bhopal, R. (2007). Mortality from all causes and circulatory disease by country of birth in England and Wales 2001-2003. *Journal of Public Health, 29*(2), 191–198.

Williams, P. (2013). *Paul Gilroy*. Abingdon: Routledge.

Wingerd, J. (1992). *Urban Haitians: Documented/undocumented in a mixed neighbourhood* (Ethnographic evaluation of the 1990 Census, Report No. 7. Final Report for Joint Statistical Agreement 90-10). Washington, DC: Bureau of the Census.

Wohland, P., Rees, P., Norman, P., Boden, P., & Jasinska, M. (2010) *Ethnic population projections for the UK and local areas, 2001-2051* (Working Paper 10/02). Leeds, England: School of Geography, University of Leeds.

Wong, D. W. S. (2003). Spatial decomposition of segregation indices: a framework towards measuring segregation at multiple levels. *Geogr Anal , 35*(3), 179–194.

Wong, D. W. S. (2004). Comparing traditional and spatial segregation measures: a spatial scale perspective. *Urban Geogr, 25*(1), 66–82.

Woodbridge, J. (2005) *Sizing the unauthorised (illegal) migrant population in the United Kingdom in 2001* (Home Office Online Report 29/0). London: Home Office.

INDEX

A

African HIV Policy Network (now
African Health Policy Network),
96, 209, 237

Annual Population Survey, 17, 59

Annual School Census, xi, 80, 84, 90,
98, 101, 107–10, 137–40, 224, 226

Aspinall PJ, xi, 24, 25, 28–30, 33, 47,
48, 57, 58, 63, 64, 72–4, 80, 91,
92, 99, 106, 137, 140, 148, 162,
182, 183, 194, 202, 228, 236

asylum seekers, viii, 43–8, 52–6, 61, 64,
65, 99, 100, 106, 111, 122, 126,
165, 170, 171, 173, 181, 198, 200,
210, 211, 220, 230, 231, 233–5

B

Bass Line African Health and Sex
Survey, 25, 96

Bécares L, 127, 163–4, 168

Bhopal R, viii, 91

Black African ethnic and migrant
sub-groups, 26
country of birth groups, 13–16
educational attainment, 136–41

fertility, 22, 23

household composition, 26, 28

household size, 29, 30

housing circumstances, 132–4

labour market participation,
160–2

limiting long-term illness, 165–7

migration, 38–41

national identity, 71

religion, 78

variations in patterns of residence,
106–13

Black African presence in Britain, 1–9

African slave trade, 2–4

arrival for study, 6

Britain's colonial campaigns, 5, 6, 8

18th and 19th century baptisms, 4, 5

era of mass migration, 8

First World War, 7

government social surveys, 8, 9

19th century African performers, 5

pan-Africanism, 6

Roman times, 1–3

Second World War, 7

Y-chromosome and mitochondrial
DNA, 2, 3

© The Editor(s) (if applicable) and The Author(s) 2016
P.J. Aspinall, M.J. Chinouya, *The African Diaspora Population in
Britain*, DOI 10.1057/978-1-137-45654-0

Printed by Printforce, the Netherlands